GENDER VIOLENCE
AT THE U.S.-MEXICO BORDER

GENDER VIOLENCE
AT THE U.S.-MEXICO BORDER

Media Representation and Public Response

Edited by Héctor Domínguez-Ruvalcaba and Ignacio Corona

The University of Arizona Press   Tucson

To the women of Ciudad Juárez
and to the memory of Jesús Tafoya

The University of Arizona Press
© 2010 The Arizona Board of Regents
All rights reserved

www.uapress.arizona.edu

Library of Congress Cataloging-in-Publication Data
Gender violence at the U.S.-Mexico border : media representation
and public response / edited by Héctor Domínguez-Ruvalcaba and
Ignacio Corona.
    p.   cm.
Includes bibliographical references and index.
ISBN 978-0-8165-2712-0 (hard cover : acid-free paper)
    1. Women—Crimes against—Mexico—Ciudad Juárez.
2. Gays—Crimes against—Mexico.   3. Transvestites—Crimes
against—Mexico.   4. Murder—Mexico.   5. Mass media and
crime—Mexico.   I. Domínguez Ruvalcaba, Héctor, 1962–.
Corona, Ignacio, 1960– .
    HV6250.4.W65G475   2010
    362.88—dc22   2009039564

Publication of this book is made possible in part by an Arts &
Humanities Publication Subvention grant from The Ohio State
University and a grant from the Department of Spanish and
Portuguese at the University of Texas at Austin.

♻

Manufactured in the United States of America on acid-free,
archival-quality paper containing a minimum of 30 percent
postconsumer waste and processed chlorine-free.

15   14   13   12   11   10   6   5   4   3   2   1

Contents

Acknowledgments

As coeditors, we wish to thank our respective institutions, the University of Texas at Austin and The Ohio State University, for their generous support of this book. We also thank the contributors to the volume and the following colleagues who, at one point or another, were part of the academic discussions that led to this work: Susana Báez, Jorge Balderas-Domínguez, Derek Petrey, Jennifer Rathburn, Ileana Rodríguez, César Rossatto, and Jesús Tafoya (in memoriam). Without their intervention, this book would not have been possible.

The authors would like to thank the editors of *La Crónica* and Frontera.info for their authorization to reprint the articles cited in the book.

We also would like to acknowledge many other colleagues, graduate students, and friends from both sides of the border for their ideas, encouragement, and enthusiasm regarding this project. Finally, we thank Joseph Pierce for his editorial assistance.

Gender Violence: An Introduction

IGNACIO CORONA AND
HÉCTOR DOMÍNGUEZ-RUVALCABA

IN RECENT YEARS THE PHENOMENON of violence and its sociological and cultural implications has emerged at the forefront of academic discussions about the U.S.–Mexico border. And yet there are few serious studies devoted to one of its most disturbing manifestations: gender violence.[1] To address this specific issue, in April of 2005 we brought together a group of scholars at an interdisciplinary symposium—Dialogues on the U.S.–Mexico Border Violence—held at the University of Texas in Austin. Participants examined the complex roles that place, gender, and ethnicity have come to play in relation to the increasing violence along the border. The conference focused specifically on violence inflicted upon women and sexual minorities. The original triple concentration on place, gender, and ethnicity expanded in several directions. New perspectives emerged on various fronts, including the implications and connections between gendered forms of violence and the persistent mechanisms of social violence; the microsocial effects of economic models; the asymmetries of power in local, national, and transnational configurations; the particular rhetoric, aesthetics, and ethics of discourses that represent violence; the structural factors that perpetuate such discourses; and the economy and culture of fear. In other words, the approaches to the problem were—and we believe they must be—interdisciplinary.

As evidenced by the diverse perspectives included in this book, when we look at violence along the U.S.–Mexico border, we are not dealing simply with violence in the abstract. Rather, this book explores concrete instances of gender-based or gender-motivated violence, which requires interpretive and analytical strategies that draw on methods from a range of fields and disciplines. Political science, sociology, and anthropology appear as necessary in studying gender violence as do literary, cultural, and media studies. The conversations across disciplines that started at the 2005 symposium continue in this book as the contributors examine how such violence is the object of (re)presentation in a diversity of texts: oral narratives, newspaper reports, films and documentaries, novels, TV series, and legal discourse.

Border Violence

Even before the signing of the North American Free Trade Agreement (NAFTA) in 1992, but more vehemently after it came into force two years later, diverse groups of intellectuals, artists, academics, and social activists on both sides of the border have called attention to the subject of violence. They have found a correlation between regional economic transformations and the increase of all kinds of violence. A number of scholarly works have addressed border violence from different angles, including gang-related issues, governmental coercive policies (from both Mexico and the United States), the dehumanizing effect of the *maquiladora* system, conflicts related to undocumented workers, organized crime, and drug smuggling.[2] The U.S.–Mexico border has been studied as the space where the fluctuating booms and downturns of the global, regional, formal, and underground economies and markets have a direct impact on such fundamental issues as the preservation and reproduction of human life.

Throughout this book the contributors have tried to resist the fascination of explanatory arguments that favor geographic exceptionalism. Systematic research has confirmed that social ills, such as gender violence, can hardly be contained by any given urban environment in exclusivity. Nonetheless, most of the chapters are responsive to the many strands of violence that concentrate on spatial conjunctures. Mexican border cities have come to represent a territorial manifestation of an overlapping of many different symbolic and material processes encompassed by globalization. From Matamoros to Tijuana, parallel to the increase in criminal activity, there has been an upsurge in gender violence. In response to the lingering question why Ciudad Juárez has become the central node of gender violence, the contributors have identified a number of circumstances. These include the characteristics of a gun-toting culture that is encouraged by the lethal mix of a corrupt judicial system and the social catalyst of impunity (Quinones, *True Tales*, 140).

There are considerable levels of crime and drug trafficking in Ciudad Juárez (three of Mexico's five most important drug cartels operate in the area), exacerbated by an ill-reputed and complicit local police. The city's infrastructure has not kept up with the numbers of migrants who have arrived to cross the border or to stay indefinitely. In fact, not only in Chihuahua but in other Mexican border states as well, the population has doubled in the past decade to 16.5 million (Laufer, 14). Across the border from Ciudad Juárez is El Paso, Texas, a city known in the past as the world's blue jeans capital. The per capita income in El Paso is one of the lowest in the nation ($20,129), despite being a metropolitan area (Blumenthal, 20). Although purely quantitative indexes may not show the border region to be one of the most critical areas among major urban settlements in the Western hemisphere, a condensation of multiple types of violence makes this region different from many urban areas that deal with high rates of criminality.

At the literal contact zone between the so-called First and Third Worlds, multiple and polymorphous processes of physical, economic, ecological, symbolical, and psychological violence seem to be amplified: violence exerted by the legal system and its deadly toll on scores of undocumented border crossers; economic violence perpetrated against different populations and its effects on the displacement of people; ethnic violence against migrants; industrial violence against the environment and the border populations; violence between criminal organizations that not only affects the members of the mafias, but also society at large; and gender violence and its ever growing number of casualties. By a tropological substitution, "border" and "violence" appear now inextricably associated in the media. The "border" acquires ipso facto an ethical and political meaning, equally relevant to its representational deployment and study.

The fact that the border has appeared as a place of violence by a myriad of narratives compels us to reflect on the concept of violence in relation to notions of place, ethics, international law, and even aesthetics. This reality also urges us to address processes of social class and gender identity–formation. As the anthropologist Renato Rosaldo (635) has claimed, interpreting the border "involves the simultaneous analysis of the theater and its symbolic dimensions, as well as the actual violence." The core problem of representing border violence is then immersing oneself in conflicting representations and a diversity of proposed significations.

Gender Violence

We define "gender violence" as psychological and physical harm that is inflicted on individuals on the basis of their gender or sexual orientation. Such a concept becomes central to the articulation of different critical views on a phenomenon that seemingly erodes social equality and puts into question notions of human value. Beyond the mere use of force or verbal and psychological forms of aggression, gender violence may also be understood as an extended set of conditions that impedes the realization of an individual's full life potential. Therefore, it is akin to a wide variety of historical forms of oppression and repression. The exploration of its latent and manifest aspects is one of the themes that bind the chapters in this collection. In none of the chapters is "violence" defined in a limited way; rather, the contributors consider it to be a widespread phenomenon. In exploring such conditions, the authors have felt compelled to use inclusive concepts, such as that of "symbolic violence." This is helpful in analyzing not only how violence manifests itself in a given context, but also, and most important, how it is engendered as "symbolic action." To examine such a widespread phenomenon contained within a specific geopolitical context, the contributors have maintained a geo-cultural focus in their exploration of the sources and the cultural and political codification of such gender violence.

Violence against women or sexual minorities is of course not a new phenomenon nor an uncommon one. It is particularly evident when patriarchal structures are stressed by fundamental changes in the social and economic framework that challenge their very existence. Amid the cultural conditions and socioeconomic developments of the border, there are thousands of young female workers drawn by the irresistible call of job opportunities in the foreign-owned assembly plant called *maquila-dora*. Most migrate from poor rural environments to help their families, and they eventually find themselves caught in the process of adapting to life in an urban environment without immediate support networks. Scholars have observed how these women's new economic role is quietly but profoundly transforming the traditional Mexican labor force and subsequently changing the face of society, which might also cause acute resentment among the patriarchal stakeholders (Quinones, *Dead Women*, 151). Such an interpretation of "context" is only one of the many hypotheses that insistently circulate among activists, journalists, and scholars, aspiring to produce usable insights to the phenomenon.[3]

This rendering of violence and its relationships to the broader community and cultural context is important to the analysis. Violence might be understood then as an action that implicitly testifies "to the entailments of identity at work, such as that of gender and social class" (Campbell, 110). If that is the case, these women are not killed in random acts of fury, but because they constitute or "symbolize" a particular group of women: those on the fringes of a community implicitly defined in social, economic, and even ethnic terms due to the predominance of the mestiza or indigenous phenotype among the victims. More important, from an economic perspective women have come to personify social change and ultimately liberation from the traditional webs of institutional and social control. For this, they are perceived as doubly threatening.

To increase awareness about the femicides, or any other form of violence for that matter, we must go beyond the physical manifestation of the phenomenon and treat it as a heuristic problem at the intersection of disciplines and institutional frameworks. Such a proposition also implies some form of textual or semiotic interpretation. In *Formations of Violence* the scholar Allen Feldman (18–19) has explained that violence is normally treated as a surface expression of a deeper cause. Such a search for intelligibility in the violent act requires attributing meaning to that kind of action. In some way violence denotes a relationship between bodies and signs: it is the threshold where discourse becomes body and body becomes discourse. Condemning the ghost of the enemy and consecrating the innocence of the victims—against a local conservative discourse that blames them for their own death—has been the collective endeavor of a literary discourse in which "fiction" is crisscrossed by references to factual events.

A Manichean narrative introduces the victim sacrificed by an often unknown perpetrator who, as an empty signifier, is always (re)invented by different social actors. Each hypothesis that tries to define a category of perpetrators is also imagining an ideological enemy, a criminal to be blamed and punished on an ideological basis. Perpetrators become allegorical figures of a "killing society," or a society in which killing increasingly tends to normalcy—that is, where murder is minimized or becomes a mere instrument of economical and political interests. This explains, in part, reiterative logic at work: it reveals traces of a social pathology. In this recurrent manifestation of violence, there is a general crisis of representation in its epistemological and political aspects. This means that the actors can neither construct a satisfactory truth-discourse about violence and crime, nor can they speak on behalf of the victims, as victimization is constructed in terms of moral or political assumptions that shape the imagined killer into ready-made forms. Likewise, as revealed throughout this book, murder, rape, kidnapping, and torture nurture socially and aesthetically produced discourses. These discourses proliferate and defy our sense of amazement through collective familiarization with violence. Bloody events presented as a public spectacle represent violence as a performative act for media consumption rather than as a problem for the community, whose solution requires the participation of the authorities as much as that of civil society.

Bridging Community and Academia

From our specific locus of enunciation, we are also reminded of the limitations inherent to our own professional practice, and at times we share the feeling of frustration of those affected by the collective tragedy of the femicides. And yet it is their struggle, undertaken with limited means, that serves as a moral example to inspire social change. In more personal terms this struggle empowers us to act from our own professional practice. Activism is not only taking these issues to the streets, almost a precondition to draw media attention, but also addressing them in a diversity of critical forums that can be established even in classrooms, where they need to be heard and discussed. For most of us, interpreting and discussing textual representations constitutes our primary professional practice. In relation to such an urgent issue as gender violence, the profession can foster a direct connection between theory and practice. Like those scholars who were devoted to the testimonial genre in the eighties, the study of violence establishes a collaborative agenda with local organizations, which constitutes another form of critical intervention and linkage between community and academia. The fact that this intervention may efface epistemological limits and distort the analysis is something that can matter only if we remain interested in a false sense of impartiality and critical distance. Writing about the present is always a risky business, but one that can offer the rewards of more direct social involvement.

Through the topics covered in this book, we offer a multifaceted analysis of the situation, but we do not claim to have come up with a ready-made set of solutions from our apparently safe haven in academia. Proposing solutions from a vantage point that is not integral to the community's needs might seem unrealistic and ultimately self-defeating—not dissimilar to the hollow promises of political candidates as they make cyclical stops and promise quick solutions to historical problems. Yet the families and local communitarian organizations expect from institutions of higher learning not only a research interest but also practical collaboration. More important, they look for guidance in confronting criminal actions in a context of social injustice and, at times, hostility from the local authorities and diverse interest groups. They recognize that the accumulation of knowledge about their own community takes place in educational institutions. These institutions are all too often deemed alien reservoirs, however; the knowledge obtained by a host of researchers and scholars rarely returns to benefit the affected communities, often confined to hegemonic circles in both Mexico and the United States. This book operates in relation to this criticism and consequent social demand as much as it is motivated by our reciprocal desire to contribute to solving the problem of gender violence in the border.

Is the scholar turning into a preacher or a social activist? Such a difficult positioning is part of our critical proposal. It seems clear that effective intervention is not possible without questioning and even strategically suspending artificial boundaries and limits: those established by professional practices that discourage cooperation and solidarity; those imposed by legal frameworks that categorize social phenomena as "city" or "state" problems; those imposed by national ideologies and economic models that may allow the free flow of some processes and impede other interactions—trade and the transfer of wealth are seen as transnational, but crime, pollution, and poverty are considered local issues. In addition to this critical operation, our proposal's centerpiece is a strategy for "building bridges": between public and private entities; national and local communities; all sorts of secular and religious organizations and institutions; the academia and the media; and civil society and the government.

Most of the book focuses on the relationship between violence and another ubiquitous concept: power. Regardless of the alleged features of violence against women—be they of an economic, misogynist, ethnic, or classist nature, or a combination of all these—femicides are virulent and misguided expressions of power, making power a physical and deadly force. Given the relevance of the concept of "gender" in the analysis of violence and the critique of the government's inefficacy in guaranteeing its citizens—particularly women and sexual minorities—public security, violence is analyzed as an asymmetrical relationship of power. Although it is not possible to generalize that such asymmetry is a precondition in all contexts for the appearance of violence, it is certainly a factor that contributes to explain its pervasiveness and recurrence in many groups, communities, and societies.

For some observers the authorities and civil organizations contribute to increasing the conjectural universe that encourages the proliferation of crime and delinquency (see González Rodríguez, *Huesos*, 76). By underscoring the authorities' indifference toward the families of the disappeared and the murdered, such documentary films as *Señorita extraviada* by Lourdes Portillo (2000) and *La batalla de las cruces* by Rafael Bonilla (2005) and chronicles like *Huesos en el desierto* by Sergio González Rodríguez (2002) and *La cosecha de mujeres* by Diana Washington (2005) suggest that authority figures are the main culprits for applying violence. This violence is not applied within the constitutional framework, however, but within unwritten norms of patriarchal domination. The scenario of pessimism is generalized: on the one hand, the authorities are defined as de facto offenders because of the prevailing impunity along the border; on the other hand, mutual disqualification and distrust among the government, NGOs, and civil and international organizations impede any sense of real progress in the solution of the femicides.

What underlies this politics for bridging the fragments that constitute the sociopolitical is a reconstitution of what has been separated and, in many cases, isolated in social or communitarian forms of life mostly due to macroeconomic transformations and what cultural theorists and political scientists have conceived as the crisis of the nation-state. They ultimately affect our identity and roles as subjects and citizens. It is therefore important to explore different paths for reorienting political actions that aim for a society more aware of gender violence and more conducive to its prevention. We propose confronting gender violence with a diverse agenda amplified throughout the social universe—necessarily beyond geopolitical borders and disciplinary fields—by forging a participative democracy where political citizenship is conceived not only as the right to receive protection from the State, but also as an individual responsibility for demanding such a protection for all citizens.

To start with, this new citizenship can be based on a frontal fight against silence, injustice, and inaction regarding gender-based violence, themes that many women's rights organizations have already advanced. As a group, the contributors of this book intervene in the politics of representation of violence (a) by analyzing the representational web that shapes and reproduces a discourse of violence in the media and (b) by revealing the discourses of power at play and the communitarian dynamics of inclusion and exclusion that operate transnationally on the basis of gender, social class, and ethnicity. We aspire to provide an understanding of gender violence and its different contexts, particularly those provided by media representations.

The Structure of This Book

One of the volume's main arguments is that in the study of gender violence we are, in essence, dealing with a cultural issue rather than with isolated criminal acts. These crimes are the undesirable result of a *machista* culture channeled by ingrained forms of pernicious representations of gender-based violence that multiply themselves throughout the local culture. This happens from their most innocent forms (such as jokes or song lyrics) to their antisocial manifestations (such as rape, torture, and murder) and by media and institutional practices that mislead the interpretation of violent events. Hence, this work analyzes textual representations and the embedded forms in which gender violence is codified and contextualized. Doubly victimized by criminals and the system of impunity on the one hand and by available systems of representation of violence on the other, the victims become a morbid source of image production as the material evidence of psychological and physical violence. For most citizens the media have been the main source of images and information about the femicides in Ciudad Juárez. This fact affords them an important role that could be used to avoid further production of discourses that perpetuate violence.

Civil society and academia increasingly assume the role of "lie detector" rather than "truth teller." They support the decentering of information through alternative channels of social communication. In writing about gender violence, it is necessary to explain social interaction departing from the interpretation of these casualties. Above all, this endeavor involves a political and an academic commitment: a profound review of the *fronteriza* society's ways of interaction, institutional frameworks, economic foundations, and cultural patterns.

The book is organized around four ways of enunciation. Two chapters are articulated around oral testimonies: from victims of homophobia (by Debra A. Castillo, María Gudelia Rangel Gómez, and Armando Rosas Solís) and from the mothers of the murdered women of Ciudad Juárez (by Patricia Ravelo Blancas). Two chapters explore audiovisual media: television (by Héctor Domínguez-Ruvalcaba) and film (by María Socorro Tabuenca Córdoba). Two chapters deal with written discourses on femicides: journalism (by Ignacio Corona) and literature (by Miguel López-Lozano). The final chapter (by James C. Harrington) revises the legal status of femicide cases in international courts. The interpretation of these different voices related to the phenomenon of border violence is one of the main achievements in this book.

Chapter 1, "Violence and Transvestite/Transgender Sex Workers in Tijuana," finds in both public officials and clients the source of violence against transvestite sex workers. Violence is perpetrated by those who are supposed to protect the citizens from it. An argument that is reiterated throughout this book is that the agent or perpetrator of violence is the very representative of public order, be it policemen who harass and extort transvestites or government officials who neglect their responsibility of preventing crimes and enforcing the law. This perception of members of the government as perpetrators—and therefore at the heart of corruption and impunity—is prevalent among activists and the larger community at the border. Chapter 2, "We Never Thought It Would Happen to Us," explores how this negative perception of the government has necessarily led to an empowered collective subjectivity, which has triggered an emergent grassroots activism.

This book also addresses the hypothesis that the prevailing representations of violence are founded on and by patriarchal views. Popular film, television, and the press predominantly represent violence as a failure of traditional morality. Policemen are seen as the heroes of B-movies, while immigrants and working-class males are frequently portrayed as victimizers who fail to fulfill their patriarchal duty: that of protecting women. Chapter 3, "Death on the Screen," discusses how the representation of violence in local television broadcasts constructs the prevalent image of Ciudad Juárez as a violent city and its perpetrators as poor immigrants, thus establishing a view that the city is victimized by foreigners. But the insistent complaint that traditional morals have been relaxed calls for a consolidation of patriarchy as a way to stop the femicides.

This is also the basis of B-movies that explore the same phenomenon, as is argued in chapter 4, "Representations of Femicide in Border Cinema." Contrasting the hypotheses that point to the patriarchal system and the negligence of government representatives as responsible for the femicides, local television and B-movies rely on the institution of the police and traditional morality for the protection of women against "evil men" or "male monsters." Chapter 5, "Over Their Dead Bodies," offers a case study on the problematic representation of violence in border newspapers, which often function as an instrument of terror production. For Corona, the sensationalist stories deployed by the press, far from inspiring the population to organize and participate actively in deterring systematic gender violence, provoke apathy and pessimism.

Literature written by nonborder writers and their concerns about human rights on the border is the object of analysis in chapter 6, "Women in the Global Machine: Patrick Bard's *La frontera*, Carmen Galán Benitez's *Tierra marchita*, and Alicia Gaspar de Alba's *Desert Blood: The Juárez Murders.*" López asserts that globalization is the main factor contributing to violence along the border. An international view concerned with universalizing human rights has been one of the most promising attempts to provide legal frameworks and approaches to confront, legislate about, and ultimately reduce gender violence. Chapter 7, "Alto a la impunidad," deals with the paradoxes of international law that make difficult the extension of human rights to citizens as well as the pursuit of those responsible for the impunity on the northern Mexican border.

These two chapters pose the central question of an antiviolence and anti-impunity politics discussed throughout the book: how can we break the borders that impede the plenitude of human life? The authors' own conclusions echo that of the volume as a whole. It involves a radical critique of national political boundaries that further deepen important legal vacuums, economic globalization's dehumanizing system—or "necroeconomics"—that tacitly produces expendable populations; the patriarchal features of governmental, social, and religious institutions; and the media's dominant discourse that contribute to support a cultural system in which gender violence often becomes deadly invisible.

Notes

1. Among the studies that delve into the subject, we could mention *Bordeando la violencia contra las mujeres en la frontera norte de México*, edited by Julia Monárrez and María Socorro Tabuenca Córdoba; *Entre las duras aristas de las armas*, edited by Patricia Ravelo and Héctor Domínguez-Ruvalcaba; *Violence and Activism at the Border*, by Kathleen Staudt; and diverse essays and articles by Patricia Ravelo, Héctor Domínguez-Ruvalcaba, Rita Segato, Sam Quinones, Kathleen Staudt, Cecilia Balli, Alfredo Limas Hernández, María Socorro Tabuenca Córdoba, and Julia Monárrez, among others.

2. Some of the works dealing with these topics are Ted Conover's *Coyotes: A Journey through the Secret World of America's Illegal Aliens*; Peter Andreas's *Border Games*; Luis Humberto Crosthwaite, John William Byrd, and Bobby Byrd's *Puro Border: Dispatches, Snapshots, and Graffiti from La Frontera*; Luis Alberto Urrea's *Across the Wire: Life and Hard Times on the Mexican Border*; Charles Bowden's *Down by the River: Drugs, Money, Murder, and Family*; James Diego Vigil's *Barrio Gangs: Street Life and Identity in Southern California*; Chad Richardson's *Batos, Bolillos, Pochos, and Pelados: Class and Culture on the South Texas Border*; Devon G. Peña's *The Terror of the Machine: Technology, Work, Gender, and Ecology on the U.S.–Mexico Border*; and Alejandro Lugo's *Fragmented Lives, Assembled Parts: Culture, Capitalism, and Conquest at the U.S.–Mexico Border*.

3. In their article "La batalla de las cruces: Los crímenes contra las mujeres y sus intérpretes," Héctor Domínguez-Ruvalcaba and Patricia Ravelo Blancas report thirty-two hypotheses regarding the femicides in Ciudad Juárez. In contrast, it has been difficult to ascertain a number for homophobic crimes in the region, as the Comisión Ciudadana Contra Crímenes de Odio por Homofobia has asserted.

Part I

Oral Testimonies on Gender Violence

Introduction to Chapter 1

Although femicides in Ciudad Juárez, the largest city in the northern state of Chihuahua, have called the attention of the international press, intellectuals, activists, and society in general, we cannot discuss gender-based violence without considering homophobia, which has become one of the most tolerated human rights violations in Mexican society. Despite the fact that the number of crimes reported against lesbians, homosexuals, and transgenders is significantly lower than the recent number of femicides, this type of hate crime is often left unreported or may even be instigated by authority figures and public discourses. Widespread intolerance against sexual diversity combined with internalized homophobia in the homosexual population make this topic of fundamental interest to the discussion of gender-related violence.

Based on a series of interviews conducted with transvestites, this chapter documents the different forms of violence that the transgender condition implies in Tijuana. By discussing this issue, the authors offer valuable insights regarding the victim's self-construction as an undervalued subject and the predominance of patriarchal ideology over human rights in the social consciousness and in public institutions. Two main sources of violence are discussed. The first is that which takes place between transvestites and their customers, including rape, kidnapping, and sudden aggression after sexual intercourse (this is generally a result of a client discovering the transvestite is not a woman). The second category of violence is inflicted by the authorities: from the different kinds of police extortion to the implementation of discriminatory city regulations. Authorities, clients, and even the homosexual population violate human rights of transvestites, making this one of the most extreme forms of gender violence. In fact, one of the main questions this chapter addresses is how the interviewees conceive their way of life as "normal" even when it is not unusual that they suffer rape, extortion, and kidnapping.

CHAPTER 1

Violence and Transvestite/Transgender Sex Workers in Tijuana

DEBRA A. CASTILLO, MARÍA GUDELIA
RANGEL GÓMEZ, AND ARMANDO ROSAS SOLÍS

ALTHOUGH THE TRAGIC MURDERS of young women in Ciudad Juárez have become the most internationally recognized example of gender-related violence along the Mexico–U.S. border, and rightly are the main focus of this book, it would be a gross oversimplification to presume that gender-based violence is limited to this single city and to these specific women. This chapter examines another form of gender/sexuality-based violence, through an empirically based study of the effects of quotidian violence on the lives of trans (transvestite/transgender) people in another border city, Tijuana.

Transvestite shows in Tijuana have formed an important part of the panorama available to sex clients who flood the city. In fact, many people understand transvestite sex work as limited to the presumed glamour of drag shows. In recent years, however, there has been an increasing recognition that the performance environment alone cannot absorb the growing number of sex workers who have begun to move from their respective establishments to massage parlors and into the streets and public parks. There are more of them (perhaps two hundred to three hundred, although no census has yet been conducted), and they are currently more visible than ever. Violence against this population is also migrating into the streets and into the public eye. Yet, except for scattered reports in human rights–oriented publications, there has been little recognition of this serious problem, and almost no understanding of the world in which these individuals live.

The Place of Transvestites

In a study for the World Policy Institute, the scholar Andrew Reding (*Sexual Orientation*, 3) has noted that in general "transvestite sex workers bear the brunt of societal hostility and face a very elevated risk of violence and murder across most of Latin America." Nevertheless, he surprisingly finds little reported major violence against transvestites in Mexico. In fact, Reding has argued the opposite. Since 2000, "repression by federal, state, and municipal authorities is now the exception rather than the rule," although he is quick to add that "the social environment in most of Mexico remains repressive and often dangerous" (Reding, *Mexico: Update*, 1). In support of this rather unexpected finding, Reding cites Víctor Clark Alfaro, the director of Tijuana's Binational Center for Human Rights. Clark Alfaro notes that although transvestites in the city have complained about frequent extortion and harassment by police, Tijuana is a cosmopolitan center that enjoys the benefits of the thriving gay culture in neighboring San Diego, ameliorating the more virulent antigay manifestations. There are, he writes, no complaints of violence against transvestites among the population he serves (ibid., 23).

Clark Alfaro's comment occurs in a context that includes an increasing, albeit small, percentage of men who are writing to the predominantly heterosexual Web site http://alt.sex.prostitution.tijuana to inquire about opportunities for gay clients to hook up with transvestites when they head across the border. This growing phenomenon hints at several new questions about the effects of queer sex tourism on local cultures. The scholar Ian Lumsden (142), reporting research results that echo Clark Alfaro's ideas, suggests that the diffusion of U.S. mass culture and cooperation between transvestites and U.S. Latinos from the area have begun to significantly affect the perceptions of and about gays in the area. Marta Lamas, from Mexico City, seems to agree, noting that there is more acceptance of homosexuality in cosmopolitan cities like Tijuana, where the term "gay" is associated with a modern, international—if still somewhat extravagant—lifestyle (Reding, *Mexico: Update*, 16).

Two main elements are conflated in Reding's summarizing comment, however: (1) harassment and abuse by police officers and other authorities, and (2) complaints from sex workers of assault or other aggression on the part of clients or other civilians. At the same time as a presumably positive U.S. influence is highlighted, both of these mostly local sources of violence are downplayed. It is almost impossible to know the reason for this lack of careful attention—whether relying too heavily on a dearth of reporting (transvestite sex workers almost never make formal complaints to authorities) or whether it rises from misunderstandings because of a lack of a common vocabulary (this point is discussed further below).

Sex work is always fraught with danger, says longtime gay-rights activist Emilio Velásquez of the Frente Internacional para las Garantías Humanas en Baja California (FIGHT), but the most difficult lives of all are those of transvestite and transgender sex workers. While Reding and Clark Alfaro paint a somewhat more optimistic picture, Velásquez and the activist Max Mejía have documented in *Frontera gay* a series detailing allegations made by transvestites of police abuse, especially by the Fuerzas Especiales (Special Forces) branch, including robbery (of both the sex workers and the clients), sexual assault, beatings, regular extortion, false arrests, breaking and entering, and illegal searches of their homes without a judge's warrant ("Brutal asedio policiaco"). The editorial published in November 1999 made a passionate appeal: "Who do the municipal police or the Special Forces think they are to hide behind the law as if they owned it? Since when are they the owners of the street and the citizens' right of passage and freedom of expression? Since when is it a crime or a misdemeanor against police regulations to stroll around dressed as a woman? Since when is it a crime that some transgender people work as prostitutes in the city's red zone? What? Women, yes, but transgenders, no? Is it a declaration of war against sexual diversity?" ("Abuso y corrupción policíaca," 3).[1]

This brief look at existing secondary material reminds us that, with the exception of these scattered reports and journalistic articles, there is very little accurate, published research to help understand the real issues of violence facing the transvestite individual along the border. Consequently, this study is intended to offer a preliminary analysis of some of the more pressing areas of concern for this vulnerable population. Much of the material here derives from ongoing work, primarily in education and public health policy, with both male and female prostitutes in Tijuana. We do not want to imply that all transvestites are employed in prostitution; nevertheless, these individuals are the most visible segment of the transvestite population and are generally thought to be frequent victims of violence perpetuated by authorities, clients, acquaintances, and random individuals (such as members of street gangs). For this reason we have gone to them for their assistance in exploring this area of concern. In addition to published research, information for this chapter comes from a two-phase quantitative and qualitative project, consisting of questionnaires as well as in-depth interviews that ask transvestites working as prostitutes about the level of violence they have experienced.

The first phase involved ethnographic work that was carried out in 2001, including interviews with forty-seven transvestite/transgender individuals working in Tijuana, along with a similar number of interviews of female prostitutes, the latter of which is cited here only when relevant for making a comparative point. One of the objectives was to understand how sex workers became involved in behaviors with a high risk of HIV transmission. Along with basic sociodemographic variables, the study also looked at violence perpetrated against them during their workday (by clients, police, unknown assailants, and so on). HIV tests were also performed on the questionnaire subjects. The transvestite individuals were asked to identify themselves according to two categories: (1) by gender (either as *hombre* [man] or *transgénero* [transgender]; those who identified as "woman" or other designations were assigned to the *transgénero* category), and (2) by sexual orientation (heterosexual, bisexual, or gay).

The second phase took place in July 2005 and consisted of extensive follow-up interviews with four transvestite individuals. It is important to note that these were face-to-face interviews conducted in the transvestites' workplaces by longtime human-rights activist Emilio Velásquez, with the interviewees' informed consent. Material drawn from these interviews, along with an earlier in-depth interview with a transvestite sex worker conducted by Gudelia Rangel in a public health clinic as well as video-taped interviews from the documentary film *Las paraditas*, serve as the basis for the discussion in this chapter. The findings are consistent with ongoing research and with the individuals' responses in workshops and meetings organized for and by them in Tijuana.

Sex Work

Whether a male sex worker identifies as a transvestite or not, as of yet, there is no systematic understanding of either the numbers or motivations of male sex workers. Contributing to this problem is a lack of in-depth research, as well as ambiguous results from existing studies, partly because of inadequate samples and partly because of cryptic responses on the part of interviewees. When asked why they go into sex work, men generally tend to give the same response as women: they need the money. Thus the perceived rise in recent years in the number of sex workers in Mexico, both male and female, can be directly tied to the lagging economy and the lack of opportunities for other employment. The employment situation is particularly difficult for men perceived as effeminate: "Employers in most trades, conscious of the impression their business makes with the public, seek to avoid the embarrassment of having obviously effeminate or homosexual men on their payrolls. That tends to constrain such individuals to trades that have traditionally been considered fit for women and (by association) homosexuals, such as cooking, the arts, hairdressing, and, unfortunately, prostitution" (Reding, *Mexico: Update*, 14).

Tijuana transvestite "Gabriela" agrees that although she first entered prostitution "out of despair, out of pain" (*por despecho, por dolor*), her attitude changed with time: "I told myself, no. I am going to be the prostitute that I always could have been. From the beginning I did it out of anger, and then I liked it and kept on." Another transvestite, interviewed in the documentary film *Las paraditas*, attributes her choices to early childhood sexual experiences: "I had my first sexual experience when I was nine years old with two boys that were friends of my brother. They proposed a game to me, that was the game of dad and mom. We had sexual relations. They asked me not to say anything." She describes how she and these boys continued playing, almost daily: "At first I felt very strange, I told myself that for me this was not a game, it was more than a game. With time I began liking the game and it could be for that reason that I came to the sex industry. But I feel that I was born this way." These preliminary accounts point to a complex and mixed rationale, which includes both economic and psychic factors. Thus the transvestite is *born* and she *becomes*; in this view, prostitution is both a free choice and a necessity for survival.

Comments from men working in prostitution in general emphasize their high degree of flexibility and also tend to show that a significant number of clients want to play an active role (also known as "international") with men they perceive as hypermacho. Similarly, a significant number of clients want to be penetrated by a transvestite. A study conducted in 1991 of men who frequented gay bars in eighteen cities found that flexibility of sexual roles was the rule: 95 percent of self-defined homosexual men and 77 percent of bisexual men had played the passive role in anal intercourse; 88 percent and 95 percent, respectively, had played the "active" role (García García et al., 53–54).

The same is true for the sex workers in our small sample, who frequently define themselves as "gay" or bisexual—or even "heterosexual," as was the case of two of the men in the survey and one of the in-depth interview subjects. The complexity of their identities and the inadequacy of survey categories are uncovered in the in-depth interviews, where, for instance, Karla (a self-defined "heterosexual") also indicates her plans to get breast implants. Another interviewee, Rosa, seems confused by the choices, asking the interviewer for assistance in deciding, at one point calling herself a "little fag dressed as a woman" and at another: "I consider myself a woman." Despite their personal preferences and sexual orientation, transvestite sex workers generally describe their range of sexual practices as including both active and passive, oral and anal sex, as well as active vaginal sex (with the rare woman client). In the larger sample captured by the survey, one respondent who had had sex-reassignment surgery also included passive vaginal sex.

One common theme among researchers in the scant extant secondary material is the passing narrative. In this story the transvestite passes, or attempts to pass, as a female prostitute, and the client may imagine that he is having vaginal or anal intercourse with a woman. The situation can become very dangerous for the sex worker if the client realizes he has been tricked, or if he pretends he did not know his partner was a man and ultimately "discovers" the deception after the sex act. Mexican American border transvestite Muñeca tells of being severely beaten by a Mexican client: "I told him to leave me alone, that if he was not satisfied with what I had done or if he felt I had tricked him into thinking I was a woman, that I was sorry. I told him I thought he knew I was a man. He was one of those people who appear to be nice but after they've had their pleasure they react in a strange way. He must have known I was a transvestite, otherwise why would he have gone to that gay bar?" (Martínez et al., 299).

Gabriela says: "Sometimes they have realized it, but from the beginning I behave as a woman." "Robinson," an experienced Tijuana sex tourist, using an amused, insider tone, describes what happened to a "newbie" he took on one of his trips: "A young fellow who worked for me, unknown to me . . . actually did his business with her and never knew the true gender of his date. I won't go into too many of the gruesome details and speculation about how it was done, but the next day I found out he had went with her when he asked why I didn't take her, and said it was the best piece of ass he ever had. He was pretty upset when I finally convinced him that he was officially no longer 100 percent straight. Best thing is probably just don't dwell on it. A BJ from a pretty little thing is a BJ after all. . . . Try not to worry about it next time. It takes all the romance right out of it" (Robinson, online posting, September 7, 1998).

In this narrative Robinson seems to unconsciously drift between the suggestion that his companion engaged in penetrative anal sex and the assertion that he received oral sex, marking a slippage from a more prohibited activity to a lesser violation of heterosexuality. He also hints at the potential for violence from his coworker ("he was pretty upset"—whether about the sexual act or about his cohort's knowledge of it). He also advises readers of his own, more cosmopolitan perspective: "A BJ . . . is a BJ after all." But of course, in Robinson's jocular comment about the BJ, he completely elides his earlier description of the transvestite prostitute as providing his coworker with, not oral sex, but "the best piece of ass."

In another, expanded version of this story, the transvestite and a straight man fall in love with each other, but the man does not know his beloved is a transvestite. When the transvestite reveals his gender, the man leaves in disgust, sometimes after beating up the transvestite for the deception (Prieur, 164, 251, 255–56). The revealing of one's gender to chosen clients in the world of prostitution is similarly fraught with danger, although as "Gabriela" notes, the results can often be anticlimactic. She says that she confides in her repeat clients: "Afterwards, I can confide in them, for example, if he has come to me once or twice, or more times I tell him the truth. And afterwards they say, so what?"

Yet on the street, among the individuals we surveyed, it seems that often the goal is not passing, but rather in being immediately identifiable. Among the Tijuana sex clients, for every story of gender confusion, there is another story of a very obviously masculine-looking transvestite. Not all sex workers want to pass as women; in fact, the obviously masculine transvestite appeals to a particular group of clients. Transvestites register a common complaint against them: female prostitutes don't like them because they don't stick to accepted and traditional practices among their female colleagues, but also because they are men, so presumably they are more in touch with male sexuality and thus more appealing to customers. In the typical passing narrative, clients will often say that they are looking for a woman when they mistakenly hire the services of a transvestite, but transvestites argue that this is not usually the case. Many of their clients prefer the passive role; others are specifically looking for the fantasy of sex with a woman with a penis (as in the earlier case of Karla). It is not that their clients are fooled by the illusion of femininity and become violent when they discover their mistake, but that these clients actively seek out the services of a transvestite and may become violent out of their own sense of frustrated guilt about desires they perceive as perverted.

Traditionally, too, the client feels licensed to engage in rougher sex with a transvestite than with a woman, with a greater risk of violence to both participants. Yvonne, quoted by Laura Ripoll in *La Jornada*, argues that to some degree the transvestite suffers from more violence because she accepts less: "A woman is more submissive, we transvestites have been brought up as men and we are stronger, no one can force us to do anything that we don't want to do." In the in-depth interviews with Tijuana transvestites, they speak of the popularity of their services among masochistic men, which also increases the level of violence. In those cases, "I initiate the sexual games," comments Yadira. Many of them also speak openly and frankly about beatings and knifings among members of the transvestite community, between transvestites and their clients (in both directions), as well as widespread robbery: of the clients (if they decide they do not want to pay the agreed-upon fee) or of the transvestite (with or without rape). Thus, if it is indeed true that transvestites suffer the brunt of physical assaults and violence, they are by no means always passive victims.

In fact, so pervasive are these aggressions that words like "violence," "kidnapping," and "rape" have lost their meanings among many members of this population. For example, Yolanda mentions that she has not suffered from violence but that the police "beat you up"; that she has not been kidnapped but that "some men have taken me in that way by force that I didn't want and they have left me outside the city"; and that she has frequently been forced to have sex with police ("they force me to do things without paying me"). When the interviewer comments on tape that these actions constitute rape and police brutality, Yolanda's answer is a calm "well, yes," but she clearly does not get the point, because later she describes similar behavior by potential clients. Here is a typical exchange: Emilio: "Have you been raped?" Yolanda: "No, but yesterday one guy forced me to give him the service."

Rosa tells the interviewer about a complaint she made to a judge about a police officer who was continually harassing her. "He has a mental problem," she explains. "That officer is suffering from some trauma. 'With all due respect,' I told him, 'or you like me, and if you like me, let's do it, sweetheart,' I told him. But if they like me, they are not going to get me that way. On the contrary, I will hate them more each day." Rosa's complaint is not so much about rape or the abuse of authority, but about wasting her time when she needs to be out earning a living. The problem, as she sees it, is that the police officer refuses to recognize his own desires, so he seeks her out for harassment and sexual abuse.

One of the transvestites in the film *Las paraditas* comments: "I feel that prostitution is not a safe job for one here in Mexico." This is *trabajo inseguro* in more than one sense: both uncertain and unsafe. Thus, for instance, prices for services are both more fluid and lower than for a female prostitute. It depends on whether the police let him work on a given day, or if he is able to keep the money he has earned. Because twenty dollars is the standard bribe each time a transvestite sex worker is approached by the police, adding up sometimes to sixty dollars a day, sex workers have commented that they have to steal from clients occasionally just to pay the bribes (Velásquez). The sex worker from *Las paraditas* adds: "I don't have an exact amount when I say I'm going to work that I am going to earn. It depends on what the client asks for and what he has with him. If he wants oral sex and has $20 or $30 in his pocket, then I'll do it. If he wants anal sex and has a little more—say $30, $40, $50—then I'll do it as well." He adds that if the clients want him to penetrate them, he does that too: Mexicans, Americans, policemen, doctors, engineers, anyone.

One of the transvestite sex workers comments on another all-too-frequent phenomenon: the transvestite is made guilty of the violence perpetrated against her. When a client turns aggressive, and the transvestite attempts to defend herself, the client may beat her up, take her money, and then call the police, manipulating the report so that the police arrest the sex worker, fine her, and take her to jail for the standard thirty-six hours (*Las paraditas*). Although this story may sound a bit self-exculpatory, this brief glimpse into the dangerous and unsettled night life of transvestites working in Tijuana is confirmed from an entirely different angle, when Tijuana sex client "Rust" notes to one of his Internet "research" buddies: "It might be reassuring to know that, if worse comes to worst, the authorities are not as likely to haul you away for physically fighting off a transvestite in the situation you describe, as for, say, punching a local in a bar" (Rust).

The predominantly heterosexual Tijuana sex tourists who post messages on the Usenet site http://alt.sex.prostitution.tijuana typically define the "shemales" as aggressive and frightening. One client describes "a trio of truly frightening exboys" in one of the Zona Norte establishments (Erip, February 1, 1999). Another, identified only as La_vida_loca, leaves a bar after only a few minutes because "the shemales were kind of scary." A client who patronized Bambi noted that "there is a good deal of gender confusion here" (Erip, September 2, 1997), and a day later described spending the "expected scary 10 minutes. The Chargers could use some of these guys" (Erip, September 3, 1997). There is in this community an acute awareness of the possibilities of the body for transformation and display, as well as of its limits—for work, for pleasure, for pain.

The majority of the survey respondents, as well as all four of the recent interview subjects, confess to using drugs or alcohol while working. The prevalence of drugs affects the levels of violence and the adherence to safe-sex practices. One of the transvestites from *Las paraditas* explains that if he really needs the money and has a Mexican client who does not like using a condom and if he himself does not have one, he will do it for the money because he needs the cash for food and drugs. In an interesting switch from first- to third-person in his account, he adds that if that client is infected with HIV, "it's sad for the guy who went with him, right?"

This association of the transvestite with disease, assault, and theft comes up again and again in the net postings. "Elsuertudo" warns that "the she-males can be very aggressive. The last time I walked through one grabbed my crotch and wouldn't take no for an answer. I had to remove his/her hands at which point she became verbally abusive." "MuleLip" adds: "Watch it on the T.V.'s as he said a lot are nothing but thiefs [*sic*]." In a later post he clarifies: "They grab your hands and place them on their cold fake tits or they pull you and make you kiss them. This way, your hands are occupied while they are free to slip your wallet out of your pants" (MuleLip). "Robinson" (September 7, 1998) corroborates: "A big burly lineback looking transvestite grabbed my johnson with one hand and wallet with the other, trying to kiss me (Ewwwww) at the same time. I successfully defended myself, my pocket, and my honor, and kept both my wallet and my virtue intact, but the tooth cut on my hand got infected so I guess he had the last laugh." Several of the transvestites interviewed corroborate with even more extreme stories of violence accompanying theft, with fists, with knives, or in this case, a broken bottle: "Once I was with a guy drinking in a bar and then the person realized that I had pickpocketed his money, and then without any warning, he hit me in the face with a bottle and I still have the scar" (*Las paraditas*).

Robinson (February 8, 2000) further warns that the Tijuana police are more likely to harass clients who look gay or solicit transvestites: "The cops do seem to pick on anybody they think is a little light in the loafers." His suggestion is to stick to more traditional heterosexual pleasures. *Frontera gay* mentions that one typical form of police abuse is to wait until the transvestite has been picked up in someone's car, then stop them a few blocks ahead and steal all the money of both the client and the sex worker ("Brutal asedio policiaco"). Mexican American transvestite Muñeca comments that in her experience transvestite prostitutes from Mexico often come to the United States to work because they see it as safer and freer from police harassment, even though soliciting prostitution is illegal: "In the United States I can walk on the street dressed like a woman and they will not throw me in jail, although I will be arrested if I walk around the square trying to make money. In Mexico they pick you up just for walking around." She concludes that she no longer "walks around," and only goes about in Mexico from the safety of a vehicle.

One open question is the degree to which sex tourism, and especially the subset of sex tourists actively seeking gay and transvestite opportunities, is shaping local experiences, practices, and even identities. For the sociologist Leonel Cantú (146), the growing popularity of the label *internacional* "has transborder connotations. Clearly, then, Mexican sexualities are being transformed through transnational processes and links, including tourism." For Cantú (148), Mexico's appeal to tourists in general is double and contradictory: "it is 'just like home' and it is exotic." For gay sex tourists the stereotypical descriptions of macho men found in gay travel guides suggest an erotic fantasyland of "butch hombres" who are "breathtaking in their beauty" (Cantú, 149). The easiest place to meet these men is, of course, the gay bar. Significantly, the gay bars that Cantú (144) describes as a feature of the international gay tourist industry tend to be located in *"zonas de tolerancia"* ("zones of tolerance"). In this context it is surprising that Cantú's survey of exotic Mexican males does not include a discussion about transvestism, because transvestites are a prominent feature of gay bars in Tijuana—perhaps hinting at his own investments in a particular image of gay tourism rather than a more general or complete picture.[2]

The few discussions of transvestite prostitution on the Internet are hedged with prohibitions. The individual who calls himself "La_vida_ loca" (June 11, 1999) describes a trip in which he searched out "some obvious shemales, some very old, and one (who I almost chose just because I was in a sick, twisted, tequila-induced stupor) who was severely cross-eyed." This online poster sees the transvestite not only as exotic but repulsive. In contrast, on one of his trips to Tijuana, MuleLip (January 20, 1999) spent time in Sans Souci with the person he considered the best-looking woman in the place: "She took me in the dressing room upstairs and flipped out what I swore she didn't have." MuleLip immediately departs for other pleasures. In both cases, however, the transvestite serves as a marker of the client's ability to test the limits of his sexuality, while remaining within a safer, heterosexual space.

Authorities

From 1999 to 2000 the gay activist Emilio Velásquez coordinated a series of meetings with transvestite sex workers to document and denounce harassment of transgender sex workers in the city. In this ongoing and systematic form of harassment, the police continually extort money from sex workers with the threat to arrest them and lock them up for disturbing the peace. The police also frequently tell the sex workers that dressing as a woman is illegal and that it is also illegal to prostitute oneself. Neither of these statements is true, of course, but even transvestites aware of their constitutional rights tend to find it easier to pay the twenty-dollar bribe rather than being locked up for thirty-six hours in the "20 de noviembre" jail (the November 20th Memorial Prison).

Velásquez says that the police were "just basically trying to extort money from these people that never spoke up for their rights, that never organized; they were used to that. It was a gold mine for many years for these different police organizations and groups to exploit the young and the weak and the ignorant and those caught in the grip of alcohol and drugs." He adds: "The police will also engage in pressuring people that they search on the streets and when they find condoms in their pockets or their purses, they immediately accuse them of prostitution, or, as they call it, 'bothering people on the street' and either take them to jail or get money from them. They also take their condoms, which is very unnerving for us, considering some of the young men, especially at the park [Parque Teniente Guerrero], are HIV positive." Velásquez comments on another difficult reality: "Another terrible aspect of the police abuse is the sexual abuse. Men, women, underage kids are forced by the police, sometimes at gunpoint, to perform all types of sexual activities. Many times they are left out in the hills surrounding Tijuana to find their way back. We fear that if this type of activity continues, we'll start finding bodies, dead bodies, up in the hills" (*Las paraditas*).

Harassment deriving from state and municipal officials is still the rule, often intensifying at the end or near the beginning of the *sexenio*, as political players jockey for maximum spoils (Lumdsen, 57–58). In general, physical abuse by authorities is an intractable problem, and transvestite activists note that it is hard to complain when the justice system as a whole is so pervasively, overtly homophobic. And yet, curiously, among the most common forms of abuse is rape, or forcing the transsexual to provide oral sex. They are also prey to sexual assault in jail, not so much from fellow prisoners (although that is also a frequent occurrence), but from the prison guards. Says Yadira, for example: "In jail and in the prison the guards want sexual favors. The *celadores* come, you do it. In the jail they take you to the bathrooms and in the prison when the lights go out the guard goes and wakes up the chosen person."

Authorities have acknowledged that the legal system gives a lower priority to the investigation and prosecution of the homicides of homosexuals, and particularly of transvestites (Ruiz Harrell, as quoted in Research Directorate Immigration and Refugee Board, 8). Other continuing concerns mentioned by Mexican activists are the abuse, especially of boys perceived as effeminate, by their own fathers (Jiménez, as quoted in Research Directorate Immigration and Refugee Board, 8). Participants in this project confirm the scattered published reports that the transvestite remains unusually vulnerable to police abuse and extortion, typically in the forms of demands for money and oral sex (Research Directorate Immigration and Refugee Board, 9–10). Likewise, their experience concords with other reports from elsewhere in the country that violence, beatings, rape by police, and abuse by fellow prisoners in jail are also common (see Prieur, 87, for Mexico City).

The scholar Victor Janoff has noted that the murders of twenty gay men in Chihuahua and Tijuana have remained undocumented since 1991. Currently in Tijuana gay men fear violence, are still frequently harassed by police, and are often arrested for "immorality." *Frontera gay* in 1998 reported on a March police crackdown consisting of "constant arrests of young men dressed as women or simply wearing makeup, abuse during arrests, two and three hour trips in police vehicles, body searches that include ripping off clothes, insults, and sexual harassment for the enjoyment and diversion of officers. . . . These abuses signal the ominous intention of police to divide gays into 'acceptable' and 'unacceptable,' 'discreet' and 'shameless,' with prejudice against the most vulnerable groups within the community" ("Legal Survey, Mexico"). Other similar incidents of abuse were documented in February 1999 (Research Directorate Immigration and Refugee Board, 10). Two years later, in August 2001, a group of Tijuana transvestites, with the support of the Binational Center for Human Rights, held a news conference to once again denounce police abuse and demand an end to extortion. "They know our addresses," said Javier Martínez, who claims that police demanded twenty to forty dollars a day in protection money from him. "They wait for us to leave our home or be on our way to work" (Reding, *Sexual Orientation*, 61).

Yadira adds that she does not even need to be going to work, because "ya te conocen" ("they already know you"). Karla notes that if she has her health card, "they tear it up in your face. So that way, even if you aren't working, you are walking in the streets with pants." Ominously, the police harassment is contributing signally to making sex work less safe: being a registered sex worker with a health card in order and a pocketbook full of condoms is *more* rather than *less* likely to get the individual fined and jailed. One of the interviewees in *Las paraditas* speaks on this topic more at length:

There is no safety in prostitution work among us here in Mexico. There are different branches of the police and for the simple fact of being homosexual they put you in jail. Things that the police say to me when they arrest me, often in front of people, I don't know if they want to look good for the people, that they are superior to us, or that the work they have, or the uniform. So you get dressed, go out as a woman, go to work, many times we don't arrive even to the bar, for example, when you, without dressing as a woman, just go out to the store to buy the food you need to feed yourself. For the simple fact that you're homosexual, they pick you up in front of people or even ask you for money. And then they take someone in. They pick him up shoving and kicking, they put him in the car, and you're even forced to give yourself to them or they take you to jail. It's not just one car; it's two or more. They've beaten up many of us; they have taken our money by force and forced us to have sexual relations with them. Burnt. I've had bad experiences in this life of mine. I have burns, scars like the ones you see on my arm. Other experiences: assaults even with the threat of loss of life. (*Las paraditas*)

More recently, in 2002 the neighboring town of Tecate, Baja California, promulgated an amendment to the Police Act providing for jail terms and fines leveled against "the male who dresses as a woman and walks in public causing disturbances" (Reding, *Sexual Orientation*, 61). Tecate councilman Cosme Cazares argued that the ordinance's intent was to avoid prostitution and prevent the spread of AIDS (BBC, "Mexico's Transvestite Ban"), and he pledged to accompany police patrols to enforce the law, adding: "I respect fashion. But if a man is wearing women's pants and walking across the park, I don't know that I would be able to defend him" ("Mexican Town Cracks Down").[3] The same BBC report commented on the precipitating factor for this regulation as the "rise in number of transvestites who have moved to Tecate in recent years to escape Tijuana's violence."

Study Results

The more provocative findings of the preliminary survey are summarized here. As is typical of the city's highly transient population, only six of the forty-seven individuals interviewed are from Tijuana; the rest immigrated to the city from a wide range of other states, so very few of them live with close friends or family (only 17 percent total) in a community-oriented setting. In the in-depth interviews, however, all of the individuals report good relations with their immediate family and comment that they visit them frequently. Fifty percent of them live in rooms or apartments that they rent, and a strikingly high number (thirty-one of forty-seven) have been at least temporarily homeless in the three months before the survey. There is a surprisingly high level of education reported by our interview subjects, more among those self-defining as men than as "transgender," with many of them completing middle school and some attending high school. Nevertheless, only a little more than half report having another stable source of income outside of prostitution. Tellingly, those who define themselves as "transgender" have a much lower employment rate (only four of twelve, compared with twenty-two of thirty-five for the men), a figure that seems to correlate with the anecdotal sense that employment opportunities outside of prostitution are extremely restricted for males perceived as effeminate.

Although knowledge of English is extremely helpful in this border city, only one-third of the interview subjects report knowing any English; this, despite the fact that more than two-thirds report having crossed or attempted to cross the border into the United States. One suggestive but still unexplored result is that fourteen of the thirty-two individuals who did attempt a crossing reported a reason other than work or family for making this attempt.

Among the interview subjects who define themselves as men, more than 74 percent define themselves as bisexual or gay, with 20 percent saying they "don't know" and two individuals defining themselves as "heterosexual." Evidence shows clearly that their main client pool is overwhelmingly a local one. Non-Mexican clients are very much in the minority among both groups, although there is an interesting potential intersection among those who identify as "men" with white gay clients from the United States. At the same time it is obvious that their response as to the client's orientation is speculation on the part of these individuals, as most typically the interview subjects do not have any way to know this information for certain about their clients. Although the transgender group was quite definite in their answers to these questions, the men were far more diverse in their responses. This richness of response suggests that they are more apt to calibrate themselves with respect to the nuanced cultural understandings on the constructions of macho identity, following more traditional gendered lines.

Those who define themselves as men also have a richer repertoire of sexual partners—they describe their clients as divided relatively equally among "men," "men and women," and "gay" individuals. By comparison, the women interviewed overwhelmingly describe their partners as men, although a couple of them report having relations "with men and women," suggesting they may participate in highly sought-after threesomes in the *ambiente de noche*. In an interesting contrast, of those who self-identify as transgender, 100 percent define themselves as gay and yet none of them report having sexual relations with gay men. Their repertoire of sexual activities with clients also matches the anecdotal reports from other sources. While they emphasize both active and passive anal sex as their principle service, both the men and the transgender individuals report occasional vaginal and oral sex as well. Since one of the transgender individuals is postoperative, she also reported passive vaginal sex. Here again, the contrast with the women interviewed is absolute and reflects the transvestites' general perception from other sources that they offer a wider range of services than their female counterparts. Fifty-two of the fifty-three women interviewed report that they only have vaginal sex, and only one of them reports having oral sex. None of them admit to offering anal sex as a service.[4]

Alcohol and drugs are very much a part of the lives of both men and transgender individuals, adding to the potential for violence. Of them, 61.7 percent reported using some kind of drug in the past six months, and almost the same number acknowledged drinking to excess. The reported experience of violence among these individuals is significantly higher than for their female counterparts. Where none of the women interviewed reported any incidents of violence from police, and relatively little violence with clients or other individuals, the situation is very different for the transvestite sex workers—34 percent of them report violence with clients; 36.2 percent have experienced police violence; and 25.5 percent of them have been assaulted by people unknown to them. An exceptionally high number of them have been jailed—60 percent of the men and 83.3 percent of the transgender individuals, as opposed to only 7 percent of the women—again, an important result for further investigation.

Conclusion

It is important to recall that this is a nonprobabilistic study, and hence the conclusions cannot be extrapolated to the population as a whole. They merely provide suggestive information about various aspects of the interviewees' individual situations. Nevertheless, as a first exploratory study, this project offers important insights into this seriously abused population, focusing on streetwalkers and the transvestites who work in gay-identified establishments. There is also another, smaller population of transvestite sex workers who are better treated and more isolated from these abuses—several of them in each of the primarily heterosexual establishments, as well as a few who provide services in their clients' homes, arranged through telephone or Internet contacts. The history of violence and abuse has made transgender/transsexual sex workers highly distrustful of outsiders, including members of the gay human rights community. Many of them are people who, even if they wish it, have not been successful in finding other kinds of work. Some of them may encounter discrimination because of their effeminate appearance, and this prejudice is enhanced by the admittedly high levels of drug and alcohol abuse, assault, and robbery.

The results of both the qualitative and the quantitative elements of this study effectively indicate that violence in all its different modalities is deeply rooted in this population, both as part of their work lives as well as outside their work. One important finding is that the most common experience of violence is with police, followed by violence perpetrated by clients, and only to a lesser degree by colleagues and by people unknown to them (often youth gangs). Police frequently threaten them with guns or other weapons, threaten or perpetrate physical violence, and rape and rob them. Because violence is perpetrated so frequently by the authorities, the sex workers subsequently and quite reasonably have little trust in the legal system. Moreover, if they complain to authorities, their perception is that it goes worse for them in the streets, since the police officer or his friends might take revenge (as interviewee Rosa explained). Furthermore, while they are a growing and fluid population, transgender/transsexual sex workers are still only a couple of hundred people. The *zona de tolerancia* is small enough that the police know them and they in turn know the police officers. They recognize each other no matter how they are dressed.

The problem of police corruption and abuse is not the only reason that discourages sex workers from filing formal complaints. There seems to be a profound difference of terminology—their vocabulary does not match the vocabulary of formal complaint, even in NGO terms. Their experience has been that they find themselves turned away both by the government and nongovernmental systems. Although there may be many factors in this lack of connection to human-rights support groups, including the reported and acknowledged prejudices of gay men against transvestites ("Transfobia dentro de la comunidad Lésbico-Gay-Trans Género"), one of the concerns that future research can help to resolve is the issue of incompatible vocabularies.

Further qualitative and quantitative study is needed to create a wider picture of the problem of violence in the transsexual/transgender sex worker population. We have noted the dramatic underreporting of rape, kidnapping, and violent assault, strong language from the interviewer's perspective, but unreflective for them. Because the actions represented by these terms seem to be so much a part of daily life, these kinds of assaults are no longer noteworthy. How, we might ask, do we approach or think about reality with a group of individuals who have suffered such constant violations of their bodies that they are separated from what we consider reality? How does their trauma affect the way we theorize about them?

Police violence has conditioned behavior in ways that are of urgent importance to public health authorities. Registered sex workers are required to carry a health card and can be fined if they fail to carry it when engaging in their work. Nevertheless, interviews suggest that if a transvestite carries her card, it is taken as proof that she is a prostitute and she is subsequently arrested. If she does not carry her card, however, she is arrested for working without a license. So the question arises, why bother to go to the clinic for the exams and the stamp? Similarly, sex workers report being arrested for carrying condoms, which are taken as proof that they are working as prostitutes, so many transvestites avoid carrying them. This means that at least some members of the population, even though they understand the importance of safe-sex practices, only use condoms if the client happens to have one—a troublesome concern for pubic health workers trying to reduce sexually transmitted diseases and especially AIDS rates through safe-sex education.

Notes

The authors are grateful for research support from the following sources: the National Science Foundation, Colegio de la Frontera Norte, and Cornell University. In this chapter we use the term "transvestite" to refer to any biological male wearing clothing socially defined as female. We do not make a categorical distinction between *vestidas*, transvestites, and transgender individuals. Where distinctions exist, they are often class-related. In general usage, vestidas tend to work the streets as prostitutes; transvestites are performers in establishments or sometimes closeted middle-class men who get together in exclusive establishments or private parties to dress in female clothing; "transgender" describes the ideological position of certain educated activists. In Tijuana the individuals interviewed sometimes identified themselves as men, sometimes as transgender, sometimes as women. They were frequently confused by the interviewer's categories for gender and sexual orientation—*jotita* is a more common term for many of them. We are deeply indebted to Emilio Velázquez for conducting these interviews among a population that is deeply and rightfully distrustful of outsiders but that has known and worked with Emilio for more than twenty years.

1. All translations in this chapter from the original Spanish-language sources are ours.

2. A number of the gay bars and discos run regular advertisements in such international publications as San Diego's *Gay and Lesbian Times*, including Paradigm, Mike's, Noa Noa, Terraza, Los Equipales, El Ranchero, and El Taurino. Clients have also identified Sans Souci, Bambi, El Zorro, and Regine as locales with a high population of transvestite prostitutes.

3. An ironic side note to the controversy surrounding this ordinance was the widely reported plans to enact a similar amendment in Tijuana. The Tijuana council members backed down, however, when Tijuana transvestites threatened to reveal the names of public officials who had been their clients ("Mexican Town Cracks Down" and BBC).

4. In an earlier publication, "Border Lives," we noted the inconsistency between women's reported sexual services and the actual services they provide their clients. We wrote: "Evidence suggests that in Tijuana, as elsewhere, the most commonly offered service is the half-and-half (oral stimulation followed by vaginal sex), which most efficiently gets a client out of the room in twenty minutes" (Castillo, Gómez, and Delgado, 387). We do not follow up on this argument here, as it is tangential to the main concern of exploring the situation of the transvestites in that city.

Introduction to Chapter 2

Patricia Ravelo Blancas analyzes the work of civic organizations and the testimonies of the mothers of the murdered women of Ciudad Juárez to demonstrate how violence along the border engenders community activism. Examining the construction of grassroots organizations becomes crucial to the understanding of the nature of the politics of resistance in this violent context. Ravelo underscores the significance of emotions in the formation of political agendas and shows how the interpretation of emotions is related to the ethics and praxis of a gender-based politics. Although this chapter closely reflects the views of both concerned mothers and activists, Ravelo's main concern is the political responsibility of public institutions for their often unrestrained patriarchal bias. How can a politics be effectively conducted by suffering mothers against a patriarchal state? Are emotions a distinctive element of a female-centered politics? What is the state's reaction to this emergent activism?

Through the conversations Ravelo discusses, we become aware of both the government's and the media's continual redefinition of their views of the victims. This process points to the core of gender politics, which consists of defining in corporal terms those social subjects who are excluded from claiming fundamental human rights. Feelings of mourning, desperation, and confusion inspire these women's actions, but they also form the basis of the definition of both victim and perpetrator, which is central to the political conflict of the border region.

The emotional basis of gender politics can help us understand and reconstruct the idea of humanism in relation to the rationality of the state and media politics. That is, by insisting on the human value of a victim, emotion-fueled activism reveals the need for humanizing laws and institutions and brings to light the violent nature of the border's sociopolitical system. This humanist perspective catapults the struggle against violence from a regional or national concern to a global phenomenon. The connection between localized and individual feelings and an empathic international politics makes emotions an effective discourse for transnational cohesion. The grassroots politics that Ravelo addresses is not free of internal or external obstacles, however. As she implies in her chapter, conflicts and differences among and within advocacy groups may arise, as was the case for several NGOs over the past decade. In the end Ravelo maintains that these obstacles should not impede the configuration of a collective agenda, ultimately based on a universal discourse of human rights, which may crystallize in umbrella-like civic organizations or comprehensive citizen networks against violence.

We Never Thought It Would Happen to Us

Approaches to the Study of the Subjectivities of the Mothers of the Murdered Women of Ciudad Juárez

PATRICIA RAVELO BLANCAS

THIS CHAPTER IS BASED PRIMARILY on interviews conducted in Ciudad Juárez, from the end of 2003 to the beginning of 2004, that were compiled for a project called Social Protest and Collective Action Regarding Sexual and Gender Violence in Ciudad Juárez. Specifically, it examines the construction of subjectivities as structures of meaning. The interviewees—six mothers, one aunt, and representatives from two NGOs—have all lost a loved one to gender violence. The discussion centers on how these women are constituted as historical subjects, understanding their subjectivities as a manifestation of conflicting emotions: on the one hand, suffering, fear, insecurity, anger, and discouragement, and on the other hand, strength, dignity, courage, and endurance. The analysis focuses on the subjects' social interactions to better understand the configuration of their respective subjectivities, intersubjectivities, and sense of morality. This focus on gender and subjectivity helps us understand the recent emergence of grassroots political organizations, whose common goal is to fight against the femicides along Mexico's northern border.

Subjectivity and Maternal Emotions

The escalating violence and recurring disappearances of women along Mexico's northern border have provoked a wide range of complex emotions from those women who have lost a daughter, sister, niece, or friend. Anguish, fear, insecurity, and apprehension, among other feelings, intensify their sense of personal vulnerability and transform their sense of belonging to a collectivity. As a result of the structural inequality currently in the region, many border residents have been forced to live in poverty and have suffered discrimination and abuses of their human rights.

The violence these subjects experience in their daily life has paradoxically changed their worldview by stimulating feelings of strength and dignity as well as of resistance and willingness to fight for justice. Among them, many women have become able to think for themselves and have also begun to question authority in an attempt to transform their surroundings for the better. On a foundational level two main groups of feelings are present: on the one hand, melancholy, nostalgia, and existential crises; on the other, desperation, impotence, and the inability to explain the violence perpetrated against their daughters. Despite the diversity of individual interviewees' responses, several women rejected the lethargy and inaction that can be a product of melancholy and depression. On the contrary, these women feel mobilized and have become active.

Not all the affected families and mothers have become activists, however. Not all have become independently operating subjects or members of groups that demand justice. Although some of the participants in recent street protests in northern Mexico acted for various personal reasons, many others participated despite fear, hopelessness, distrust, and anguish. Some were involved as a result of their respective individual or collective interests, while others were simply committed to fight for social justice.[1]

One interviewee, Ramona Morales, is a member of the group Nuestras Hijas de Regreso a Casa (NHRC, Our Daughters Returning Home) and is the mother of Silvia Elena Rivera, who disappeared on July 7, 1995. On September 1 of the same year, Silvia Elena was found murdered in Lote Bravo, Chihuahua. On the participation of mothers in public demonstrations, Morales comments: "I have learned much of the suffering of the other mothers who have fought together with us, with me. Two friends that I had decided to give up because they became quite frustrated. We insist everywhere, and they ignore us. [. . .] I have worked so much, and they don't pay us any attention. [. . .] Whatever comes out, may God help us so that one day all these things are cleared up."[2] Here suffering is resignified through action—fighting against impunity—and the emotions that provoked that action. This is even more evident when what galvanizes these families is such a powerful cause: to find the true killers of their daughters and relatives. This search for truth, often resulting in partial or incomplete answers, is inspirational for border women whose loss is not experienced in isolation, but as a public, social, even globalized act.

Marisela Ortiz, another representative of the NHRC, is a journalist and the former teacher of Lilia Alejandra García Andrade, who disappeared on February 14, 2001. Lilia Alejandra was found killed a week later. Ortiz recounts how she became involved in this fight: "Unfortunately, I was just one more citizen who believed in what they said in the newspapers and that there was no way to ever solve these murders. Yes, I was estranged from what was happening. I wrote about it and criticized it, but it was not like what happened in February 2001. When Lilia Alejandra disappeared on the fourteenth of February, I only had one thought: I was sure that they had kidnapped her and that there was no hope of ever seeing her returned alive. I could not get that thought out of my head. Even so, I worked very hard to find her final location. The search time was very short because exactly seven days later, her body was located."[3] In Ortiz's case we can identify her development from being "one more citizen," uninformed and isolated from the overarching problem, to being energetically involved in political activism. Ortiz expresses her transition from exclusion to inclusion, which is also marked by the jump from writing about to participating in antiviolence activism.

While the previous examples demonstrate a strong emotional connection to subsequent political activism, this original emotional impetus can gradually fade away and diminish these women's motivation over the course of their political struggle. This is especially evident when the relationship between suffering mothers, society, and the state is distorted by official (governmental) efforts to co-opt these women's struggles. The testimony of Benita Monárrez, the mother of Laura Berenice Ramos Monárrez, who was reported missing on September 21, 2001, and whose body was found along with eight other corpses in an old cotton field in a central area of Ciudad Juárez two months later, illustrates the state's co-optation of her political struggle: "When I set myself to think about all this, [when] I decided to participate in something, I mentioned it to Rocío Urías [at the time a civil employee in the government's Sexual Crimes Unit], and she told me, 'Go ahead, Benita, go ahead.' By then I knew some other organizations were well established and had begun to request donations for the mothers of the victims, and I realized the money never arrived to our hands. I did not request money, nor do I request it now. The only thing that I request is respect for the memory of my daughter and respect for my pain."[4]

One of the most telling instances of state co-optation is evident in the label given to the murder victims on Mexico's northern border: "Las muertas de Juárez" (The dead women of Juárez). This designation has been converted into one of the elements in the chain of victimization (suffering mothers, society, state) that currently serves to sustain the mass media's dominant discourse rather than the interests of those affected by border violence. With the repetition of this label, the media disorients the population in a way that can paradoxically corrupt political action or restore validity to it. This label can actually become a mechanism of victimization because it is rehashed in public speeches that sap the slogan of its original call for social justice instead of encouraging political action. A similar process has been noted regarding the concept of femicide, since it has also been appropriated by media discourse. The process of internalization/externalization of these labels in which the mothers take the prescribed characteristics as inherent to their feminine subjectivity shows how offensive the term "The dead women of Juárez" has now become.

Rosario Acosta, the aunt of Cinthia Rocío Acosta, a ten-year-old girl who disappeared while at a playground on February 9, 1997, and was found murdered eighteen days later, reflects on the use of this terminology: "'The Dead Women of Juárez,' as they call them. This is in the end everybody's and nobody's business. It seems to me that, rather than constrain it to a particular issue, you would have to place it in a context of impunity that goes beyond the women—that is, this is a state of generalized impunity. The dead, murdered, and disappeared women come to give voice, color, and form to this generalized state of impunity that we all live in, men and women, not just the women of this border strip."[5]

Benita Monárrez gives her own interpretation of this issue from another point of view: "All this has already been handled politically, because one party as much as another is far from solving any of this. They come out saying that it's just one more death, or it's the 'Dead Women of Juárez.' They are not merely dead women from Juárez; they are our daughters, and they had names, dreams—they had everything. I think that I don't understand it now, nor will I ever."[6] The connection between suffering mothers and political control is posited here in a context of pervasive organized delinquency and illegal drug trafficking, in which impunity, insecurity, discrimination, and social conflict are seemingly ever-present. The relationship between these mothers and the government could be based on solidarity, or it could be produced by co-optation. In both cases the suffering of women functions as a means of control that is assimilated by the hegemonic discourse. That is to say, a humanitarian cause can prompt social cohesion when intense suffering becomes the subject of international interest. As women's suffering crosses cultural and geopolitical borders and blurs seemingly artificial sociocultural divisions, it reinforces human connections—mainly related to gender—in the same globalizing context that dominates the political scene.

The testimony of Evangelina Arce, whose daughter Silvia Haro Arce disappeared on March 11, 1998, is an example of this gender-centered solidarity: "Indeed, other colleagues and organizations listen to us, because when I spoke of this in Washington, when [then president Vicente] Fox said that the issue of Ciudad Juárez was already resolved, I said it was a lie because he has resolved nothing, a lady from Virginia approached me and told me: 'What can I do for you? I feel so sorry about what has happened with your daughter and that nothing has been done. If you have flyers, clippings'—it happens that the newspapers have hardly mentioned my daughter—'my name is also Silvia' [this lady from Virginia said], 'and it bothers me that they are doing nothing. What can I do here except to continue speaking of your daughter with flyers and to take what you speak or say to see what we can do?' When I was in Ireland, all the people ran up to me. They embraced me, [and told me:] 'We are with you. We didn't know what was happening in Ciudad Juárez.' They embraced me. They told me they were sorry."[7] The internalization/externalization process experienced by these women involves a wide range of emotions, but it also creates memories that form part of their value system. In this process women generate feelings, thoughts, and moral judgments that trigger their political practices.

In the case of the mothers of the women killed in Ciudad Juárez, the local society has assigned them a stereotype permeated with religious and moral prejudices. According to the dominant discourse, they must endure the burden of guilt for failing to fulfill their societal role as good mothers. The following sentiment expressed by Benita Monárrez reflects this culpability: "I believe that we all feel guilty. I think that there is not one of us who says there is no blame for not knowing how to care for my child; that I didn't know to do this. There is always a feeling of guilt."[8]

In addition to the pain of losing a child, many of these women have endured a life of seemingly endless suffering, a characteristic that has resulted in some cases in their being compared to saints. The woman is repeatedly characterized as one who suffers. The words of Norma Andrade, another member of the NHRC, underline this suffering: "They have reminded me that I still have one daughter living and wasn't I afraid that she would be murdered? They told me I should soften my tone. That was what the ministry agent who was responsible for my daughter's case told me. They summoned me at eleven at night, supposedly to give me information, but they gave me nothing when they brought me into custody to give evidence. I was at my husband's funeral, and all they wanted to give me were copies of my daughter's report. I turned around and told the officer: 'I think you could have sent me this at the funeral home. What is it that you wanted? To see me cry? Did you want to see me broken and in pain? Of course you did.'"[9]

Besides Andrade, few women have been recognized for their ability to deal with powerful political figures, demand justice, and confront the disillusionment of the border region's generalized impunity. This means that bringing together demands for social justice and women-centered political action will certainly be a long-term undertaking. There is much room for improvement, and we must keep in mind that developing a new ethics that respects the morality of political action is a difficult process. Actively participating in national and international politics requires a great deal of training, evaluation, and planning (Hierro, *De la domesticación*, 77–83).

Internal strength, resolve, and the zeal to fight against impunity and violence has changed the lives of many mothers. Paula Flores, the mother of María Sagrario González Flores, a young worker who disappeared on April 16, 1998, and who was found murdered thirteen days later, expresses many of these feelings in relation to political action: "I have learned simply that I must help myself with the little that I already know. I did not know what a community representative was; there are many legal things that I am currently learning. I learned that I do not have to remain in that hole. Working in the community helped me a lot. When it happened to my daughter, my mind was focused only on Sagrario, thinking of all the rather disagreeable things that could have been done to her, that could have happened to her, remembering her when she was small. But nothing hurt me more than [thinking] that she wanted to defend herself and that she couldn't. Nothing hurt me more than [thinking] that she couldn't [defend herself]. When I began to work in the community, it served as therapy for me."[10]

The testimony of Rosario Acosta, another mother, leaves no doubt about the political and emotional impact of the loss of a daughter: "Definitely, Cinthia's death changed my life. Cinthia's death transformed my life even when my every move and all my energy were directed at demanding that they search for her and they find the guilty party, it was more than that. It was a question of personal dignity, of the dignity of her name."[11] Their participation as subjects able to control their own history underlines both their individuality and their focus on the collective. That is, in positioning themselves within a specific social reality, they participate in the construction of emotions in which the idea of the future or of what is possible empowers these women. Justice, as a utopian project, is the principle that conditions these women's feelings and their will to fight.

The testimony of Esther Chávez Cano, director of the Centro de Crisis Casa Amiga (the House of Friends Crisis Center), redefines her militancy and her strength: "The bravery of the women who come here has made me stronger. I can withstand many things, because if they come here after having been beaten, raped, their value diminished, they strengthen me to keep on fighting."[12] We can see in this example how Chávez Cano internalizes the experiences of the women she comes in contact with through the Centro de Crisis Casa Amiga. This internalization is then transformed into political militancy, by moving from the subjective to the historical. To understand this, according to the sociologist Hugo Zemelman (24), it is important to consider three sociocultural moments that have their own temporalities and spaces: necessity, experience, and a vision of the future.

In the case of the politically organized mothers, the connection of apparently isolated crimes in a social context of marginalization and violence that has been established as a form of political and economic control creates first an immediate need for survival, but also a future need, one that also involves the elimination of any form of discrimination from human existence. This movement produces an array of emotions that can lead to other future political possibilities. It can lead to imagining a just world and a new reality. In this sense a vision of the future actually frames the possible life that is discontinuous with these women's daily reality (Zemelman, 24–25). What is currently lived is not the same as the life one wants or the life that is possible in the future.

Esther Luna, mother of fourteen-year-old Brenda Esther Alcántara Luna, who was found seven months after disappearing in 1997, offers a harsh assessment of the state's ability to administer justice: "A moment arrived when I wanted to take justice into my own hands, but I said no, we must see what the law does, although we didn't believe in these men. As I tell you, they scurried me out of the police offices, and they laughed at me. Instead of doing you justice, they mock your pain. Maybe because you're poor, they don't practice justice like they should. I have realized that of all the girls who have been lost, they are all the same way—they are poor. How is it that no rich girl has disappeared, not that I wish it on them, but why is it only the poor ones? For this reason I think and say that the evil is in the law."[13] In the case of Esther Luna, effective political practice was discouraged by the generalized impunity of the border region, not to mention the classist prejudice of the law.

Rosario Acosta, an activist with a remarkable humanist profile and the founder of the NHRC, questions the meaning of political practice in this fight and observes not only classism but also a total lack of political representation: "I decided to involve myself in this matter, as it was a question primarily of dignity and the dignity of the life and death of my niece. When I did this, I thought that all of this could change. I really believed that it was only a matter of lack of will, of people who had been there and hadn't had the will to say: 'Here, senators, change the law,' and so I did it. Not only did I do it locally, I mean in the state. I did it at the federal level and said, 'Here.' But in the chambers of the representatives as well as of the senators, they were busy with something else, with partisan politics and the simple things that they tell you there. Now, the law itself says that you as a citizen cannot promote any law, nor can you make it. You can propose it and say, 'I, Rosario Acosta, say that this should be,' but you can't promote it. You can't make it happen, so that in the end you can't do it unless there is an important force of civil society behind you that is also responsible, that feels responsible along with you that this should be."[14] For Acosta, political practice requires a collective force, an opening of individual subjectivity toward the group. This is a process previously referred to as intersubjectivity, the articulation of different subjectivities that act on an instrumental objective, through reciprocity, or even through subordination to the collective ideal. In the majority of women's organizations, however, the fight for justice has been negatively affected because cause itself becomes sublimated to political action.

Paula Flores, a battle-hardened activist for social justice, has tried to overcome pain with intense community activity: "In part, before, when cases happened, people were quiet. They handed over the body and thought that that was it. They found their dead daughter, they buried her, and that was it. But in our case, for the family, when we found Sagrario there, the fight began. Since my husband belonged to a civil association, he saw how they were petitioning the government. Since I was giving interviews, I was demanding justice and all that. At the association meeting, they asked me if I could help them to represent the community committee. I started to think because in Poleo [the name of the community] we didn't have electricity, and I thought about the risks taken by the other girls who worked at night. That was when I got involved and accepted the job of president of the community committee."[15] Here we can see how pain leads to political action that is aimed at resolving the needs of a specific group. This awakening of consciousness provides the tools that make change possible in the community.

Norma Andrade for her part highlights how, when viewed from an international perspective, this social struggle challenges the government to fulfill its treaty obligations: "I told [President] Fox that we weren't ignoring him, that we were hoping that he would put things in order. There are instances that could obligate him. They signed some treaties for the eradication of violence against women and torture. Just as they can go to The Hague, we have the right to demand that these courts condemn my government for allowing this to happen. I told him, as a show of goodwill, that if you wish to resolve this situation, you would have to start by dismissing those government employees who have been working there and have been accused of murders in Ciudad Juárez."[16]

Andrade's political action reveals the construction of an intersubjectivity specifically through her repeated references to justice, an idea molded to the attitudes espoused by representatives of the political hegemony, from the lowest-level state employee to the president of the Republic.

These women are aware of their human rights, internalizing the local and national versions and projecting them onto the international stage. Although their political action originates in feelings of pain and loss, women like Norma Andrade look to transcend this purely affective dimension by turning emotions into political action. Some have even based their activism on denouncing and attempting to restructure current political strategies in order to obligate the state and mainstream society to first recognize and then eradicate widespread impunity.

Loss and Impunity

The loss of a loved one often leads to the internalization of complex emotions and the intensification of a mother's perceived deficiencies, which can powerfully alter her affective links. This loss produces a deep pain that can drown out her existence. Only by facing this loss can a woman shed the yoke of suffering. This outlook allows us to view loss in political terms because it reveals the fragility of a woman's affective nexus. If a mother remains frozen in a state of melancholy and drowns herself in depression, she will lose her sense of vitality. However, if anger and indignation take over her subjective structures, she is more likely to take action. As women internalize feelings of hopelessness and injustice, they begin to confront an ineffective judicial system, not only understood as an intolerable abuser of authority but also as a system that promotes exclusive and discriminatory policies (Suárez, 7).

Evangelina Arce considers the disappearance of a child the saddest experience one could ever endure. She reveals the feelings of hate produced by injustice: "It's hatred, anger; it's a great pain that one feels in not knowing where your loved one is, of losing a daughter without knowing where she is, where to find her. And to see the injustices done in the special prosecutor's office. The government, those who perform the investigations, [say] that everything is solved. It's a lie, for me it's all a lie—because they are doing nothing. I think that it is very sad and painful to lose a person and not know where to find her. Like I told all of my companions, you know where to see your daughter and I can't. It is the saddest to have a disappeared daughter and to not know where she is."[17]

Benita Monárrez explains the uncertainty and anxiety that she experienced when her daughter disappeared and how she felt when her daughter's corpse was found: "Who do I go to? Where do I go? What do I do? 'Go home'—the officer told me—'we need to wait seventy-two hours before we can take the report of a disappearance.' And I asked what else could I do? Where else I could turn? Because you think that this will never happen to you. I felt very sure about everything, and seeing all this made me feel like the most insecure and destitute woman. They called me on the phone, and they told me: 'We have found some bodies, and it looks like [one] might be Laura's. We need you to come and talk with us.' I think that this is when you begin; it is the most suffering feeling—there is hopelessness in not knowing where she is."[18] Esther Luna describes the hopelessness, rage, and impotence provoked by injustice: "Like my husband says, I felt like taking justice into my own hands, but how? One doesn't have the means to pay for that, even if they were to find the guilty ones and give them life in prison, so they could never do this again. You feel a rage, a hopelessness, an impotence."[19]

In another instance, Norma Andrade experienced denial when she learned of her daughter's death: "When we found my daughter's body, first there was denial. I said, 'It's not true, it's not here.' When we were mourning her, I was saying, 'It's not my daughter, it's not Alejandra. She was thinner, she had a longer hair.' Not until they took the lid off of the coffin for me in the mausoleum was when I said, 'I can't keep on denying it.'"[20] Paula Flores also recognized that the loss of her daughter grieved her heart, but when her daughter was found murdered, she dealt with the situation by rationalizing it: "We went out to the street to look for her. I saw my daughter's face in every girl's. One time they told me that they had a girl on the bridge, and they just passed her. I saw some of Sagrario's features in her and I went running and running, but when I got there, she wasn't her. I felt so deeply that I was going to see her. I didn't know if I even ate. I knew nothing; I only wanted to find Sagrario. When we found Sagrario [her corpse], the fight began there."[21]

Ramona Morales also speaks out of sadness and hopes that all this violence against women will be stopped. By focusing on the collective, she shows the possibility that other mothers may avoid the same pain: "I felt a lot of sadness that my only daughter would have died in this way. They may never return our daughters to us, but at least they have to stop all this so that other mothers do not suffer like we have."[22] Meanwhile, Rosario Acosta reflects on the emotional puzzle found along the border, which overlaps life and death, certainty and uncertainty: "The funda-mental feeling is the need to know that it is death for sure. It is rather terrible, all the feelings—anguish, uncertainty, the need to be certain, even when that certainty means death. It is a feeling totally impossible to put into words. It is a feeling that saps you bit by bit and destroys your faith, your physical condition, and your existence. You finally want with all your heart the certainty of death to arrive, to pass from the lethargy of anguish to mourning. It is so unexplainable at times to put it into words that necessarily you have to wait years to come to an explanation. It is like hoping for something and not wanting to acknowledge that preferably that *something* is death. That you would prefer to find that spent body and that life ended in a given place, from a given deed, and then go on to something else. That certainty of death can become a need during the uncertainty that the disappearance [of a loved one] can mean."[23]

The emotions produced by the loss of daughters and relatives are inevitably linked to a sense of impotence and the lack of justice; to the lack of a rational explanation for the disappearance of a loved one; and to the subsequent impunity of those who committed the crime. These are complicated feelings coming from a subjective dimension that are difficult to understand rationally. But what is it that these women have in common? Indeed, they have all lost someone of value while living in an ineffective political system. There seems to be nothing that can eradicate this system of impunity, especially when civic action is obscured by a stig-matizing and exclusive moral system in which society implicitly blames the mothers and families for the victim's death. This only feeds their guilt and results in a type of self-flagellation.

The Inexplicable

A thought commonly expressed in the interviews, and evidenced in the quotations included in this chapter, is consistently reiterative: "We never thought it would happen to us." Such a phrase seems to show that a per-son's idea of reality is not constituted solely by his or her own lived experi-ences, but by the experiences of others as well. Perhaps fear prevented these women from internalizing their own individual reality, or perhaps the struggle for survival of daily life played a part. Regardless, although women search for rational explanations for the tragedies that have afflicted their lives, they find no such certainty.

The thoughts of Josefina González recreate the atmosphere in which she lived after the disappearance of her daughter and establish a moral system in which mothers are primarily responsible for their daughters' well-being: "Well, since Claudia disappeared, I have advised the girls that come here, but they don't pay attention to me. It's worthless for me to advise the mothers if they don't care for their daughters. I never thought it would happen to me. From 1995 on I have known about the murders. Then my girls were young, and I said: 'Those poor mothers.' We never thought it would happen to us. I warned my girls, and they were quiet, as if they weren't paying attention. Well, then God may help the mothers. . . . I watched the TV, and I said I wasn't going through that, as many mothers were. When Voices Without Echo [an organization of mothers founded in 1998 by Paula Flores and her family] marched, I never thought [I would ever be in that situation], the idea never occurred to me, but I never called them old whiners. On the contrary, I said, 'Poor mothers they came from so far away to have their daughters murdered.' There was one from Veracruz whose boy was killed, and through all this, I never thought for one moment that the same thing would happen to us."[24]

Ramona Morales also thinks that the mothers must take better care of their daughters, although she recognizes that if her daughter were to "end up badly," she would accept it: "My husband and I could not sleep. I thought that she [our daughter] had gone away then with a guy. A lady, a clairvoyant, asked me if I would receive my daughter as she might come. I told her, 'Yes, I would receive my daughter with all my heart, however she might come.' I never imagined that she would be found dead. I thought that she had gone away with a guy or she had ended up badly, right? Whenever I meet the children of my friends, I tell them: 'Be very careful.' To the mothers I would say, 'Take care of your daughters. If they are in school, well, go with them. Take them there and don't let them walk alone, because here there is much danger. [Do it] so they don't suffer like we did when we lost our daughters.'"[25]

Norma Andrade reiterates a previously mentioned theme by claiming that she never imagined the violence would affect her life: "I never thought that they would kidnap her from me. I did not see the news, and I did not watch TV. I had my stories [soap operas]. My husband said I wore rose-colored glasses. My daughters were everything to me. This was when I was working outside the city. When I come here, I am with my students and the news doesn't grab them at all. I knew that there was violence, the violence worried me, but on a general level, I didn't care at all, even about intrafamily violence, because it did not occur in my house. I knew that [this violence] was there through my students, but I never felt that it was something that would affect me directly. I never thought that they would steal her from me."[26]

Paula Flores never thought that she would undergo this same trauma. She had other expectations for herself and did not feel implicated in this climate of violence. Nevertheless, she feels troubled by the pervasiveness of this dangerous situation: "I never thought I would come to this, you know? I never watched the news, or read the newspapers. On the TV, I would watch the news, but I would change the channel quickly. I didn't know about what was happening or about these things. Nevertheless, even in my hometown in Durango, over there, the rumor arrived that here in Juárez girls were being killed. There were serious crimes. When my sister-in-law invited us, I got to thinking that same thing: 'It would not happen to us.' I never mentioned to my daughters anything about that [the murders]. When we arrived here [in Juárez], I asked my sister-in-law why they killed the girls. She told me that they got into strangers' cars. Then I started taking Alicia to primary school. I took the precaution to take her directly there along with her little friends and to go get her and to look after her until she got to school. I still thought to myself that if somebody grabbed a girl, she wouldn't be able to defend herself alone."[27]

Rosario Acosta describes the knot of confusion and the torment of everyday life under these conditions: "You begin to put together a series of things and circumstances in your mind that allow you to follow along or to remain in a primary state of hope. This is like going from less to more, depending on the time that passes. With this you can live or survive at least one week, just telling yourself, 'She is coming right now, right now somebody will call you with good news, right now somebody will bring her.' There is confusion, an error. The first thing that comes to mind is to say: 'This has passed through my mind many times. I've seen it on the television, on the posters in the street, but to me it can't be happening.' You begin to exclude that possibility that it might even end in tragedy. When the days pass, you begin to equip yourself with more tools that can allow you to continue waking up, to keep sleeping, and to continue existing. You say, 'Well, good, she hasn't come yet, no one has brought her yet, no one has called yet.' From there you begin to think that something could have happened to her."[28]

These sentiments are submerged in the incomprehensibility of such violence. Women do not understand why someone has murdered their daughter or relative, and there is no moral or rational explanation that can appease them. The only survival mechanism that they possess that can help cope with this violence is the repetition of their stories. By converting their individual stories into a collective discourse, these women can reshape suffering into political action. They also have to confront the misogynist culture in which these deeds are to understand the patriarchal moral system that dominates their actions. This is a consciousness-raising process that will take time to develop given the border region's deeply rooted discriminatory and sexist societal practices.

Final Reflections

The subjectivities of all these women have been irreversibly altered by the conflicting emotions produced by the loss of a loved one. As we have seen, this conflict can lead to direct political action that is in turn represented via media outlets across the globe. Today we must be alert to manipulation by those powerful groups that control the mass media (see Héctor Domínguez-Ruvalcaba's chapter in this book), for they dictate how and in what way both violence and political action are portrayed. As the ethnographer Roger D. Petersen (3) has reminded us, action drawn from emotion may be simplistic, but this does not reduce its value.

Following Petersen's analytical approach, this chapter considered objective reality by exploring the world of emotions, understood as mechanisms that work to transform predominant societal structures. This transformative process is evident in the mothers and representatives of nongovernmental organizations when they demand the nightmare of everyday life end, that their city be a safe place again, that basic necessities be satisfied, and that ingrained systems of discrimination and impunity be terminated. This chapter's theoretical direction considers subjectivity and personal experiences as constituent elements of human consciousness within a patriarchal culture. This is a culture that is permeated (consciously or unconsciously) by elements of misogyny, domination, and sexual and gender oppression. These characteristics have made possible a reevaluation of the feminist project of autonomy of women and men, as proposed by the anthropologist Marcela Lagarde, as a way to attain gender democracy, ethical political participation, and social justice.

The knowledge extracted from individual subjectivities and lived experiences shows the inner workings of broader social knowledge, as has been discussed by the feminist philosopher Susan Sherwin. It is important to know how and why these movements are enacted by the waking of (or coming to) consciousness.[29] Women can gain a sense of self-consciousness by sharing both lived experiences and emotional responses. When they reflect on their emotions, they can analyze how their experiences gain meaning. This meaning is grounded in historical, racial, and patriarchal identity categories and requires interpersonal connections. These connections, established through shared emotions and political action, will eventually give way to a new ethics that can transform truth and justice from fleeting dreams to a concrete reality.

Notes

This chapter is dedicated to the memory of Graciela Hierro and to Marcela Lagarde, my life teachers. The results presented in this chapter form part of a wider investigation that was funded by the Consejo Nacional de Ciencia y Tecnología (CONACYT) and sponsored by the Centro de Investigaciones y Estudios Superiores en Antropología Social (CIESAS). I thank Rosario Acosta, Norma Andrade, Evangelina Arce, Esther Chávez, Paula Flores, Josefina González, Esther Luna, Benita Monárrez, Ramona Morales, and Marisela Ortiz, who kindly granted us interviews. I also thank Héctor Domínguez-Ruvalcaba and Ignacio Corona for their insightful commentary. Translations in this chapter from the original Spanish are by Derek Petrey and Joseph Pierce.

1. For more information about these protests, see Ravelo Blancas, "Entre las protestas callejeras," 21–32.

2. "Pues he sabido mucho de los sufrimientos de las demás madres que han luchado junto con nosotros, conmigo. Dos amigas que tenía [dijeron] que ellas ya no quisieron saber nada porque se desilusionaron por completo, ya no quisieron saber nada, porque anda y anda y no le hacen a uno caso [. . .] tanto que he andado y no le hacen caso [. . .] pues no, quien quite y que Dios nos ayude un día y se aclaren todas estas cosas."

3. "Desafortunadamente, yo era una ciudadana más que creía en lo que decían los

periódicos y veíamos que no había manera de solucionar los asesinatos; sí [era] ajena a lo que estaba ocurriendo, escribí acerca de ello y hacía una crítica pero no era similar a lo que ocurre en febrero del 2001. Cuando desapareció Lilia Alejandra el 14 de febrero no tenía otro pensamiento, estaba segura de que a ella la habían secuestrado y no tenía esperanza de que la volviéramos a ver con vida y no me podía quitar ese pensamiento de la cabeza. Aún así, trabajé muy duro para dar con su paradero. Fue muy corto el tiempo de búsqueda porque exactamente 7 días después fue localizado su cuerpo."

4. "Cuando yo me pongo a pensar en todo esto yo decido participar en algo, lo comento con Rocío Urías—en ese entonces funcionaria de un área de la Unidad de Delitos Sexuales del gobierno—y me dice: adelante Benita, adelante. Ya algunas otras organizaciones que ya estaban bien establecidas, que sé yo empezaron a pedir donaciones para las madres de las víctimas, como se ha dicho siempre, primero, que nunca llegó a manos de cada una de nosotros. Yo no pedía dinero, ni les pido, lo único que pido es el respeto a la memoria de mi hija y el respeto a mi dolor."

5. "'Las muertas de Juárez,' como les llaman, ese es un asunto de todos y de nadie, finalmente. A mí me parece que esto habría que, más que encerrarlo, habría que ubicarlo en un contexto de una impunidad que va más allá de solamente las mujeres. Es decir, este es un estado de impunidad generalizado, no solamente por el hecho de las mujeres. Las mujeres muertas, asesinadas y desaparecidas vienen a ubicar o a darle voz y a darle color y darle forma a este estado de impunidad de manera generalizada que vivimos todos y todas, no solamente las mujeres en esta franja fronteriza."

6. "Todo esto ya se ha manejado políticamente, porque tanto un partido como el otro, no sé, lejos de darle un resultado a todo esto, ellos salen con que es una muerte más o 'Las muertas de Juárez.' No son muertas de Juárez, son nuestras niñas y tenían nombre, tenían su nombre, sus ilusiones, tenían todo y creo que yo no lo entiendo ni nunca lo voy a entender."

7. "Sí, la oyen a uno las otras compañeras, otras organizaciones, porque ahora en Washington cuando yo hablé de eso, cuando dijo Fox que ya estaba resuelto lo de Ciudad Juárez yo le dije que era mentira, que no estaba resuelto nada, se arrimó una señora de Virginia . . . me dice: 'qué puedo hacer por ti, yo siento mucho lo que ha pasado con tu hija y que no se haya hecho nada, dijo, si tienes volantes, recortes—Mi hija casi nunca ha salido en el periódico—,yo también me llamo Silvia [continuó esta señora] y a mí me duele mucho si no están haciendo nada, qué puedo hacer yo acá para poder seguir hablando de tu hija con volantes y sacar lo que tú hablas o dices para ver si así podemos sacar algo.' Ahora que estuve en Irlanda, toda la gente corría, me abrazaba, estamos contigo, 'nosotros no estábamos enterados de lo que está pasando en Ciudad Juárez.' Me abrazaban, me decían lo sentimos."

8. "Creo que todas nos sentimos culpables. Creo que todas . . . no hay una que diga que no existe esta culpa de yo no la supe cuidar, yo no supe hacer esto, siempre hay una culpabilidad."

9. "Me han dicho que me queda una hija viva y que si no tengo miedo que me la asesinen, me han dicho que le bajara a mi tono. Eso me lo dijo la agente del ministerio que estaba encargada del caso de mi hija, que ya no está. Me citan a las 11 de la noche,

según ellos para darme información, no me daban nada cuando me llevaron detenida a declarar. Yo estaba en el funeral de mi esposo y todo lo que querían era darme copias del expediente de mi hija, yo voltee y le dije a la fiscal: creo que me lo podías mandar a la funeraria, qué era lo que querías: ¿Verme llorar? ¿Querías verme doblada y dolida? Claro que sí."

10. "Yo he aprendido simplemente que debo de capacitarme a lo poco que ya sé. Yo no sabía qué era un representante de una comunidad, muchas cosas legales que ya las voy conociendo. Aprendí que no debo de quedarme en ese hoyo. Me sirvió mucho trabajar en la comunidad. Cuando pasa lo de mi hija mi mente estaba enfocada nomás en lo de Sagrario, pensando puras cosas desagradables que le pudo haber hecho, que le pudo pasar, recordándola de chiquita. Y pero más que nada me lastimaba mucho eso de que ella quiso defenderse y no pudo, pero más que nada me lastimaba mucho eso y no pudo. Cuando yo empiezo a trabajar en la comunidad, me sirvió de terapia."

11. "Definitivamente la muerte de Cinthia cambió mi vida. La muerte de Cinthia transformó mi vida, yo aún y cuando la fuerza mayor de cualquiera de mis movimientos y de cualquiera de mis acciones pudieran estar encaminadas a demandar que se buscara y se encontrara al responsable, iban más allá, era una cuestión de dignidad, de dignidad personal, de dignidad en nombre de ella."

12. "El valor de las mujeres que vienen aquí me ha hecho más fuerte. Puedo resistir muchas cosas porque si ellas vienen aquí después de haber sido golpeadas, violadas, minimizados sus valores, me dan fuerza para seguir continuando la lucha."

13. "Llegó un momento en el que quería hacer justicia con mis propias manos, pero dije no, hay a ver qué hace la ley, pero no, nosotros no creemos en esos señores. Como le digo, me llegaron a correr de las oficinas de la policía, y se burlan de uno, en lugar de hacerle justicia, se burlan del dolor de uno, será porque uno es pobre, que no ponen en práctica la justicia como es debido, yo me he dado cuenta de que todas las muchachas que se han perdido son de la misma calidad de uno, de pobre, cómo no se ha perdido una rica, que tampoco se lo deseo pero, por qué nada más a uno de pobre, por eso yo pienso y digo que el mal está en la ley."

14. "Yo decidí enrolarme en este asunto que era una cuestión eminentemente de dignidad y de dignidad por la vida y la muerte de mi sobrina. Cuando yo hice eso pensé en que todo eso podía cambiar, creí verdaderamente que era falta de voluntad, de gente que ya había estado ahí y que no había tenido la voluntad de decir: 'aquí está senadores, modifiquen la ley,' y así lo hice. Y no solamente lo hice localmente, quiero decir en el estado, lo hice a nivel federal. Y dije, aquí esta, pero en las cámaras, tanto de diputados como de senadores, están ocupados en otra cosa, en pugnas partidistas y en cosas que sencillamente te dicen así. Ahora, la misma ley te dice, tú como ciudadano no puedes impulsar ninguna ley, tampoco lo puedes hacer, puedes proponer y decir: 'yo Rosario Acosta digo que esto debería ser,' pero tú no lo puedes impulsar, tú no lo puedes avanzar ahí, para que finalmente que no puedes, a menos que detrás de ti esté una fuerza importante de sociedad civil, que también esté responsable, se sienta corresponsable junto contigo de que eso exista, de que eso avance, a menos que detrás de ti esté una fuerza ciudadana importante que se sienta parte de un problema y de una solución."

15. "En parte, lo que pasa es que antes cuando pasaron los casos como que la gente se quedaba callada, les entregaban un cuerpo y creían que ya terminaba todo, encontraban a su hija muerta la sepultaban y ya. Pero en el caso de nosotros, la familia, cuando encontramos a Sagrario ahí empieza la lucha, cuando nosotros la encontramos a ella. Como mi esposo pertenece a la asociación civil y veía cómo les reclamaban al gobierno, cómo es que daba yo entrevistas de los medios y exigía justicia y todo eso. A mí en la reunión de la asociación me pidieron por qué no les ayudaba a representar el comité comunitario. Y empecé a pensar porque en el Poleo no teníamos electrificación y me puse a pensar en el riesgo que corrían las otras hijas que trabajaban de noche y entonces es que yo me involucro y acepté trabajar como presidente del comité comunitario."

16. "Yo le dije a Fox que no lo habíamos brincado, que esperamos que ponga un poco de orden, hay instancias que lo pueden obligar. Firmaron algunos tratados para erradicar la violencia contra las mujeres y la tortura. Así como ellos se sienten en la libertad de ir a la Haya, tenemos el derecho de exigir a esas cortes condenen a mi gobierno por permitir lo que se permite. Yo le dije a él, como una muestra de buena voluntad, que si usted quiere resolver esta situación habría que empezar por destituir a los funcionarios que ya tiene trabajando aquí y que ya están acusados de asesinatos en Ciudad Juárez."

17. "Es odio, coraje, es un dolor muy grande que siente uno al no saber dónde está su ser querido, que pierde uno una hija sin saber donde está, dónde encontrarla. Y ver las injusticias que hacen en fiscalía especial. El gobierno [dice que] que ellos siguen las investigaciones y de que todo está arreglado, eso es mentira. Para mí todo es mentira porque ellos no están haciendo nada. Creo yo que es muy triste y doloroso perder a una persona y no saber a dónde irla a visitar. Como yo le digo a las demás compañeras, ustedes tienen a donde ir a visitar a su hija y yo no tengo, y es mas triste que tener a una hija desaparecida y no saber a dónde se encuentra."

18. "¿A quién me acerco? ¿A dónde voy? ¿Qué hago? Váyase a su casa—me dijeron en la fiscalía—necesitaba pasar 72 hrs para que lo podamos tomar como desaparición. Y yo me preguntaba que más puedo hacer a dónde acudo qué hago. Porque uno piensa que nunca le va a suceder uno eso. Yo me sentía muy segura de todo y viendo todo esto me sentí la mujer más insegura y desvalida. Me llaman por teléfono y me dicen: hemos encontrado unos cuerpos al parecer es el de Laura y necesitamos que venga a hablar con nosotros. Creo que es la parte donde empieza uno, en el mayor sufrimiento y la desesperación de no saber dónde está."

19. "Como dice mi esposo, con ganas de tomar uno justicia con sus propias manos, pero de qué manera. No halla uno la manera de cómo pagar esto, de que ya encontraran a los culpables y que les dieran cadena perpetua para que ya no hicieran ese mal. Una rabia que siente uno, una desesperación, impotencia."

20. "Cuando encontramos el cuerpo de mi hija primero fue la negación, de decir no es cierto, no es, cuando la estábamos velando yo decía no es mi hija, no es Alejandra. Ella era más delgadita, tenía un cuello muy largo. Hasta que me la destapan en el panteón que ya la van a bajar es cuando digo: 'no me lo puedo seguir negando.'"

21. "Salíamos a la calle a buscarla, en cualquier muchacha yo veía el rostro de mi hija. En una ocasión me dijeron ahí en el puente que tenían una niña y que la acababan de

pasar y yo le vi las características de Sagrario y yo me fui corre y corre, pero ya cuando llegamos no era. Yo llevaba dentro del corazón que ya la iba a ver. Yo no sabía si comía, no sabía nada, yo nomás quería hallar a Sagrario. Cuando encontramos a Sagrario ahí empieza la lucha."

22. "Sentí mucha tristeza que siendo mi única hija, muriera en esa forma. A nuestras hijas ya nunca nos las regresan pero, cuando menos, que se parara todo esto para que las demás madres no sufran lo que uno ha sufrido."

23. "El sentimiento primordial es la necesidad de la certeza de la muerte. Es muy terrible, todos los sentimientos que se relacionen sobre todo con la angustia, con la incertidumbre, con la necesidad de una certeza, aún y cuando ésta sea la muerte. Es un sentimiento totalmente inexplicable a las palabras, es un sentimiento que acaba y merma poco a poco tu fe, tu condición física y tu existir, porque finalmente deseas con todas las fuerzas de tu corazón que llegue esa certeza que puede ser la muerte, para pasar de ese letargo de la angustia al duelo. Y es tan inexplicable a veces, te digo a las palabras que, necesariamente tienen que pasar a veces años para que puedas tratar de explicar. Es como esperar algo y como no querer reconocer que ese algo es preferiblemente la muerte. Y que prefieres ubicar ese cuerpo y esa vida ya consumida en un lugar determinado, en un hecho determinado, y de ahí pasar a otra cosa, pero se llega a convertir esa certeza de la muerte en una necesidad durante esta incertidumbre que puede significar la desaparición."

24. "Bueno, desde que desapareció Claudia yo les aconsejo, muchachas que vienen aquí, yo les decía, pero como que les valía. Pues ya para qué les digo a las mamás, no las cuidan. Porque yo nunca pensé que me iba a pasar eso a mí, porque desde el 95 para acá miraba, mis hijas estaban chicas y decía, pobrecitas mamás. Nunca pensamos que nos iba a pasar a nosotros. Y yo a las muchachas las aconsejaba y sumisas, como que me ignoraban. Ya por eso, bueno pues Dios que las ayude a las mamás . . . . Yo miraba la tele y decía, yo no estaba pasando por ese momento como muchas mamás, cuando andaba Voces sin Eco [organización de madres fundada en 1998 por Paula Flores y su familia]. Yo nunca pensé, nunca se da una idea uno, pero yo nunca decía 'viejas gritonas.' Al contrario, decía, 'pobrecitas mamás de tan lejos venir a matarle a sus hijos.' Que ya ve que el niño que mataron de Veracruz, y todo eso, yo nunca pensé, ni por aquí me pasó que íbamos a pasar por lo mismo."

25. "Yo y mi esposo nos desvelábamos. Yo pensaba que se había ido pues con un muchacho, y una señora, clarividente que va uno y me dijo que si yo recibía a mi hija como viniera y yo le dije que sí, que recibía a mi hija con todo mi corazón, como viniera, pero yo nunca me imaginé que fuera a aparecer muerta. Yo pensaba que se había ido con un muchacho o que había salido mal, ¿verdad? Yo siempre que me encuentro niñas que son de mis amigas, 'Pues cuídate mi niña.' A las madres yo les diría, 'Que cuidaran a sus hijas, que si están en la escuela pues, que las acompañen, que las traigan y que no las dejen andar solas porque aquí hay mucho peligro, para que no sufran tanto como nosotras al perder a nuestras hijas.'"

26. "Yo no veía noticias, yo no veía televisión. Yo, mis cuentos. Mi marido decía que vivía en un mundo color de rosa, con mis hijas y nomás. Esto fue cuando trabajaba fuera

de la ciudad. Cuando vengo aquí, estoy con mis alumnos y las noticias no las agarraba para nada. Sabía que había violencia, me preocupaba la violencia pero en general, pero todavía ni siquiera violencia intrafamiliar, como en mi casa no se daba, ni siquiera esa. Sabía que la había como en mi caso con mis alumnos. Yo nunca lo sentí como algo que me afectara directamente. Nunca pensé que me la fueran a secuestrar."

27. "Yo no pensé llegar a esto, ¿verdad? Yo nunca veía noticias, no leía periódicos. En la televisión veía noticias y luego luego le cambiaba. No estaba enterada de lo que pasaba ni de esas cosas. Sin embargo hasta allá, mi pueblo en Durango llegaba el rumor de que aquí en Juárez se mataba a las muchachas. Había crímenes. Cuando a nosotros nos invita mi cuñada yo llegué a pensar que no nos fuera a pasar lo mismo. Yo a mis hijas nunca les comenté nada de eso. Cuando llegamos aquí cuestionaba a mi cuñada. Yo le preguntaba por qué mataban a las muchachas, ella me dijo que se subían a carros de desconocidos. Y para ese entonces yo traía a Alicia que iba a la primaria y tenía la precaución de ir a encaminarla con sus compañeritos y de irla a recoger y divisarla hasta que llegaba a la escuela, pero yo dentro de mí pensaba que si alguien agarraba a una niña, pues ella no iba a poder defenderse sola."

28. "Empiezas a armar como una serie de cosas y de circunstancias en tu mente que te permitan seguir o permanecer en un estado de esperanza primario, porque esto va como de menos a más, dependiendo del tiempo que transcurre. Y bueno, con esto puedes vivir o sobrevivir yo creo que una semana, con este hecho de decir: 'ahorita viene, ahorita alguien habla, ahorita alguien la trae.' Hay una confusión, hay un error; lo primero que se te viene a la mente es decir, esto ha pasado por mi mente y por mi cabeza muchas veces, pero en la televisión, en posters que he visto en la calle, pero a mí no me puede estar pasando. Empiezas a excluirte de esa posibilidad, que además termina en una tragedia. Cuando más van transcurriendo los días, empiezas a armarte de más herramientas que te puedan permitir seguir amaneciendo, seguir durmiendo y seguir existiendo, y dices bueno, ya no vino, ya nadie la trajo, ya nadie llamó, y de ahí pasas a pensar que algo le pudo pasar."

29. In another work I return to the proposal of Graciela Hierro on the process of construction of consciousness. For further information, see Ravelo Blancas, "Aportes para una epistemología," 14–19.

Part II

*Audiovisual Representations
of Gender Violence*

Introduction to Chapter 3

By analyzing the images of violence constructed by diverse local and binational television broadcasts, chapter 3, by Héctor Domínguez-Ruvalcaba, argues that television commodifies violent events, which are brought to a marketplace of emotions. Furthermore, the representation of violence functions as an instrument of manipulation in the ideological and political struggles between interest groups, like those comprised by entrepreneurs, politicians, religious organizations, media consortia, and civil organizations. As studied with respect to print media in chapter 5, by Ignacio Corona, the representation of violence on television also reveals the ways political interests are deployed in the public sphere, which is one of the factors that reproduces a violent culture.

In this arena the issue of the city's public image, a valuable commodity for politicians and the economic elites, becomes a central debate that echoes previous intellectual controversies about the marginality and cultural value of the border region as a whole. On the one hand, media in the Ciudad Juárez–El Paso area usually support a conservative view when it represents violence as a symptom of the decadence of patriarchy. On the other hand, local media campaigns suggest that the community should develop a strategy of self-defense because the state no longer seems to be able to control the use of violence against citizens or hold the so-called monopoly of violence. This means that the audiovisual media actually helps to solidify the idea of a general state of terror, which far from helping to reduce violence, instills fear in the population about their use of and interaction with public spaces. This in effect leads to surrendering the city, which is then perceived as a place of collective risk and danger.

CHAPTER 3

Death on the Screen

Imagining Violence in Border Media

HÉCTOR DOMÍNGUEZ-RUVALCABA

IN AN ARTICLE PUBLISHED in the cultural magazine *El ángel* in March 2005, Eduardo Antonio Parra, a novelist known for his depictions of Mexican criminal environments, considers that violence is essential to the country's history, that Mexicans have been exposed to it and have practiced it since the pre-Columbian era, and that most of their cultural expressions show an attraction to violent images and events. According to Parra, Mexicans enjoy violence when reading it in history and in fiction and even when dancing to *corridos* about bloody events and watching television news programs. For Parra, national identity is enacted—and delighted—in representations of violence. However, when violence is experienced in one's life, this fascination evolves into fear. Hence, we can distinguish two forms of violence: one that is represented, whose effect is fascination, and one that is experienced, which produces fear.

Beyond the enjoyment of the "México bárbaro" ("barbarian Mexico") that Parra suggests, the border stages fear in daily life; it allows people to experience disorder and crisis: a destabilization of the social and cultural order. In this climate of fear, border media depicts the border space as a concrete site where violence is experienced as a continuous series of disturbing events every minute of the broadcasting clock. Violence is a bloody spectacle where the border's inhabitants play the role of either perpetrators or victims. This chapter argues that media representations of violence in Ciudad Juárez imply a dispute over the city's image in which strategies of control and the domination of television are visible when focusing on this perpetrator-victim community.

The Image of the Border

Disputes over the image of the border have constituted a major public issue beginning with Mexico's postrevolutionary literature, in which the idea of the North as a place of primitive culture and people is related to the revolutionary assaults and the elemental way of life in the region. Intellectuals like José Vasconcelos and Salvador Novo, among others, propagated the idea that the border fringe was uncivilized and therefore should be marginalized from the modern Mexican nation. Yet in the 1980s we saw this same criterion of civilization in the intellectual debates about this region fostered by the Programa Cultural de las Fronteras (Castillo and Tabuenca, 19).

Borderland writers—who congregated in Hermosillo, Ciudad Juárez, La Paz, and Tijuana—rejected depictions of the Borderland and its inhabitants, the "Borderlanders," as barbaric and uncontrolled, as centralist Mexican critics (Carlos Monsiváis, Néstor García Canclini, Carlos Fuentes, for instance) and even Mexican American writers (Guillermo Gómez-Peña) had proposed at one time or another. In those debates one of the main proposals of borderland writers was to destereotype such depictions of the border as its supposed lack of national identity or "authentic culture." Today, it seems that border television and national and international networks continue to dispute the border's image in terms and contexts that can overcome the existing frame of nationality with globalization and transnational migratory movements.

It can be argued, however, that the image of the border as an uncultured and marginal dimension can fulfill the Mexican cultural identity that Parra proposed. If the border is part of the fascination with violence, then showing the border as the place of daily fear is nothing but the reiteration—or better: an extrapolation—of a fatalistic imagination that has been present in the Mexican arts and intellectual sphere practically throughout the country's entire history. The center and the margin is no longer a fundamental question, since the border is no longer a marginalized element in sociopolitical processes, but the problematic center that generates contradictory realities. Being a site of concomitances and disparities, the border is a scene where differences and inequalities deploy the symbolic and material contents of contemporary history (Rosaldo,

635). We can summarize this process in terms of the denationalization and reconstitution of a multiple and continually changing collectivity (Hardt and Negri, 60).

At present, the contradictions regarding the question of the border's image are no longer problems solely disputed in literary and intellectual debates. Rather, the battlefield about this image has been displaced from lettered environments to the mass media–consuming public. This broader public context provides the border image with other connotations than the ones that nourished writers' discourses. On the one hand, this recontextualization invokes questions related to globalization, immigration, and postnationality, rather than insisting on the problem of belonging or not to a national culture. On the other hand, questions about self-representation and representations produced from so-called nonborderlanders introduce the problem between national and transnational positions that restructure the arena that allows this dispute. If, as we discuss in this work, violence is overrepresented in the border media, narratives of abuse, crime, and insecurity depict the catastrophe of national integrity and the reconstitution of the collectivity in terms of a mediated community, to rephrase what the communicologist Jesús Martín-Barbero (25) has called the mediated city—that is, the city deployed on the television screen. It means that television produces and distributes identities of violence.

Regarding identity, the border has been imagined, on the one hand, as the site of contamination (that place where the cultural devastation of the global empire corrupts nationality), and, on the other, as the site of cultural enrichment by the process of hybridization (see the work of Néstor García Canclini, Gloria Anzaldúa). Both images overcome national and local cultural boundaries. The questions I want to pose against the grain of these corruption or hybridization theories will be the ones that the media suggest to the public at large: Is violence produced by the immigrant's hybrid culture? Is sexual violence related to the general propagation of global hatred? If so, can we interpret violent events as symptoms of a broader social crisis that is produced not on the border, but in a larger geopolitical scenario?

I focus on the moral-political debate implicit in some television programs from the El Paso–Ciudad Juárez area and then contrast that debate with representations from the national networks from Mexico and the

United States, attempting to grasp the meaning of sexual violence in the media. If television produces and disseminates images, then broadcasting can be thought of as the core of the cultural and political processes where violence plays a central role. The voices of the community, experts, and authorities referring to violence are subjected to the technologies of media entertainment.

Patriarchal Concerns

Two groups of crimes nurture border television: on the one hand, the kidnapping and killing of women, domestic violence, and rape; and on the other, gang-related violence and executions related to organized crime. Violent events have their root, according to television's perspective, in the general decadence of values, which we can interpret as a crisis of patriarchal principles. The literary critic María Socorro Tabuenca (418, 420) has pointed out that representations of female victims in the campaign undertaken by the Dirección General de Policía (the General Office of the Police) in 1995 were based on a common assumption that takes for granted a patriarchal ideology to explain violence as a response to women's transgression of the patriarchy.

The moral content of this common sensibility is reiterated in the television campaign Ponte Viva, broadcast on local television between 2001 and 2002. In one of its ads, Ponte Viva addressed its male viewers, those charged with protecting women as part of their moral duties in society. This campaign invokes the archetype of a superman who defends the "weaker sex." The female speaker says: "Fathers, brothers, male teachers, take care of your women," using a possessive adjective to indicate their dominion over females. According to the scholar Norma Pecora (63), in the narratives of supermen, masculinity is characterized as benevolent, powerful, controlling, confident, competent, and successful. These attributes are supposed to entitle men to a privileged role in the efforts to solve cases of abuse against vulnerable women. Misogynist violence must be fought with violence. Ponte Viva suggests a male-centered value system that reduces crime to a dispute between males over the bodies of women. With this patriarchal view the Ponte Viva campaign commands the population to self-defense against the criminals, which implies that the state is no longer responsible for society's security.

The Aesthetics-of-Violence Broadcast

Women's self-defense is the main topic of another ad in the same campaign. It prescribes how women should dress, what they should do, where they can go, and even proposes the idea of inducing vomit in case of sexual assault to discourage the rapists. Empty streets and unwatched spaces are the stages of Ponte Viva. This desolate urban landscape depicts the absence of the state and the proliferation of perpetrators lying in ambush. In Ponte Viva, both the state and would-be murderers of women are not considered the addressees of the campaign. This separation recognizes the existing conditions of impunity and places the responsibility of solving the situation on patriarchal values.

Ponte Viva summarizes the politics of fear that border television seems to disseminate in the following terms: (a) if women's victimization is a symptom of the patriarchy losing control of women, then it is crucial to reinvigorate the male's responsibilities of domination; (b) violence should be fought with violence, which is validated as a coercive endeavor that proposes a violent moral system; (c) this coercive morality of violence is understood as a masculine commitment to confront perpetrators and as a feminine responsibility of self-defense; (d) provided that the population is entitled to exercise defensive violence, the state's role in this aspect is exempted; (e) the perpetrator is a subject to be punished and the community is in charge of determining who is the perpetrator. If, in fact, it is recognized that state institutions are losing control, the community should develop the ability to define, detect, intervene, and prosecute those subjects prescribed by the media as perpetrators.

While border media seems to generate a highly participatory community, its promoted consensus undoubtedly constitutes what the late scholar Susana Rotker (7) called "citizenship of fear," which is defined as a violent, self-defending community. It could be argued that building a society of fear is not the expressed will of local television. In fact, the main function of television should be, according to the logic of the consumption of images, the saturation of aesthetic experiences (Jameson, 11). Values represented in the abundance of violent images, rather than undermining the asymmetry in the roles of males and females in misogynist violence, induce a paralysis of any political project intended to fight terror. Seemingly, the ideology of punishment is not questioned, leaving unexamined the propagation of hatred in border society. By failing to challenge these structural generators of violence, the media coincide with the agenda of patriarchal supremacy and the ideology of criminal-ization, supporting propaganda of terror and oppression in the name of security.

As television broadcasting depends on the mass production of repre-sentations of violent events, especially in news programs, the audience is forced to focus on the quantifiable recurrence of violence in society. Our analysis of border news aims to find the fictional form of violence in its reiteration on television. In the same way in which the historian Hayden White (9) has observed fictional structures shaping one's account of his-tory, we can find in television news the rules of fictionalization that make sense of the proliferation of violence. Media serves as a mediator between an event and its reception. It is this mediation that we consider the appa-ratus for imagining violence; it structures the perception of these events and provides the public with a sense of the implications of killing. Being the producers of the social consensus is in fact the principle element of media hegemony.[1]

In border narratives the predatory sexual attack is an omnipresent form of killing whose monstrous image is embodied by a man who abuses women. Both the victim and the perpetrator are protagonists in the nar-rative that represents our image of reality. Beyond the naiveté of the melodramatic extrapolation of the evil and the innocent, we can explore the web of power relations that are manifested when images of violence come to the screen. This apparatus of power allows us to conceive of the media as a "vehicle for hatred" in the way that the philosopher Paul Virilio (13) has defined the pervasive destructiveness of techno-science.

Mass media are not apolitical or amoral; rather, it is a machinery that conceives society: the concepts of media society or commercialized culture (Jameson, 206), the mediated city of Martín Barbero (25), and the society of consumption of García Canclini (29) have been some of the terms proposed to describe this politics. If media constructs society through this interrelation of violence, which is a product of consumption and fear, then hate is constituted within the politics of the media market. What kind of politics is the one based on the propagation of fear and hatred? Is there any supporting rationale for hate? What is the role of the media in this politics? If, according to the philosopher Renata Salecl

("Worries in a Limitless World," 105), a speechless, hateful act is one form of communication, then we are confronted with a new breed of sexual politics that is inseparable from killing. Rape becomes a practice of war, a way of establishing sovereignty, the ultimate act of domination. What sexual violence reveals is a practice of domination that makes visible a power relationship whose battlefield is the sexualized body. We have to admit that the difficulty of knowing the political sense of killing is the absence of a discourse that articulates hate.

Because we cannot determine who is the subject of most crimes against women in Ciudad Juárez, we cannot make any assumptions about his or her sexuality. Our only position toward this drama is to interpret the remains of the killing action. News programs use the remains, incomprehensible residuals projected on the imagination of both television producers and the receptor. That very moment of signifying the scarcely recognizable corpses exacerbates the anxiety, which is the engine of the melodramatic imagination. Although the identity of the perpetrator is protected by the clumsiness of the investigations and the proliferation of hypotheses of who are the actual killers of women in Ciudad Juárez, the image of fear—and its precariousness translated into insecurity and the threat of disappearance—is propagated in civil society by the media.

Hence, the remains of victims of sexually abusive crimes are metonymies of the border population to which they belong. The effect of this metonymy is that the spectator can be included along with a number of possibly imminent victims. There is a political resource of the representation of violence that has to do with the communality of the stories of killing. This rhetoric consists of representing the community with the corpses and produces a document that evidences the possession of a reality, in the form of macabre fetishes, which in this case is a commodity consumed by the mediated society.

Television news programs reach a large daily audience. In their visual content we can find the most impressive images that record furtive moments of violent actions: fights between gangs, shootings, and panicked screams. These images are the most precious visual products for the audience and the television companies. Extraordinary events of daily life are reiterated to the point that they become the expression of the ordinary to the eyes of the audience. Violence is highly profitable in the emotional industry not only as a commodity, but also as a symbolic product in political and moral discourses. In short, these images are key instruments in the machinery that consolidates neoliberal hegemony. How is it that the violent events that plague border inhabitants and the profitable images that follow can be instruments of neoliberal ideology? In its passage from the local to the national and the transnational media, we can distinguish the different agents that are struggling to impose their meanings—that is, their power of representation.

The Politics of Precariousness

The news programs of Channel 56, the local branch of the Televisa consortium in Ciudad Juárez, are structured under a polyphonic feature by which the editors assign a role for each social actor in a violent narrative. Leaders of civil organizations accuse, suspect, and denounce; victims and witnesses are perturbed and imprecise, thus the television anchors of the program disqualify them; official authorities make defensive statements; experts are invited to the opinion segments to fulfill the role of moral-cognitive authority. The entire population seems to fit on the screen. The news program represents the community with this gesture of convening different sectors of society to a public forum.

During the first week of November 2004, Channel 56 news reported that two girls had been murdered. Investigations had not produced results at that time, but the authorities offered their conjectures to the public. Officials at the Department of Justice of the State of Chihuahua suspected that the parents were the murderers in one of these cases, based on the fact that they did not find traces of sexual abuse on the victim's body. "It is frustrating to have good intensions but not to be able to accomplish them," said the director of the Justice Department to a Channel 56 reporter, referring to the shortage of resources that prevents the police from performing their duties effectively. The authorities' official statement attempts to explain their ineffectiveness, allowing their investigation to function as evidence of the precariousness of public service. It also serves to create scapegoats, who are constantly revealed as these murders go to trial. In this way the institutions of justice can dictate who the murderer is to circumvent more strenuous investigations.

One such scapegoat was depicted on screen during the early weeks of November 2004, close to the third anniversary of the discovery of eight female bodies in a cotton field located near an industrial area of Ciudad Juárez (November 6 and 7, 2001). In addition to the horror of this tragedy, the subsequent investigations are suspected to have been faked via the invention of scapegoats. Gustavo Meza, known as La Foca, and Víctor Javier García Uribe, known as El Cerillo, were accused of these murders. Their trials were full of irregularities, with evidence of torture purported by the media. La Foca died in prison during a minor surgery and García Uribe's attorney, Mario Escobedo Anaya, was reportedly killed by seven undercover agents of the Policía Judicial under dubious circumstances in February 2002. In a Channel 56 special report that aired on November 8, 2004, El Cerillo insisted on his innocence.

Very often, local television news produced in El Paso suggests the inability of public security forces in Juárez to combat misogynist violence. In *Noticieros Univisión*, El Paso's Spanish-speaking news program, in a report on La Foca's case, just days before his murder, his attorney declared that the state government was protecting corrupt police agents. Similar statements were broadcast by Channel 9 in El Paso in March 2002 in a report on the organization Friends and Relatives of Killed Women, positioning criticism of police corruption and criminal activities as the main preoccupation of antiviolence activism. The staging by local television of these cases confronts local media with the statements of officials who argue that El Cerillo had confessed his guilt. It is evident that the Policía Judicial cannot make reprisals against television. This fact implies a restatement of the notion of hegemony.

According to Ernesto Laclau (Butler, Laclau, Žižek, 53, emphasis in the original), understanding the notion of hegemony in the globalized present needs "to move from a purely sociologistic and descriptive account of the *concrete* agents involved in the hegemonic operation to a formal analysis of the logics involved in the latter." If this is so, we must penetrate the logic of the hegemonic operation of media instead of reducing our scope to the description of corrupt activities of the police. *The police kill attorneys to maintain their particular version of the murder* is a statement unquestioned by the public, or at least the voice of the authorities appears doubtful to the public. Therefore, the media is hegemonic when it demonstrates that its statements are convincing when confronting authorities' declarations. The media claims to represent a specific community, its procedures are constitutive of the social consensus, which consists of generalized views of how to perceive violence—that is, who is defined as perpetrator and who is considered a victim.

Hegemony is not precisely located in the statements of government agents or organizational leaders, much less in the hesitation of victims and witnesses when talking to the cameras, but in the role of mediation by anchors and guest experts, who perform the censorship that creates and propagates social consensus. This censorship molds the city's image through an excessive visual documentation of crimes. By this allegorical process (the images of killing are equivalent to the city's image), we find a paradox that characterizes local television: on the one hand, its visual content is saturated with macabre iconography, and, on the other, it sanctions official opinions, academic research, and those voices that denounce and propagate their knowledge of violence. Television functions according to the logic of the sensationalist market, but it also validates the pertinence of the different expressions produced in the public sphere. This double frame of representation exposes the television's strategy for constructing its hegemony: (a) television is saturated with narratives of fearful events, producing an image of the city as a site of terror, which demonstrates that security is precarious; (b) security institutions are conceived, paradoxically, as enemies of security, an idea directly related to the obsolescence of the nation-state model; (c) the voices of the authorities are subsumed to the consensus sanctioned by media; and (d) media are then the dispositive for imagining a community that will "restratify and transcend the nation" (Sinclair, 56).

What then becomes the role of the voices of community leaders and the general public regarding violence that is represented in media? While the nation-state is disregarded as the guardian of security, the plural motion of the multitude is organized under the command of desiring security (Hardt and Negri, 60, 66). Not only do media orchestrate this social desire, but they also create a community based on it. The population is represented in the news of Channel 56 in three different ways: (1) as witnesses or victims of crimes as represented in short interviews conducted by street reporters, (2) as callers in live sections where the anchors receive and comment on input from the audience, and (3) as perpetrators—or alleged perpetrators—detained in the police station or in prison.

We can observe these different representations, the different roles assigned to specific actors, in the reports and commentaries related to the case brought against José Luis Montes, in October 2004. In the neighborhood of Colinas de Juárez, public transportation does not complete its regular route after dusk because of the area's insecurity. José Luis Montes was wandering the streets under the effects of cocaine and alcohol after a fight with his homosexual partner. Montes followed an adolescent female who had to walk a longer distance to her house because of the limited bus service. She knocked on a few doors, but the neighbors did not come out to help her. In her despair, she unknowingly ran down a dead-end alley to escape. In the street interviews transmitted on Channel 56 news, some neighbors admitted that they had heard her cry out but did not intervene because they thought it was a couple fighting, implying that they would not help in cases of domestic violence. Others called the police, but the agents arrived too late. A young man who was walking in the area saw Montes having sex with the already dead body of the victim. He subdued Montes until the police arrived.

"The police say that they cannot go further because the gangs don't allow them to. There is only one patrol for all this sector," explained one woman who lives near the crime scene. This discourse of defenselessness dominates in street interviews. Most murders have witnesses, but the climate of insecurity and the ineptitude of public security forces often discourages them from speaking out. Instead of filing complaints in police offices, they use the media to speak out. The local television news programs become the public arena where criminal issues are disputed. Television is taken as the substitute for the courtroom. The public is a massive plaintiff; the anchors refer all complaints to a deaf authority or simply reiterate commonsense principles, a melodramatic morality that is nurtured by the claim of being victims. Manuel Gómez, one of the Channel 56 anchors, is emphatic with calls out to the citizens to "rescue Ciudad Juárez." But what does rescuing the city mean in terms of concrete actions? Is Gómez calling on society to fight gangs and murderers and neglecting—even criminal—police agents? Is he calling on politicians to propose effective actions to recover security?

When news anchors forcefully address the public, when they call for action, they speak before an abstract multitude that can be defined as lacking citizenship—that is, lacking guarantees, access to law, social services, and many of the benefits that the state is supposed to provide.

Television functions as a wall of lamentation, a forum where the multitude manifests and even proves that no real democratic action is possible. Personal testimony takes the form of an expression of grievance, an individual recrimination rather than that of a fight against the pain of loss. In the series of short interviews in the Colina de Sol neighborhood, the speech act becomes a fatalistic depiction of defeat: public force is not acting, there is no community to prevent the crime, there is no leadership that seeks to reconstitute citizenship. Rather, all actors that have witnessed or indirectly allowed the murder Montes committed can be considered, like him, a perpetrator. Defining violent society in these terms leads to the general erosion of democracy. Melodramatic mood turns out to be an overwhelming diatribe. The aesthetics of television news in Ciudad Juárez propose that pain is a symbolic act of violence that repeals any political ideas aiming to recover community. Then the media's slogan "rescuing Ciudad Juárez" does not imply any political sense but represents a pale cosmetic that cannot dissimulate the multitude's immersion in a climate of terror.

How is it possible that news broadcasting, with such broad public participation, especially evidenced by those citizens who call the live programs, is not a means of democratization, but that of a fatalistic consensus? The excess of representation consists of being overwhelmingly present in the daily life space and the fact that there is not any force—either from the state's institutions or from civil society—capable of fighting the proliferation of crimes. Common sense, the ideological horizon that provides sense to the audience's speech, cannot simply be referred to as popular wisdom, but also as a pervasive conscience of horror.

Phrases like "disturbed subject attacks a woman," "terrifying screams of a woman," and "excessive crime" indicate the impossibility of understanding the motives of such violence. Going beyond the harmonious transforms violence into something illegitimate that gets expelled from pertinent discourses. The incomprehensibility of violence, expressed as it exceeds the line of senses (what makes sense, what is meaningful, what is sensual), reaches the level of the unspeakable. It poses the idea of "Evil as ethical," where failing to recognize or understand the sense of violence becomes a social duty (Žižek, *Tarrying with the Negative*, 47). When the audience views television, a perplexing web of insoluble horror is weaved throughout, making stronger the impediment to true knowledge.

This impediment to understanding the violent acts does not mean that television refuses to show the voice of perpetrators, but that their voices are incomprehensible. José Luis Montes was interviewed on a special program broadcast in November 2004, on Channel 56 news. "Let's understand what was in the mind of Montes," Manuel Gómez says. Then the screen shows a close-up on the face of the murderer. The audience scrutinizes Montes's gestures, but also his social class, his race, and even his "problematic" sexuality that cannot be categorized with one specific identity, but only as an execrable pathology. He is not presented as homosexual, but as a man who had an affair with a homosexual. He cannot love or be loved because he is a necrophiliac. This depiction of Montes implies that he can only be known as a monster, as an "other," as a nonsubject, unable to make sense of his actions. But Montes speaks, trying to deal with his hesitation and the panic of the scene. He is like a beast in a cage, trapped there as the star in this spectacle of horror. His voice trembles:

Montes: I thought I could seduce her. I started doing well: "Where are you going? Where do you live? Can I accompany you?'"and so on. . . . She slapped me, and in the moment that I tried to grasp her hand, she got mad. I remember she asked me not to bother her. Immediately after saying that, she started to call out to the neighbors. I think this was one of the causes that forced me to subdue her. There was a person a block beyond. . . . She continued to scream asking for help.

Reporter: But you strangled her, and then you sexually attacked her.

Montes: Everything was at the same time. I wanted to cover her mouth, and I told her not to scream, but it did not happen. I pulled her hair, but she did not stop screaming. I thought I better leave her there and run away, but I was afraid.

Reporter: Why so cruel? Why asphyxiate a person?

Montes: I myself don't have a clue. It may be like you say. Maybe because of the problem I had with the other person I had just seen before this happened. I guess so. When I followed her, I was thinking about seducing her. Truly, I don't know why I deceived myself. It had been a year since I had sex with a woman, and I never thought I would do something like that. . . . I did something unforgivable.

After this interview a psychologist analyzes Montes's words to offer the public a profile of the homicide: "a low self-esteem," "deficiency or absence of values," "a sexual disorder where the subject is satisfied through controlling the situation," "this is the beginning of a psychopath."

The pertinence of the expert in the media, according to the historian Michel de Certeau, consists of his ability to translate ordinary language. The expert's specialized discourse is an authoritative action that validates, evaluates, and puts the ordinary language into another context, so it can make sense in the scientific discourse (de Certeau, 11–12). When the expert speaks, the ordinary subject becomes an object of science. In the psychologist's explanation of Montes's actions, we can recognize that we will never be able to understand the reasons that contributed to the perpetration of this violence, but we confirm our preconception of the violent subject. This preconception is actually a strategy to introduce a moral judgment. The expert condemns not only Montes, the assassin, but also the category of males that he represents.

Mirna González, a Channel 56 anchor, then comments: "When we see this man, who was a construction worker, we cannot imagine how many like him are out there . . . he had been with his homosexual partner before." Low social class and nonhegemonic sexuality are suggested as factors that produce violence. With these portrayals, Channel 56 does not propagate the need to understand the subjective processes that produced the crime but rather the lynching of certain social categories—an ethics of Evil, if you will. By blaming the "other" subjects (lower class, homosexual, immigrant, and so on) for the production of violence, television blames one supposedly pathological social group for the city's bad image. Pathologizing the other is a process that creates scapegoats out of marginal subjects.[2] When the bishop of Ciudad Juárez expressed, regarding the May 2005 murder of another girl, "go out from Juárez, we don't want you here," he implied that the assassins could only be foreigners. For the oligarchy, the government, an important sector of academia, and the media, the city's image (destroyed by those "others") is the main concern that should be considered by the good citizens of Juárez.

Defending the city's image is an omnipresent slogan in all the local television broadcasting. But what image is defended? Who is concerned with this defense? In the program Patricio contigo (Patricio with you), produced by the Chihuahua state government until December 2004, the governor insisted that defending the city's image is society's priority. Officials and entrepreneurs say that the local economy suffered because of the stigma of violence. Two controversies help us to understand the political background of this image issue. The first occurred in 2003, regarding the song "Pacto de sangre" (Pact of blood) by the Mexican American band Los Tigres del Norte, where, like the Ponte Viva campaign, there is a summons for men to protect women against evil. The second controversy occurred in 2004, when the local chamber of commerce protested against TV Azteca for broadcasting the soap opera *Tan infinito como el desierto* (As infinite as the desert) and a series of special reports on violence in Ciudad Juárez.

Local consortia invited the population to boycott the Salinas Pliego Corporation, which owns TV Azteca. Taking care of image is a main concern of a market-ruled society. Local television uses violence to nurture the emotional market, to produce a politics of hate against those who represent the "other" for the local hegemony, and to censor the representations of violence that other agencies produce. We have seen campaigns against journalists like Sergio González Rodríguez and Diana Washington, whose work has accused such mainstream groups as local entrepreneurs, officials, and police agents of participating in illicit activities. Inconformity with external researchers, film makers, artists, and popular singers (like Los Tigres del Norte) has to do with the kind of perpetrator those social actors represent: they do not coincide with the segregating and hating profile of the murderer as portrayed by Juárez's hegemony.

National and international voices have produced a large number of works depicting a circle of victimization that emerges within the process of globalization: a vision that interprets violence in Ciudad Juárez in terms of economic and cultural turmoil, where the act of killing is part of a structural phenomenon. *Juárez: The Laboratory of the Future* by Charles Bowden (1998), *Señorita extraviada / Missing Young Woman* (2001) by Lourdes Portillo, *Huesos en el desierto* by Sergio González Rodríguez (2002), and more recently *La batalla de las cruces* by Rafael Bonilla and Patricia Ravelo (2004) and *La cosecha de mujeres* by Diana Washington Valdez (2005), are some of the pieces that have been blamed in local media for disseminating a negative image and therefore victimizing the city.

Even though this defense of the city's image is a discourse that unifies

Juarenses against the foreigners, creating a motif of local identity, there is a common denominator between the outsiders and the locals: both coincide when pointing at the police and the corruption of the justice system for being a key factor in the proliferation of crimes. This is not, however, a coincidence in all of their terms. Since July 2003, the strong presence of federal security forces reproduces the local-outsider conflict that presents the federal agents as the bad police. Although the audience is allowed to denounce the abuses and negligence of police agents on a daily basis, these voices are neutralized and even disavowed by officials who pronounce statements that represent the official truth. In the same way that experts impose the authoritative devaluation of the multitude, governors, police directors, mayors, and other officials make statements meant to recover the city's good image. This fact reveals that the city's image is nothing but a question of having the privilege of telling the truth.

Chihuahua's government, local entrepreneurs, and the Juárez media agree in their defense against the outsiders' accusations leveled at the local officers. They neutralize their charges, arguing that what happens in Juárez is also happening everywhere else. Media discourses have globalized the violence. It happens here and everywhere: that means the Borderland is not the only killing machine. It is hard to reject that statement because evidence can be found in many parts of Mexico. However, preventing Ciudad Juárez from being stigmatized does not improve its image. Spokesmen from local, state, and federal governments, entrepreneurs, and a broad sector of the population say that the treatment of femicides by the media is irresponsible. This opinion points out an excess of visibility of the violence. Although the governor Patricio Martínez (1998–2004) was concerned about this image of the city, the media persisted in presenting those images, ignoring the government's will.

Imagining the Perpetrator

The main contrast between local television and national and international networks has to do with the image of the sexual criminal. Ciudad Juárez's channels broadcast detailed interviews with the murderers, as in the Montes case. The channel hosts criminologists and psychiatrists whose knowledge portrays the criminal and his environment as the city's marginalized west side. The criminal's point of view is analyzed with a therapeutic condescendence; they come from the westside shantytowns, they are immigrants from the South, drug users, and uneducated people. There is a consensus among the media on locating sexual crimes in the spaces inhabited by the *maquiladora* workers, gang members, prostitutes, and countercultural groups. The west side is a region of an unrooted multitude. The sexual predator is an enemy who does not speak or think: he is not considered human.

In the show *Tan infinito como el desierto,* broadcast by TV Azteca in the summer of 2004, police officers are portrayed as insensitive, negligent government officials, and women as their inevitable victims. Local news constructs the image of sexual offenders with characteristics of the marginal "other," detaching the "real Juárez" from the inhuman immigrant. TV Azteca points out the corrupted and premodern *machista* public forces, referring to the notion of "México bárbaro," the barbarous Mexico. In its special reports on Ciudad Juárez, TV Azteca argues against the state institutions of Chihuahua. Local channels often complain that the national network aggressively threatens local society. National television is associated with the centralist politics of intervention in borderland affairs. The discontent against immigration from the South, a xenophobic and racist local compulsion, on the one hand, and the centralist criticism of the barbarian northern politicians, on the other, has drawn two different versions of the public enemy.

The violence of Ciudad Juárez has been portrayed on international networks, making sexual killing a concern of the transnational audience. *El show de Cristina,* one of the most popular television programs on Univisión, in 2003 presented a panel with mothers of victims and leaders of organizations protesting against the victimization of women. Corpses in the desert, women crying, vibrant music in the background—such is the sequence that starts the talk show. The speed of the pictures multiplies the corpses, creating a dizzy sensation of excessive reality. In such ways the action of demanding justice is placed in the most visible arena of public life. Nevertheless, the addressee of complaints is absent. It is important to underline that this program invokes a collective and abstract tribunal. The television anchor is a mediator between the public and the plaintiffs. There is an irrefutable truth: the principle of melodrama consists of the statement "the victim is right." Acting on the stage of daily spectacle, a stage where melodrama produces the dominant moral values, allows victims to perform the role of political actors. They proclaim the divorce of the nation-state from the civil society. Either crying or scream- ing, all those interviewed point to the police agents as the perpetrators of sexual crimes.

The hypothesis of the police tends to diminish the legitimacy of the nation-state's structures, questioning their effectiveness, while the hypoth- esis of the marginal criminal tends to relate poverty to criminality. In both cases studied in this chapter, the murderers presented in the media are still imagined as extraordinary individuals and not as competent social actors. With conceptions like these, the media magnifies, damages, and stigmatizes particular subjects, preventing the audience from knowing the structural factors that propitiate the climate of terror in which the media itself plays a central role. According to the scholar Marcela Suárez (7), impunity is not only an effect of corrupt government, but also a result of these segregating politics of the media. Considering this analysis, we can conclude that violence has not only emerged in the chaos of corrup- tion and poverty, where the migrant and the unrooted multitude play out their pathological hate. Rather, we have to admit that the representation of the real in the daily dynamics of the media is one of the main factors contributing to the general condition of fear that defines contemporary border society.

Notes

I thank Aura Avila for her help collecting data for this chapter.

1. According to the political scientist Giovanni Sartori (78–79), television is currently the most effective mechanism for inducing and conducting public opinion, strongly con- ditioning the government's decisions.

2. I do not mean that Montes was falsely accused of being a killer, as in the cases of La Foca and El Cerillo, but that violence is not performed only in the marginal sector. Rather, violence is a process of hate production that spans from the privileged to the vulnerable: the upper classes to the marginal, from men to women, from heterosexuals to homosexuals, from police to civil society, and so on.

Introduction to Chapter 4

In this chapter María Socorro Tabuenca Córdoba analyzes how the victimization of women in Ciudad Juárez is represented in recent Mexican films. As with other chapters in this book, Tabuenca's work addresses the problematical representation of violence and its cultural and political implications. Her arguments help us understand the way patriarchal values are disseminated through the film industry. Based on the examination of three films, Tabuenca explores the process of representation on which the border's patriarchal culture is formed. She considers two main features of patriarchal society: (1) that such a society is constructed around a masculine figure and (2) that it is constructed around the family.

In both cases Tabuenca points out the failures of traditional views to offer a response to the problem of violence. Films plotted around the masculine figure exalt the police as a central actor, whose heroic performance will save society from bad men who kill women. In contrast with the opinions of most Mexican advocacy groups and the relatives of victims of femicide, these masculine-plotted films back the position of authority figures who justify ineffective investigations by blaming femicide victims for their own deaths, citing an exogenous violent population, and by relying exclusively on official police criterion for their investigations. As Tabuenca notes, intelligence and the capacity for action are reserved for male characters, while women are typically characterized as passive and dependent on men. Films plotted around the family emphasize the conservative view that crime is a result of the deterioration of traditional values.

It is important to underline the contrast between the depiction of a corrupt and indolent police force (as offered in chapter 2 by the mothers and activists interviewed by Patricia Ravelo Blancas) or that of homophobic abuse by Tijuana policemen (alluded to in chapter 1 by Debra A. Castillo, María Gudelia Rangel Gómez, and Armando Rosas Solís) and the selection made by Tabuenca, which focuses on low-budget films and aims to describe the conservative values that are transmitted to working-class audiences. This same view is present throughout the mass media, in television, as discussed in chapter 3 by Héctor Domínguez-Ruvalcaba, and in newspapers, as discussed in chapter 5 by Ignacio Corona. Tabuenca's particular selection of films does not imply that the film industry has been predominantly conservative, however. Feminist and nonfamily-centered works have been produced, including documentaries mentioned in her chapter and such U.S. films as *Bordertown* (directed by Gregory Nava, 2007) and *The Virgin of Juárez* (directed by Kevin James Dobson, 2006), where the investigation of femicide is conducted by women and the fight for human rights is the expressed purpose of the film.

Representations of Femicide in Border Cinema

MARÍA SOCORRO TABUENCA CÓRDOBA

> Representations . . . do not simply copy the world, they produce
> *versions* of it. Consequently, representations are involved in the
> *production* of a version of the world. They do not simply copy it.
> A further position is reached when it is maintained that the repre-
> sentation is centrally involved in the *construction* of the world.
> —Elaine Baldwin et al.

IN RECENT YEARS violence has been a topic of growing public and academic interest across disciplines and geographic boundaries.[1] One reason
for this is that the mass media saturate the public with violent images
from all over the world. The philosopher Alejandro Tomasini Bassols
(36) has described this constant bombardment as a distinctly modern
development: "There is perhaps a sense in which the great technological
revolution of our times gave a new face to violence and has gradually
modified our attitude toward it. . . . The cultural ideals that are promoted, the symbols for the masses, are certainly of violent beings, not of
gentle beings."[2] It seems that violence becomes less and less astonishing
by the day. Still, we are shocked to find out that students, ex-Marines, religious fanatics, or lonely vagabonds have fired weapons against children in
schools, patrons of restaurants, and groups of people in shopping malls,
or that someone has strategically detonated a car bomb in a crowded
market place. Hearing about the victims of pedophiles, rapists, or serial
killers is also undoubtedly disturbing. But most people quickly forget or
compartmentalize these violent events because they are considered foreign, part of a different world, despite the fact that many of us (including
myself) inhabit reputedly dangerous cities.[3]

The Pervasive Image of Violence

Violence permeates our lives whether through the media or lived experiences. But even in recent years, when certain sectors of society have shown that they are fed up with this violence and have begun to study its causes and possible solutions, it seems that we have at the same time become immune to violence and many times justify its perpetrators.[4] The scope of this violence is sometimes overwhelming. It is present at home, at school, on the streets, in the workplace, in government offices, and so on. The medical doctor Alberto Concha-Eastman (38) has described the pervasiveness of violence in contemporary society: "Violence is exercised by the fathers who abuse, beat, and humiliate their wives and children; the youths who leave home and join gangs to rob, rape, assault, or kill; the members of organized crime who mug, assault, and murder; those who traffic drugs . . . especially in urban centers; the state and the police who violate human rights; the public functionaries who abuse of the rights of citizens soliciting their help; and, in extreme cases . . . the guerrillas and the paramilitaries. . . . The conduct of corrupt politicians, leaders, and governors who are directly or indirectly enriched by the coffers of the state erode the ethics, norms, and the culture of coexistence."

Despite Concha-Eastman's extensive catalog of violence, in everyday life it seems that we are still unable to perceive or acknowledge all of its various shapes. Our exposure to violence is now so commonplace that we actually normalize and naturalize it. Examples of these processes include state-sponsored violence, domestic violence, and gender-based violence—acts that are so rooted in our society that sometimes we fail to even notice their existence. After analyzing violence and its repercussions across many different cultures, Tomasini Bassols (31) has concluded, "It would be most prudent to affirm that there is a sense in which violence is co-substantial to man, that is to say, that it has to do with a way of being of the human being, thanks to which he can, occasionally, solve problems."[5] Unfortunately, Tomasini Bassols's idea is essentialist and seems to affirm that there are few alternatives for humankind than to solve its problems through violence. Although I do not agree with this, Tomasini Bassols does offer a useful proposal that may help to explain how, along the U.S.–Mexico border, violence has been naturalized in recent years.

For the past fifteen years two types of crime have made Ciudad Juárez a staple for local, national, and international media: (1) the kidnapping, rape, and sexualized serial killing of women (femicides) that currently sum more than five hundred victims; and (2) the cyclical violence perpetuated by drug lords and members of organized crime, whose victims include drug traffickers as well as innocent bystanders.[6] It is under the latter category that we would include the news that a clandestine cemetery containing seven bodies had been discovered by the Mexican police and the U.S. Drug Enforcement Administration (DEA) in 1999, another site where five bodies were discovered in an exclusive neighborhood in 2004, and two other mass graves with thirty-six and nine bodies, respectively, found in March 2008. These stories have elicited a response from state and local authorities and businesspeople wishing to cleanse the image of Ciudad Juárez.[7]

Cities along the U.S.–Mexico border garnered a reputation for vice and lawlessness beginning with the tumultuous geopolitical separation of the two nations in 1848. This characterization was exacerbated by the role border towns played during Prohibition in the United States (1920–33) and was continued with the Bracero Program (1942–64), which imported thousands of migrant agricultural workers from Mexico to the United States. The collective weight of these historical events, combined with the current state of overwhelming impunity that plagues the border region, has eroded the area's identity and cultural production. The apparently inexplicable nature of border violence has caught the attention of artists, writers, and journalists who have traveled to Ciudad Juárez from all over the world to film documentaries, write poems, plays, novels, and articles; to set up installations; to organize performances; to design Web pages; and so on.[8] They have done whatever they felt necessary to stop this violence, and it is within this vein that the current chapter continues.

Film Realities

This chapter analyzes the imagery and discourse that represent Ciudad Juárez and its inhabitants in three Mexican films that take femicide as an important thematic element. The films are *16 en la lista* (16 on the list) by Rodolfo Rodoberti (1998), *Pasión y muerte en Ciudad Juárez* (Passion and death in Ciudad Juárez) (2002) by Javier Ulloa and Luis Estrada, and *Espejo retrovisor* (Rearview mirror) by Liza di Georgina (2002). My interpretation of these films takes into account the way in which a violent discourse constructs the images of possible victims, their perpetrators, and the urban spaces where crimes are supposedly committed. I also analyze how certain images can legitimize, perpetuate, or contest stereotypes. The main focus is to investigate how the reality of femicide is reconstructed in these films. This chapter is part of an ongoing research project, and some of my reflections have been presented or published previously.[9] My interpretation of these films is by no means impartial, for I have been living in Ciudad Juárez for almost forty years. My experiences there, my readings, and my position as a middle-class feminist scholar all influence my academic stance. I would like to add that my interest in writing about the femicide in Ciudad Juárez represents a humble tribute to the women and children who have died and continue to die in my city.

In terms of my methodological approach, I base much of my interpretation on the framework provided by the sociolinguist Norman Fairclough in *Language and Power*. Fairclough proposes a critical study of language that reveals the connections between language and unequal power relations. In this chapter I also analyze the connection between language and image. Fairclough's methodology helps us understand how little we value the meaning of language, both spoken and visual, in the production, perpetuation, and variation within power relations, and how the exercise of power is achieved through ideology—in particular, through ideological uses of language and image. With this in mind, I look at the language in use and the use of language as producer of our daily realities. I pay special attention to the way images, dialogues, silences, and voice-overs are intertwined.

I also consider sociologist Stuart Hall's theoretical account of how messages are produced and disseminated in his well-known essay "Encoding/ decoding." Hall's ideas support my analysis because he also identifies a structure of dominance in human messages. When talking about television, he suggests a four-stage theory of communication, claiming that each stage—production, circulation, consumption or distribution, and reproduction—is "relatively autonomous" from the others ("Encoding/ decoding," 128). In this sense the coding of a message may control its reception, but this is not a transparent process because every stage has its own determining limits and possibilities. Hall (ibid.) argues that actual social messages have a "complex structure of dominance" because at each stage they are imprinted by institutional power relations. For example, power relations at a point of production will imprecisely fit those at the point of consumption. In this way the communication circuit is also one that reproduces a pattern of domination.

In the films examined in this chapter, power relations are often quite obvious. However, there are times when they are not so clear. This is especially true when power relations refer to women, be they the victims of femicide or other feminine characters that support the plot.[10] I use examples of Mexican cinema because, as the historian David Maciel (xi) has mentioned, "It has been instrumental in constructing, defining, and representing [Mexican] national identity. The sociocultural evolution of twentieth-century Mexico is nowhere better represented than in its films, which have vividly captured and reflected its society and national character as well as its exciting past and complex present." Within that construction of national identity, the most popular narratives of Mexico's northern border are as follows: the border as a brothel, the border as a crossing/migratory/passing site, and the border as a place of gambling and smuggling. In other words the border is seen as a place of damnation and its inhabitants as gamblers, *coyotes* (human-traffickers), drug dealers, prostitutes, or murderers of women.

The second-tier films *16 en la lista*, *Pasión y muerte en Ciudad Juárez*, and *Espejo retrovisor* could be categorized under the genre "border cinema." For the scholar Norma Iglesias (233), "'Border cinema' is an important cinematographic genre not only because of the vast number of films it encompasses . . . but also because of its substantial audience—an audience who has a strong emotional link with the genre—along the U.S.–Mexico border and in the central part of Mexico." Consequently, the message these films project is important because of their reception by large audiences and their construction of the victims of femicide, their relatives, the perpetrators, and the authorities. As a demonstration of the dramatic growth in the interest of the border as an object of study, at the time I conducted this research, these three films were the only ones available in video clubs in Ciudad Juárez and El Paso that dealt with femicide. Several others have since been released—*Las muertas de Juárez* (2003) and *Bajo Juárez* (2006) in Mexico and *The Virgin of Juárez* (2005), *Juárez: Stages of Fear* (2006), *Juárez, México* (2006), and *Bordertown* (2007) in the United States.

Border Thrillers

In their article "La batalla de las cruces," Héctor Domínguez-Ruvalcaba and Patricia Ravelo (122–24) have identified thirty-two different lines of investigation in which both Ciudad Juárez society and the state have attempted to explain and solve the crimes against women. Their research includes an extensive analysis of newspaper articles including interviews conducted by journalists devoted to the study of femicide as well as interviews with NGOs and surviving family members. The first conclusion that they draw is placed in the symbolic-political arena that includes what they call "la imaginación cinematográfica o la política de los monstruos" ("the cinematographic imagination or the politics of monsters") (ibid., 124). The second deals with structural interpretations of victimization. The third conclusion mentions impunity and neoliberalism as its main perpetrators (ibid.). In the three movies studied, all of these interpretations are somehow present.

Another work that offers an insight as to the imagination of sexualized killings is *The Lust to Kill: A Feminist Investigation of Sexual Murder* by Deborah Cameron and Elizabeth Frazer. The authors claim that our modern taste for horror is such that, in the case of sexual killings, it becomes difficult to distinguish between fiction and reality. This is one reason why films and literature use diverse narratives that exploit sexual killings as if they were fiction. At the same time we find works of fiction that are treated as if they told the truth. For Cameron and Frazer (53), "Every major killing becomes a lurid paperback or movie; many murderers turn out to be avid consumers of literature which celebrates the pleasures of (imaginary) horror."[11]

16 en la lista (written and directed by Rodolfo Rodoberti and produced by Héctor Molinar) and *Pasión y muerte en Ciudad Juárez* (written, produced, and directed by Javier Ulloa and Luis Estrada) can be defined generically as both thrillers and border cinema.[12] In both films the main character is a detective in charge of the investigation of a murder case. For *16 en la lista* we have Charlie; for *Pasión y muerte*, Olivares. Both films narrate a series of crimes from the point of view of the investigating police officers. In both, the audience bears witness to a game of power played out between the detective, the murderer, and the victims. In the end both protagonists propose that a single serial killer is responsible for the murders. These characters are based on hegemonic schemes of masculinity and embody the prototypical Hollywood hero: young, handsome, neat, well dressed, assertive, and aggressive, but also soft and understanding when he relates to women (Gauntlett, 43). The heroes are persistent and under no circumstances willing to give up on their respective cases.

16 en la lista portrays two types of violence that are endured by the inhabitants of Ciudad Juárez: femicide and drug-related crimes. Yet the film does not connect these two phenomena; rather, they appear as separate ingredients in an overarching social crisis in Ciudad Juárez. The film separates these two issues presenting, on the one hand, warring drug lords' struggle for power and, on the other, the distress caused by the serial sexual killings. At the beginning of the film, the audience is presented with two hypotheses to explain the crimes: first, that femicide is connected to drug trafficking, and second, that the crimes have been committed by a solitary killer, a "psychopath," a "monster" (Ravelo and Domínguez-Ruvalcaba, 134). In the end the hypothesis connecting drug trafficking to femicide does not prevail. One of this chapter's main goals is to observe how these hypotheses, facts, and realities are reconstructed on screen.

16 en la lista follows the pattern of a suspense thriller; it relates to films that use the figure of Jack the Ripper (including Jack the Ripper), and others, like The Boston Strangler, The Bone Collector, Seven, and so on. Both Jack the Ripper and The Boston Strangler are based on actual serial killings: the former deals with murders that took place in London in 1880; the latter with murders in Boston from 1962 to 1964. These types of cinematographic productions lead us to turn such characters into myths. Films dealing with Jack the Ripper date back to the 1920s and continue through the 1970s. Alfred Hitchcock used the character in his film The Lodger (1926 and 1944), as did Godfrey Grayson in Room to Let (1950). Richard Fleischer would make Tony Curtis his Boston Strangler in 1968. Seven (1995) and The Bone Collector (1999) also belong to this subgenre of serial murder films while they also incorporate some elements from the classics: a lonely killer is always one step ahead of the detective in charge; an intelligent man (the assassin) is trying to hunt the hunter (the detective) by giving him leads as to where to find him or his victims. In most cases the perpetrator is never caught.

In 16 en la lista, Tony (the murderer) is constantly challenging Charlie (the detective) by sending him provoking messages and tips that lead him to the next victim. This same technique was used in *Jack the Ripper*, *Seven*, and *The Bone Collector*. The repeated image of Tony's boots reminds us of the film *See No Evil* (1971), and there is an open reference to *Psycho* (1960) in one of the final scenes, in which the audience can see Tony's shadow trying to kill Charlie with an ax. While in *Psycho* the detective dies at the killer's hands, in *16 en la lista* he is saved by Tony's psychiatrist, who sedates the killer by giving him an injection. This ending proposes the often more desirable resolution in which good triumphs over evil. Unfortunately, in reality there is no such resolution for so many of the serial sexual killings.

16 en la lista is narrated from the perspective of the police agents whose commitment to solving crime is reiterated from beginning to end. The thriller constructs an image of a police corporation devoted to the investigation of both femicide and drug trafficking. The agents are depicted as sensible, patient, respectful, and committed to solving the crimes at hand. Their responsiveness is proved not only when they question witnesses, but also when they deal with the relatives of missing women who at one point protest the lack of information available for their cases. In this scene a small group of mothers gathers to question Chief Inspector Jaimes, to which he responds in a rude manner. However, when one of the mothers confronts him with the poignant question, "Don't you have daughters?" he is visibly shaken and leaves in silence.

In private with his police team the inspector recognizes the importance of finding the killer and accepts the fact that the parents were right. Finally, the courage and honor of the police is embodied in the figure of Charlie, the detective. At the end of the film he is badly wounded by Tony when trying to save Denisse, the sixteenth and final woman on the hit list (hence the title), who also happens to be Inspector Jaimes's daughter. By catching Tony, Charlie solves the crimes and dignifies the work of the police. The message is that the police are fully committed to these cases and that in the end there was only one assassin who, now eliminated, will no longer harm the city's women. The difference between the stories projected in films and those reported in the news media is this "happy ending." In real life the crimes are very rarely solved.

In *16 en la lista* power relations are perfectly defined, yet sometimes not easily decoded. On the one hand, the film subtly protests against police incompetence, as in the scene with Jaimes and the aggrieved mothers. But on the other, almost the entire movie is spent praising the work of the police by highlighting Charlie's actions. The film also depicts the assassin as a psychopath and the victims as responsible for their own deaths. This dual discourse permeates the film and is especially evident in the use of dialogue.

The audience learns that some of the victims had gone out on a date with the killer before eventually falling victim to him. We also learn that two of the victims were his friends and had quarreled because they both liked him. However, none of the victims' friends or family members knew who the man really was. Rosario, one of the victims, is portrayed as a drug addict, while another, a teenager, lies to the police in her testimony out of fear. Finally, in the previously mentioned scene in which the mothers protest to the police, Inspector Jaimes responds sharply: "You, the parents are the ones to blame because you don't know with whom your daughters associate or with whom they went out."

Identifying these discourses and images allows us to decode a patriarchal and politicized ideology that has circulated ever since the lifeless bodies of women started to appear in Ciudad Juárez. Such discourses are registered in newspapers, in "prevention campaigns," and in official statements by authority figures (governors, mayors, district attorneys, prosecutors, deputy prosecutor, police agents, and so on) in an attempt to excuse their inefficiency in solving the murders by exculpating themselves and blaming the victims.[13] The film suggests that the victims are responsible for their own deaths because the women "went out with an unknown man" or were "drug addicts." Both of these excuses are part of the authorities' discourse. Consequently, in *16 en la lista* we see a glorification of the police and a stigmatization of the victims.

Another important issue for the construction of discourse, patriarchal ideology, and the distribution of power is the narrator's point of view. Although the plots for all three films focus on solving crimes committed against women, the narrated world is completely masculine. Homosocial bonding is facilitated by the paternal figures of police inspectors, detectives, and the rest of the police corporation. Their relations are presented as if they were members of the same family, and the police inspector in two films is depicted as a father to the detective. The chief inspector in *Pasión y muerte* covers up the faults in Olivares's investigation caused by his alcoholism. In *16 en la lista*, Chief Inspector Jaimes excuses Charlie's volatile temper as well as his excessive use of violence when arresting a group of drug lords.

Interestingly, we also see male bonding between the detectives and the assassins. In *16 en la lista*, for example, Tony Lavalle, the serial killer, is shown to have some of the same characteristics as Charlie, the detective. Tony is portrayed as young, neat, extremely intelligent, a great hunter, and as most movie villains, he dresses in black and wears boots. Charlie and Tony will always be in conflict, but their similarities establish a masculine bond. It would not be too farfetched to propose that under different circumstances, Charlie could have been Tony. This implies interchangeability between criminals and law enforcement officers. They are as two sides of the same coin, or as Tomasini Bassols (31) has described, "violence is co-substantial to men." Another connection worth mentioning is that among Tony, his mentor, and his psychiatrist, whom he has not seen in a long time. Both Tony's mentor and his psychiatrist suspect that he is the killer and attempt to stop him. Tony ends up killing his mentor; it is his psychiatrist who eventually manages to subdue the killer. These close male-centered relationships perpetuate the ideology that the world is (or should be) guided only by men.

In addition, the relationships between the female characters in *16 en la lista* are not as solid as those of the male characters. Not only does the film suggest that women are responsible for their own deaths; it also implies that they cannot establish lasting friendships when a man comes between them, as is the case for Rosario and Isela. Something similar happens with Denisse, the chief inspector's daughter, and Andrea, Tony's father's ex-girlfriend, who had been the teacher of some of the victims. The female characters serve to support the male roles and they are presented as sexual objects. Denisse, an intelligent, incorruptible lawyer who refuses to defend drug lords, is most of the time dressed in a tight miniskirt and form-fitting blouse. In the final scene, however, she is shown wearing jeans and a T-shirt. This is the same outfit worn by most victims of femicide from 1993 to 1998 and is a visual clue for the viewers familiar with recent border violence that she will be the next victim.

Another female character, Andrea, is killed by Tony for being his father's girlfriend and for supposedly identifying him to the police as the killer. She also dresses with low-cut blouses and tight miniskirts. The film makes an interesting contrast between these two women's dress and physical characteristics and that of the victims, all of whom are very young with indigenous features, dark skin, and dark hair. Andrea, on the contrary, is pale and red-headed, and Denisse is fair-skinned with light-brown hair. Thus we see a rearticulation of ethnicity and social class in these characters. On the one hand, this perpetuates the image of some victims, but on the other, suggests that dark-skinned women are more prone to be "lead into temptations" such as "going out with unknown men" or "giving in to drugs," while white women are constructed as "pure." This being said, the film does make a positive assertion by indicating that no matter whether a woman is dark-skinned or fair, young or old, she can become a victim simply because she is a woman.

This construction of female characters in *16 en la lista* follows the example given by the film theorist Laura Mulvey: "A female character has no importance in film . . . except as 'spectacle,' the erotic object of both the male character and the cinema spectators; her role is to drive the hero [and the villain] to act the way he does" (cited in Gauntlett, 38). As Hall and Mulvey suggest, this film "represents a sophisticated account of the relationship between media messages and ideology . . . and power" (Baldwin et al., 89). The world constructed by *16 en la lista* is an overwhelmingly masculine one in which relations of power are specifically defined: men are in charge of granting life, taking life, and procuring justice. In this world women are passive beings dominated by men, male power, physical strength, and patriarchal discourse.

Masculine Duties

The film *Pasión y muerte en Ciudad Juárez* follows the same thriller structure as *16 en la lista*. In the former, Detective Olivares is charged with solving a series of crimes that take place in Ciudad Juárez's red-light district. He is given the assignment by Chief Inspector García, who believes that Olivares is his best man for the job—this despite Olivares's alcoholism. As with *16 en la lista*, the environment depicted in *Pasión y muerte* is predominantly masculine with such characters as Olivares, the murderer (who is also a physician), and Chief Inspector García prominently displayed on screen. While *16 en la lista* portrays its protagonist, Charlie, as a typical hero, in *Pasión y muerte*, Olivares is portrayed as an antihero. This is made clear through his alcoholism and messy personal appearance. Still, his illness does not seem to prevent him from performing well under pressure and eventually solving the crimes.

Homosocial bonding is again one of the pillars of the film and is evident in the special treatment that Olivares receives from both Inspector García and the physician/assassin. García is like a father to Olivares in the same way that Jaimes is for Charlie. The inspector covers up for his protégé not only when he is late for work, but also when he does not appear at the scene of a crime because he is either drunk or asleep. Although this type of male-centered camaraderie within the police force may not be very surprising, the friendship that is cultivated between Olivares and the assassin is rather unexpected. In *Pasión y muerte*, in contrast with the animosity observed between Tony and Charlie in *16 en la lista*, the assassin and the detective actually become friends. The assassin is Olivares's neighbor and tries to look out for him by advising him to stop drinking. Paradoxically, as a physician, he also provides Olivares with sleeping pills upon request.

The hypothesis presented in *Pasión y muerte* is that there is a serial sexual killer on the loose who picks up prostitutes from the streets in the red-light district, takes them to an isolated place, then rapes, kills, and abandons them. This is a plausible storyline when we consider the statistics compiled by the scholar Julia Estela Monárrez Fragoso ("La cultura del feminicidio," 94) indicating that from 1993 to 1999, 162 women were killed along the border, including 19 that could be classified as prostitutes, exotic dancers, or bar waitresses.

In *Pasión y muerte* most women are portrayed as prostitutes. They are seen standing on the same corner, dressed in a low-cut blouse and form-fitting miniskirt, wearing heavy makeup, and speaking vulgarly. This construction of the future victims of violent crime exacerbates negative social stigma and perpetuates stereotypes. The idea of the prostitute as an appropriate victim of sexual crime is a stereotype that was actually promoted by the administration of Governor Francisco Barrio (1992–98) and then continued when Patricio Martínez took office (1998–2004).[14] This stereotyping absolves government authorities for their inability to prevent and solve these crimes and ultimately blames the victims themselves for the violence committed against them. During Barrio's administration he and the deputy prosecutor, Jorge López Molinar, declared that the crimes

committed against "these women" were a result of their dangerous profession. During Martínez's subsequent administration, the prosecutor
Arturo González Rascón reiterated these sentiments. In both cases the
government implied that it was normal that prostitutes be killed because
of the nature of their work.

There is, however, another female character in *Pasión y muerte*,
Carmelita, who is Chief Inspector García's nosy secretary. She is always
seen listening through García's door, especially when he is talking about
Olivares. She constantly flirts with Olivares, and he always seems to
reject her advances. As with Andrea and Denisse in *16 en la lista*, Carmelita also wears low-cut blouses and form-fitting miniskirts or slacks.
Her character reiterates the image of a coquettish, prying, and comical
woman. In general, the women in this film are, like most representations
of women on TV and film before the 1980s, "'incompetents and inferiors'
as victims or having 'trivial' interests" (Gauntlett, 44). In *Pasión y muerte*
there is no doubt that women are represented as sexual objects, not just
because all the victims are prostitutes, but also because of the positioning
of Carmelita. The construction of female characters in this film as well as
in *16 en la lista* are echoed in the activist and writer Sharon Smith's (13)
words: "Women in any fully human form have almost completely been
left out of film. . . . The role of women in a film almost always revolves
around their physical attraction and the mating games she plays with
other male characters. On the other hand, man is not shown purely in
relation to the female characters, but in a wide variety of roles."

Pasión y muerte shares with *16 en la lista* a narrative structure common
to other mystery novels and movies. Such characters as Jack the Ripper
and Robert Louis Stevenson's Dr. Jekyll and Mr. Hyde clearly resonate in
Pasión y muerte. The similarity with Jack the Ripper can be seen in the
cold and calculated way in which the assassin targets his victims and carries out his vicious plans. The murderer in *Pasión y muerte* is a devoted
physician by day and a terrible killer by night. His plan is to provide
Olivares with sleeping pills so that when the detective falls asleep, he can
eventually replace him. The assassin steals and wears Olivares's clothing
and even uses his truck to commit some of the crimes. In Stevenson's
tale Dr. Jekyll is searching for a secret formula that would allow him
to become someone else, a double, who on the one hand maintains all

his virtues and on the other can vent all his passions. This double is Mr. Hyde, who in becoming Dr. Jekyll's other half represents the fusion of two different personas in a single body.

In *Pasión y muerte*, however, instead of a single body we have a double mask. Although the physician could represent the virtuous Dr. Jekyll, he could also represent Mr. Hyde because at night he transforms into a merciless killer while dressed as Olivares. At one point this confusing game of personality exchange actually makes Olivares himself start to believe that he is really the assassin. In the end, however, Olivares discovers that the physician is the true culprit. Just before he is killed, the murderer confesses that he derives pleasure out of killing women. This is the same explanation given by Mr. Hyde in Stevenson's tale. Thus the murderer is located in a privileged position because he is portrayed as a psychopath, as a sick man who kills women because he is ill; not as a man who kills women because he knows he can exercise that ultimate power in a patriarchal society.

In both films victims and perpetrators are portrayed in two different ways. Women are undoubtedly given a negative image: either they are held responsible for crimes committed against them, or they are portrayed as sex objects that are subservient to men. Male perpetrators, however, are depicted as psychopaths. According to Cameron and Frazer (35), this type of cliché representation comes from popular tradition. Within this tradition sexual killers are seen as maniacs who find that their actions are glorified and denigrated at the same time. If viewed within the context of the literary tradition, we can see how the figure of the murderer has been mythicized in different ways. First we could look at such clinical annals as the "Monster of Düsseldorf" or the "Yorkshire Ripper," whose infamous personalities have terrorized and fascinated millions throughout history. Something similar has happened with legendary figures like Jack the Ripper and the Boston Strangler. It seems that this stereotype has its roots in clinical cases, mythology, and literary traditions. The sexual killer thus embodies a diachronic patchwork of ideas and cultural manifestations. This is why we can recognize such literary archetypes as the "Sadeian libertine, Mr. Hyde, the Gothic villain, the monster, the hunchback; or on the other hand, the social/mental deviant: the madman, the psychopath, the existential rebel" (Cameron and Frazer, 36).

Unfortunately, as Cameron and Frazer have argued, by categorizing all serial killers with these stereotypes, we are unable to perceive the perpetrator of femicide as a man who exercises his power over a woman until her death. Both films use a stereotypical assassin. He is therefore not to be held fully responsible for his own actions; his abnormal behavior exempts him from full-fledged social condemnation. The image that *Pasión y muerte* fails to project is that of a man who kills women because he knows that he can do so. This man feels that he can exercise that terrible power and will be excused by society for being a "psychopath." In fact, as the sociologist R. W. Connell has affirmed, "Most men do not attack or harass women; but those who do are unlikely to think themselves as deviant. On the contrary, they usually feel they are entirely justified that they are exercising that right. They are authorized by an ideology of supremacy" (83). This means that when we call them psychopaths, madmen, deviants, or maniacs, paradoxically, we end up normalizing violence against women.

Both films project multiple ideological discourses on screen. One of which is the excessive strength, virility, and loyalty of the male characters; another is the weakness and wickedness of the female characters. These types of discourses conjure up a historically divisive image of the border that is subsequently rearticulated and eventually reduces border residents to nothing more than drug lords, pimps, and whores. Unfortunately, when dealing with femicide in Ciudad Juárez, these films reconstruct and disseminate stereotypes of young, unchaste women and prostitutes. Because the films are narrated from the male perspective (especially that of the police), those attempting to solve the city's problems (the Ciudad Juárez police department) are rebranded as dedicated officers, efficient in the handling of femicide. In reality, however, there has been a litany of deficiencies and ineffectiveness regarding these crimes. In addition, the serial sexual crimes are ultimately presented as closed cases, when in real life, there are far too many that remain unsolved.

The final film I analyze in this chapter is *Espejo retrovisor*. Narrated from a totally different perspective than *16 en la lista* and *Pasión y muerte*, this film was written by Liza di Georgina and directed by Héctor Molinar. The film is narrated from the point of view of the city itself, taking into account its various problems and relating them to the life of the teenage protagonist, Paloma. This perspective contrasts with *Pasión y muerte*, in which the city is completely unrecognizable as Ciudad Juárez, and *16 en la lista*, in which the city barely shows up on screen. In *Espejo retrovisor*, Ciudad Juárez is depicted as pleasant and tidy; it is clean and bright and boasts plenty of green spaces. A street sign reads "Welcome to Juárez, México's Best Border City. Drive carefully," and there are also monuments, schools, parks, clean restaurants, neighborhoods, and homes, as well as wide avenues. Even when the camera focuses on the area's poverty, the scenes seem cleansed. Differing from such classic films as *Aventurera* (1949) or *Espaldas mojadas* (1953), where Ciudad Juárez's urban spaces are defined by night clubs, cantinas, and brothels, *Espejo retrovisor* limits itself to showing only one minutelong scene at a night club, where Jorge, one of the main characters, picks up his best friend, Fabián.

Ciudad Juárez is introduced to the audience as Jorge's father is driving and listening to the news on the radio. The idea of the city as "Mexico's Best Border City" is contested when the news broadcast informs its audience of the large number of children who have become victims of the city's dangers. These are children in need who have been abandoned by their parents and are now vulnerable to the abuse of tobacco, alcohol, and drugs. We find a noticeable contrast between what we see and what we hear in this film. The children mentioned have been all but forgotten by a government unable to incorporate them into society; their alienation makes them all the more likely to become the city's next generation of "criminals." Other stories heard on the radio provide details about two undocumented persons now in critical condition after being abused by Border Patrol agents, the execution of drug traffickers by hired assassins and the police's subsequent manhunt, a series of car thefts that have left the police incapable of locating the vehicles or the culprits, and finally the apprehension of a suspect after another woman's dead body (she was apparently raped and tortured) had appeared in Ciudad Juárez.

Contrary to what we (fail to) see in *16 en la lista* and *Pasión y muerte*, where the real population of Ciudad Juárez is totally invisible and the only possible plot line is that of the serial sexual killings, *Espejo retrovisor* shows the life of the city's inhabitants through a group of high school teenagers led by Paloma and Jorge. In contrast to the women depicted in *16 en la lista* and *Pasión y muerte*, Paloma subverts the stereotype of the "unchaste women of Juárez." She also brings into question the previously mentioned stereotypes advocated by Chihuahuan state authorities about the victims of femicide. Paloma is a teenager with character and strong morals. She is obedient and well behaved. A member of the school's honor roll, she loves to read and write poetry. She is romantic and idealistic, a consummate optimist. This is why Paloma turns off the radio and says "only bad news," when she hears that another woman was found dead, bringing the total to fourteen already that year. Paloma is the character who ends up teaching a lesson to Fabián and Jorge, two upper-class students whose sole aim in life is to drink, race cars, paint graffiti on park murals, and otherwise destroy school property. When Fabián is killed along with his father, a drug lord, Paloma helps Jorge find his way again. She guides him and gives him purpose, and tragically, she is one day kidnapped and later found dead, thus forming part of the city's "bad news" at the end of the film.

Espejo retrovisor draws attention to the femicide of Ciudad Juárez, bringing to light these unsolved crimes without the patriarchal ideology we saw in *16 en la lista* and *Pasión y muerte en Ciudad Juárez*. It plainly exposes the reality of the border in the radio newscast that opens the film, in another radio show that Paloma turns off, and also when the camera focuses on the black crosses over a pink background painted by some of the victims' families as Paloma and a friend are riding the bus around the city. Yet only after Paloma is kidnapped, when her family and friends are desperately searching for her, do we see people protesting in the streets and crosses erected as memorials where women's bodies have been found. We really do not understand the scope of the problem until the voice of a female narrator overlays these visuals: "To be young and poor is to be exposed to being kidnapped at any time of the day anywhere in the city; to being raped, murdered, and thrown away like trash anywhere in the city. We, the women of Ciudad Juárez, Chihuahua desperately appeal to you, and request your assistance to stop the never-ending series of murders and disappearances of young poor women that have been perpetrated since 1993. There is no exact number of bodies that have been found around the city and most recently, bodies have been found in downtown avenues in broad daylight. According to information from the press, the number of victims ranges between 230 and 408, and most of these are unsolved cases."

As with the other two movies, *Espejo retrovisor* is not a cinemato-graphic masterpiece. However, it does document the city and the problem of femicide in a way that the other films do not. It challenges stereotypes by showing the city and its inhabitants as complex and multifaceted. The masculine roles are portrayed by the characters of Jorge, Fabián, and Jorge's father. Although male bonding is certainly present between the two teenagers, they are portrayed as ordinary teenagers dealing with the problems of their age and social class. The feminine roles are played by the characters of Paloma, her mother, her sister, and her friend, all of whom are also presented as ordinary people. Even though the plot is melodramatic and Paloma's character is romanticized, she could easily be taken as one of the victims described in *El silencio que la voz de todas quiebra* (Benítez et al.), a collection of statistics, newspaper articles, and testimonies of the families of victims of femicide, which is considered the first testimonial to include the voice of these powerless people. By allowing Paloma to speak with an original voice, *Espejo retrovisor* disarticulates the stereotype that has been assigned to most victims of femicide — that they are prostitutes, exotic dancers, or *maquiladora* workers.

In another departure from the previous films, the villain in *Espejo retrovisor* is not projected as a solitary assassin; rather, he has an accomplice. He is also not portrayed simply as a psychopath or as someone with a split personality. Instead, he is presented, in a story that parallels Paloma's upbringing, as an abandoned child who has now grown up but who was denied the opportunities and privileges of the more affluent social classes. In this way the killers are presented as the product of a more complex societal problem rather than solitary psychopaths or monstrous "others."

Conclusion

In closing, I return to the theoretical framework mentioned at the beginning of the chapter. The use of language and images (as prescribed by Fairclough) and the coding of media messages (according to Hall) have been two key elements for this analysis. Institutional power relations are affected by the complex structure of language, images, and messages. In *Espejo retrovisor* the family (or lack thereof) becomes the dominant institution but remains incomplete. Jorge and Fabián are depicted as two teenagers attempting to deal with all the typical problems of their age, but we can also see how their problems stem from the lack of a feminine figure that "unites the family." Interestingly, the same critique applies to the killer—an orphan who turns to crime not only because society has denied him equal opportunities, but also because he lacks the foundation of patriarchal society: the family. Paloma, in contrast, is portrayed as the perfect daughter, having grown up with both parents, and her mother is especially exalted in the film. The police are absent in *Espejo retrovisor*, and we only see or hear about their indifference toward the femicide through the news broadcasts, the black crosses on street lights, the demonstrations condemning violence against women, the pink crosses as monuments, and finally the kidnapping and murder of Paloma. By eliminating the work of the police in this film, *Espejo retrovisor* magnifies the state of impunity that chokes the city and the inefficiency of the police department in solving these crimes.

The three films examined are connected by the common theme of the violence that is produced along the U.S.–Mexico border, specifically in Ciudad Juárez. *16 en la lista* and *Pasión y muerte en Ciudad Juárez* share the same view of the city and its problems. Power relations are well established and well defined, presenting a biased view in favor of dominant social groups by glorifying the work of the police, presenting the criminals as monsters, the detectives as heroes, and stigmatizing the victims and other women. In other words, the dominant view preserves the patriarchal ideology that persists in the cases of the femicide in Ciudad Juárez. By constructing society in this way, they support the hegemonic ideology that normalizes violence against women.

In *Espejo retrovisor*, however, even when the film suggests that someone who does not have a patriarchal nuclear family might grow up to become an outcast or troublemaker, at least it represents the problem of femicide from a different perspective. The film questions the image of an efficient and professional police force and consequently the standing regime of legality and social justice. It shows a patriarchal, classist, and deeply troubled society, while at the same time it gives a voice to the victims and privileges the lives of women of Ciudad Juárez rather than their deaths. Consequently, as a work of fiction, the film starts creating an alternative discourse to the stereotypes created by the authorities. It begins to question the reigning structures of power and supports the prevention of and end to violence against women.

Notes

This chapter is in memory of Guillermina Valdés-Villalva and Jesús Tafoya. *Epigraph*: Baldwin et al., 43.

1. For an excellent bibliography, see Monárrez Fragoso, "El feminicidio sexual sistémico."

2. "Hay quizá un sentido en el que la gran revolución tecnológica de nuestros tiempos dio un nuevo rostro a la violencia y ha paulatinamente modificado nuestra actitud hacia ella. . . . Los ideales culturales que se promueven, los símbolos para las masas, ciertamente son de seres violentos, no de seres apacibles."

3. For more information, see Domínguez-Ruvalcaba's and López Lozano's chapters in this book.

4. For more information, see Dobash and Dobash; Martha K. Huggins, "State Violence in Brazil: The Professional Morality of Tortures," in *Citizens of Fear: Urban Violence in Latin America*, edited by Susana Rotker (New Brunswick: Rutgers University Press, 2002), 141–51; and Nancy Cárdia, "The Impact of Exposure to Violence in São Paulo: Accepting Violence or Continuing Horror?" in *Citizens of Fear: Urban Violence in Latin America*, edited by Susana Rotker (New Brunswick: Rutgers University Press, 2002), 152–86.

5. "Lo más sensato es afirmar que hay un sentido en el que la violencia es consustancial al hombre, esto es, que se trata de una forma de ser del ser humano gracias a la cual éste puede, en ocasiones, resolver problemas."

6. I use the statistics from "Socioeconomic and Geo-Referential System of Gender Violence in Ciudad Juárez, Chihuahua. Analysis of Gender-Based Violence in Ciudad Juárez: Proposals for Prevention" (Sistema socioeconómico y geo-referencial de la violencia de género en Ciudad Juárez, Chihuahua. Análisis sobre la violencia de género en Ciudad Juárez: Propuestas para su prevención"), research directed by Julia Estela Monárrez Fragoso for the Commission to Prevent and Eradicate Violence against Women in Ciudad Juárez (Comisión para Prevenir y Erradicar la Violencia contra las Mujeres en Ciudad Juárez, CPEVCMCJ), which took place from 2005 to 2006 and is published by the Colegio de la Frontera Norte in conjunction with the CPEVCMCJ.

7. For more information, see Domínguez-Ruvalcaba's chapter in this book.

8. Documentary films include *Señorita extraviada / Missing Young Women* by Lourdes Portillo (2001); *Performing the Border: On Gender, Transnational Bodies, and Technology* by Ursula Biemann (2001); *Desierto de esperanza* by Cristina Michaus (2002); *Ni una más* by Alejandra Sánchez (2002); *La batalla de las cruces* by Rafael Bonilla and Patricia Ravelo (2004); and *Preguntas sin respuestas: Los asesinatos y desapariciones en Ciudad Juárez* by Rafael Montero (2005). Performances and exhibitions have been put on by the group Viejaskandalosas. Books include *Huesos en el Desierto* by Sergio González Rodríguez (2002), *Desert Blood: The Juárez Murders* by Alicia Gaspar de Alba (2005), and *La cosecha de mujers* by Diana Washington, among works.

9. My previous publications on this topic include, María Socorro Tabuenca Córdoba,

"Imagen de víctimas y victimarios," paper presented at the Foro por el Día Internacional de la Mujer, March 9, 1995; "La representación de las mujeres en Ciudad Juárez," paper presented at the first Simposio Regional sobre Mujeres, March 8 1998; "Reflections on the Juárez Femicide," paper presented at Dartmouth College, Hanover, New Hampshire, February 20, 2003; "Illegal Immigration, Prostitution, and Femicide: Narratives of Ciudad Juárez in Mexican Cinema," paper presented at Yale University, New Haven, Connecticut, September 15–16, 2004; "Baile de fantasmas al final/principio del milenio en ciudad Juárez," in *Más allá de la ciudad letrada: Crónicas y espacios urbanos*, edited by Boris Muñoz and Silvia Spitta (Pittsburgh, Pa.: Biblioteca de América, 2003), 57–73; and "Ciudad Juárez como espacio testimonial," *Entorno: Nueva época* 60–61 (Spring 2004): 18–23.

10. For more information about femicide in general, see Caputi, *Age of Sex Crime*. Also see, among other works, Jane Caputi, *Goddesses and Monsters: Women, Myth, Power, and Popular Culture* (University of Wisconsin Press, 2004); Jane Caputi, "The New Founding Fathers: The Lore and Lure of the Serial Killer in Contemporary Culture," *Journal of American Culture* 3, no. 13 (1990): 1–12; Jane Caputi, "Sexual Politics of Murder," *Gender and Society* 4, no. 3 (December 1989): 437–56; and Radford and Russell. For more information about the phenomena in Ciudad Juárez specifically, see Elena Azaola, "La sinrazón de la violencia: Homenaje a las mujeres muertas en Ciudad Juárez," in *Violencia contra las mujeres en México*, edited by Martha Torres (Mexico City: El Colegio de México, 2004), 71–82; Rosa Linda Fragoso, *The Making of Social Identities in the Borderlands* (Los Angeles: University of California Press, 2003); Alicia Gaspar de Alba, "The Maquiladora Murders," *Aztlán: A Journal of Chicano Studies* 2, no. 28 (Fall 2003): 1–17; Monárrez Fragoso, "La cultura del feminicidio en Ciudad Juárez," and "Feminicidio sexual serial en Ciudad Juárez"; Debbie Nathan, "Work, Sex, and Danger in Ciudad Juárez," *NCLA Report on the Americas* 3, no. 33 (November–December 1999), 24–30; and Melissa W. Wright, "The Dialectics of Still Life: Murder, Women, and Maquiladoras," in *Millenial Capitalism and the Culture of Neoliberalism* (Durham, N.C.: Duke University Press, 2001), 125–46.

11. For more information and a pertinent bibliography, see López-Lozano's chapter in this book.

12. For another reading of *16 en la lista*, see Héctor Domínguez-Ruvalcaba, "La cultura patriarcal y las representaciones mediáticas de la violencia fronteriza," paper presented at the symposium "El tercer sexo" in Puebla, Mexico, August 8, 2004.

13. For more information, see Monárrez Fragoso, "La cultura del feminicidio en Ciudad Juárez"; Balderas Domínguez; Tabuenca Córdoba, "Baile de fantasmas al final"; Domínguez-Ruvalcaba, "La cultura patriarcal y las representaciones mediáticas de la violencia fronteriza"; and Domínguez-Ruvalcaba's chapter in this book.

14. For more information, see Tabuenca Córdoba, "Baile de fantasmas al final."

Part III

*Representations of Gender Violence
in the Print Media*

Introduction to Chapter 5

This chapter studies the journalistic representation of violence in Ciudad Juárez. It focuses on the ways femicides are portrayed in the news, reflecting on how the rhetoric of newspapers is itself a factor that misinterprets or neutralizes those deadly events. By relating what is said and what is omitted from news to political and cultural contexts, the analysis emphasizes the role played by the press in the exacerbation of a climate of border violence. Because violence is understood as a meaningful phenomenon that can only be read by taking into account the economy and the political forces that operate in Ciudad Juárez, the press is considered a key instrument of these forces. Therefore, it is possible to talk about a violent journalism as it can be considered a medium that reproduces the border's violent culture.

This chapter argues then that the press is responsible for the frequent implementation of a politics of "not-knowing" in the media, which undermines the central role it plays regarding the strengthening of democracy and toward preventing the emergence of a state of terror in contemporary Mexico. The press's usefulness in helping the general public to cope with the impact of other crises (that is, economic or public health) contrasts sharply with its more passive attitude toward the origins, manifestation, and consequences of gender-based violence. Unfortunately, the public has been led to believe that a solution is impossible. This position is echoed in the skepticism of the authorities themselves, who, alluding to the presence of the drug cartels and the amount of illegal weapons that freely circulate in most border cities, assume that any systematic effort to combat the causes of public insecurity and violence is a lost cause. Unlike the low-budget movies studied in chapter 4 by María Socorro Tabuenca Córdoba, in which the intervention of a police hero solves the femicides with ease, the pessimistic view reiterated in the press contributes to the propagation of an image of terror that, according to chapter 3 by Héctor Domínguez-Ruvalcaba, is also present in border television.

CHAPTER 5

Over Their Dead Bodies

Reading the Newspapers on Gender Violence

IGNACIO CORONA

> To transfer an event into a news story is not the same as simply
> reproducing what happened. To transform an event into news is
> also to alter it, to digest it, to mutilate it.
> —Ciro Marcondes Filho

NEWS COVERAGE about the U.S.–Mexico border has practically exploded
in the past two decades. Primarily providing accounts of recent socioeconomic patterns in the region—especially the boom of the *maquiladora* industry, increased migration, and the new transnational dynamic
brought about by the North American Free Trade Agreement (NAFTA)—
this coverage has often been clustered around certain object-themes that
invariably include crime and violence.[1] Stories of corruption and brutality
are prominently displayed on the front-page of local newspapers, competing with the press's defining elements of social reality: politics and the
economy. A cursory search for news about the border may indicate that
a great deal has been built on negatives—pollution, the vice industry,
illicit activities, crime, drug trafficking, which add to the historical stigmatization and anxiety about the limits of the nation-state and its population.[2] The analysis of this journalistic discourse reveals the conjunction
of meanings and social processes that reproduce a "violence-obsessed
culture."

Hence, more than a preferred journalistic object-theme, violence actually becomes the dominant narrative of contemporary Mexican reality
and—more acutely—that of the Borderlands. As with all readings of particular features of social life, such a journalistic emphasis conveys ontological
presumptions without disclosing their complicity in the representational

process of violence. This chapter's main line of inquiry explores precisely this process that produces a "violent journalism" inasmuch as it depicts (in both fact and opinion) and produces (in its discursive formalization) a more violent reality. By examining such an internal formalization of a violent reality along Mexico's northern border, a first line of inquiry focuses on the press coverage of the several hundreds of women murdered in Ciudad Juárez, Chihuahua. The analysis is based on a follow-up of a local newspaper, *El Diario*, during 2004 and 2005, which is systematically compared with other Mexican newspapers from the region, such as *La Crónica* (of Tijuana, Baja California Norte), or from the center of the country, such as *El Informador* (of Guadalajara) and *Reforma, La Jornada*, or *El Universal* (all of Mexico City).[3]

A second line of inquiry addresses the press's epistemic function regarding the interplay between factuality and nonfactuality in the production of violence as a journalistic object-theme. It examines how the demand for information in constructing the typical object of journalistic attention is defied by the inability to balance "the factual" and "the contextual." This explains why the news coverage spreads a discursive network over the "factual gap" of the events—the "not-knowing." The public yearning for news necessarily generates first- and second-degree journalistic texts—more than a mere platitude, indeed in the media there is no such thing as a "vacuum of information."

An editorial politics of "not-knowing" then responds to such a demand by transferring the documented facts about particular events to the background and replacing them with "news" about social or intergroup conflicts, which may be related to or in some cases generated by the occurrence of the primary events. Such a politics infuses media "noise" to fill the void created by the public relevance or impact of events for which there is not enough proven or sanctioned information. To engage these different levels of journalistic discourse and the institutional modes of inquiry in which they are produced, it is necessary to expand the object of analysis from the basic news reports (first-degree) to op-ed columns, editorials, chronicles, published interviews, and readers' letters (second-degree) to approach their cultural underpinnings and the politics involved—that is, the analysis of the tensions that shape the "not-knowing."

Femicide and the Economic Boom on the Border

At a juncture of greater independence and economic competition, border newspapers have had to rely more on their own sources of financing and commercial strategies as they increasingly depend on the income provided by publicity rather than by the number of subscriptions. For decades the municipal, state, and federal levels of the Partido Revolucionario Institucional–dominated government supported a wide array of newspapers throughout the country with a steady influx of resources, most often in the form of paid publicity. In that predictable world a hegemonic perspective with its national and regional schemes coincided with a traditional organization of the news.

The typical "serious" press used to secure the front page for economic or political issues, or for occurrences of national relevance, reserving the interior pages of the widely read *policíaca* (public security) section for information dealing with *la nota roja* (crime news). The emergence of a new national "finanscape" (Appadurai)—in which selling newspapers actually matters—may explain the selective dosages of frontal sensationalism in a large sector of the contemporary press. The local press invariably converts the discovery of female corpses into headlines that do not disguise but underscore the commodification of women. The market value of sensationalist *notas rojas* explains the "industrialization" that follows the murders for newspapers entangled in diverse commercial competition, most important with the audiovisual media. Sales of newspapers increase when the headlines refer to a violent (preferably local) event; if they come accompanied by catchy headlines and graphic pictures on the front page, they are considered more attractive to the reader.

The media impact of news reports about the femicides has triggered complaints from local economic groups who argue that these stories represent "bad publicity" for the city and involve a high economic cost as a potential deterrent to investments (Ciudad Juárez itself provides 40 percent of Chihuahua's GDP).[4] And yet economic data does not back such complaints. Data from the last *sexenio* (the six-year-long presidential election cycle) reveals that the city attracted 57.7 percent of all foreign and national investment to the state of Chihuahua. A total of 245 new industries were established with a complete investment of more than three billion dollars and a generation of more than sixty-five thousand new jobs. The Dow Jones Corporation magazine, *América economía*, placed Ciudad Juárez among the twenty top cities for investment in Latin America (Pineda Jaimes, "Los mitos").

If anything might scare away investment and the arrival of more *maquiladoras*, it is the "unfriendly" economic atmosphere (the *high* costs of production in the locality; the difference in salaries relative to another country, such as China; the presence of unions; and so on) or increased public insecurity. Violent and nonviolent crimes committed in the city jumped from 129,000 in 1997 to 260,000 in 2003 (ibid.). But the "bad publicity" brought about by media attention to the femicides, as has been argued, has not kept business away. On the issue of security, investors and the local population may agree. In a poll conducted on September 30, 2003, among nine thousand participant adults, 33 percent estimated that the worst element of Ciudad Juárez was public insecurity; 30.7 percent delinquency; 5.7 percent public services; and 5.6 percent corruption (ibid.). The absence of the femicides among these categories—perhaps expelled from public consciousness as a sort of defense mechanism—is an issue that requires further research.

Correlations between the economy and gender violence, however, are difficult to deny. Recent changes in the economy of Ciudad Juárez, in both its legal and underground manifestations, have occurred alongside the increase in femicides. Such an increase coincided with the moving of operations to the city of one of Sinaloa's drug cartels, headed by Amado Carrillo Fuentes (aka "The Lord of the Skies") in 1993, with its consequent impact on the local economy. It also coincided with the implementation of international policies of commercial integration, such as NAFTA. The murders of women appear eerily inscribed in the local newspapers along with news about economic growth and social change in a momentous time for Ciudad Juárez's economy—a city that concentrates a fifth of all *maquila* jobs (250,000) available in the country. As a drawback of NAFTA, these murders disturb the political optimism of economic prospects with the ghosts of a dark collective reality, the roots of which are mostly unexplored by the media, which typically offer little more than a voyeuristic approach to the themes of violence and death along the border.

This apparently contradictory reality that found its way onto the front page of all local newspapers may explain the double editorial strategy regarding the continuous reports of more female corpses: "showing" (reaping the benefits of their sensationalist appeal) and "hiding" (immediately withdrawing them from the public eye). This symbolic transfer of information to the black box of the authorities' desks for their supposed investigation amounts to a second disappearance of the bodies, given the endemic corruption in the country's criminal justice system. This may explain, then, the contrast between the prominence achieved by the news reports about discovered bodies and the depth and duration of the journalistic coverage for each new case. Archival research demonstrates that the threshold for these news reports rapidly diminishes not only in the newspaper but in the other news media as well. The journalist Sam Quinones ("Dead Women," 152) has estimated that on average each case lasts only three days. Such a short duration not only responds to the fast turnaround dynamics that control journalistic production, but also suggests that it may reflect local readers' desires to place the news about the discovery of yet one more body securely in the past by quickly excluding it from the surface of the "real." This could be interpreted as a normalization of a symbolic social crisis engendered by the flagrant transgression of the traditional norms of collective coexistence that male homicides (as in mafia-style executions) do not provoke, unless they fit the category of *magnicidios* (assassination of an important person).

Because a corpse or its partial remains take time in being identified, many bodies are accounted for only as "unknown." For the purposes of surpassing the *nota roja*, the typical journalistic treatment of the murders does not provide enough elements for rational discourse, for collective memory, or for avoiding a discourse of victimization. The lack of information does not even allow fulfilling all the requirements of the traditional structure of the news report. Its collapse in many of the hundreds of killed women represents, from an epistemological perspective, a collection of newspaper cutouts that are like fragments of a large puzzle oscillating between failed documents and the possibility of a clue. As Heyman and Campbell (207) have observed on the information gathered so far: "The best data were mislaid and destroyed by the Juárez police. So after one of the worst cases of femicide in world history, we are left with speculation—powerful politicians or rich businessmen did it, satanic killers did it, a deranged gringo did it, the police did it, copycats did it, all Juárez men hate women, Juárez is a 'city of fear,' and so on—but few answers." In effect, many a hypothesis have been elaborated in relation to the murders, those motivated by organ trafficking, organized crime, networks of human smuggling, production of snuff videos, and so on.[5]

Nevertheless, the fundamental questions remain unanswered. And yet every single column or news report keeps on building on the cumulative emotional impact rather than on the informational value of the news. The informative void is filled up by the emergence of a public space of dispute of meaning and politics. Because an erotic or sexual element has been mentioned in more than a third of the cases, speculations linked to moral values abound, for instance, regarding the motivations for the killings. News stories about the femicides provide lurid details to grab the attention of readers. In more abstract terms this informational void is the space of articulation of both individual subjectivity and group interest, in which reason, interest, desire, and emotions somehow inscribe themselves.

In analyzing a journalistic discourse of violence, it is important to point out the connection between the reported event, the emotion it generates, and the accompanying circuits of cultural production and consumption. All news media, in their capacity for constructing reality through the use of images, have the power to evoke emotional reactions in the public. In due time these reactions become familiarized by the population and create a certain habitus. The repetitive representational model of violence as a unit or object-theme stimulates generalized forms of recognition of reality.[6] As the scholar Rosa Nívea Pedroso (142) has explained in her study of the Brazilian sensationalist press: "By repeating the same enunciation in each section, a cult to the magnitude of violence in society (and to the judicial power of journalism) is created."[7]

At the same time such a model exacerbates social tensions and increases a collective psychosis by alarming the citizenry, while offering few rational alternatives for coping with "the imminent danger." These are some of the narratives that instill in the public feelings of dread and anguish. Yet at the emotional level, the readers (and the TV spectators) look daily for their adrenaline rush as an addictive effect: seeking to be frightened and reassured of their fears one more time. That is why, from an economic standpoint, the news media cannot simply ignore this vicious circle of supply and demand, which explains the vivid accounts of violence and public insecurity in the local and national news.[8] Likewise, the void of information, paired with the persistence of the object-theme (violence), triggers an ambivalent reaction of further anxiety, anger, and frustration, but one that may also produce skepticism and disinterest as defense mechanisms.

The Textual Codification of Violence: The Journalistic Format

It is pertinent to cautiously address the closing of the epistemic gap between action and representation in approaching the problematic that underlies the theme of re-presentation of violence in the media. The underlying proposition is that the exercise of violence—with physical violence as the prototypical model—can be transferred to other means of performance or expression. Likewise, it can be subjected to a process of instrumental logic. Representational strategies employed through the use of language and image allow the exercise of symbolic violence to be consistently codified by the imprint of an author seeking to deliver said violence to a given target, thus conflating action and representation. However, this intentional fallacy has to be abandoned in favor of a more decentered formulation to focus not on how violence is enforced by individuals, groups, or institutions and felt by victims, but rather on how it is textualized in a given discourse, represented as a general theme and "communicated" through different means of expression, such as the journalistic format.

Violence becomes codified in various ways in the newspaper, including a selective focus on violence as a privileged object-theme; an emphasis on its textual representational strategies; the peculiarities of its discourse that assign and attribute specific roles to certain actors while omitting reference to others; and the subtraction of context. Ciudad Juárez's *El Diario* has a daily circulation of more than twenty-five thousand copies and boasts the largest readership in the city as well as an office in El Paso, Texas. It is one of the most influential dailies in the northern region, along with Monterrey's *El Norte* and Hermosillo's *El Imparcial*. After the PRI lost the state elections, through its editorials and news selection the newspaper became an ardent critic of the *"panista"* (of the PAN, Partido Acción Nacional, party) administration led by Francisco Barrio, whose government directed the first investigations into the femicides in the early 1990s.

Founded in 1985, *El Diario* is considered a "serious" or "quality" newspaper—another expression media analysts use to differentiate more professional newspapers, those that follow the rules of the professional press, from the mass market (*"popular"*) or sensationalist ones.[9] This newspaper is a good example of how the traditional dependency on governmental sponsorship has been transformed by economic pressures that require that the printed press increase profitability and competitiveness and rely more on the sale of advertisement space. Such a combination of political interests and economic conditions is reflected by the ideologies put into practice in its coverage of the femicides. Its front page invariably prefers to make a visual impact. It includes a prominent headline in bold, just slightly smaller than the very name of the newspaper, *El Diario*, which is usually accompanied by a subheadline and two smaller headlines also in bold within single-line borders. Behind the headlines in bold that announce the execution of another violent act in the city, there is a logic of reiteration and spectacular violence that seeks to compete in terms of its effects with the audiovisual media.

Like other "visual-oriented" newspapers, introductory paragraphs are limited to four or five news reports. Size reflects their value in the informational hierarchy of the newspaper. Infographic material is abundant: the larger photograph in color is linked to the main headline and five or six smaller photographs reinforce the content of the subheadlines and the leading stories of the other sections. Graphic and formatting devices—such as color framings, letters, and symbols, and so on—are also used, including a triptych header to introduce other news in smaller print, but also accompanied by photographs. All of this material is organized in a six-column vertical pattern. The frequent focus on crime news and recurrence to sensationalist headlines as the main news for the day—such as "Minor Decapitated and Raped," "Minor Was Not Raped: Autopsy," and "Assassin Confesses"—with the support of attention-grabbing graphic layouts and infographic elements like color photography make the dividing line between "the serious" and "the sensationalist" press a very fine one.[10]

For the commercial press everywhere there is a tendency to lean on police statements as a source for headlines. In fact, violent crimes are one of the three staples of commercial news, along with sports news and stories from the world of entertainment. Repetition of the informative unit "violence and crime" is considerable in the pages of *El Diario*. One of the three main headlines of the printed version of the paper is systematically taken from the *nota roja* section in intervals of frequency usually no greater than four days. By contrast, the most widely read newspaper in Mexico's second largest city (Guadalajara), *El Informador*, a conservative daily, consistently chooses a headline from national or international politics and economy and very rarely one that deals with a security issue or from the *nota roja*.[11] As a pro-business daily, *El Informador* seeks to project an atmosphere of apparent stability and control. The choice of headline is the direct result, then, of specific editorial criteria, marketing strategies, and ideologies, in which a way of framing reality and foregrounding or minimizing violence is constructed as a distinctive event in the life of the community.

Newspapers transmit a sense or order of reality and hence are creators of meaning; they are not an arbitrary collection of facts, names, and numbers. By supporting their claims, views, and inferences on a diversity of discourses (that is, academic, scientific, political, economic, legal, religious, and so on), newspapers are subsidiaries of the different fields of knowledge, disciplines, and cultural practices. They bring together and disseminate information from these fields, but always through a given ideological lens that privileges some discourses over others. Since newspapers define what public interest is from a selection of certain object-themes, the focus on crime and violence invariably relegates other topics and views of reality to the back pages. These "other realities" are subordinated to the predominant perception of a violent reality and the encoding of an entire narrative of violence for social consumption. Hence the institution of journalism, to which society turns for (neutral and objective) information, is also—in a sort of Foucauldian interpretation—part of a scheme that provides a view of a reality characterized by violence.

All possible news items produced in a city the size of Ciudad Juárez— the fourth largest urban population in Mexico—are subsumed or disappear under such crime headings as "More Picaderos [Drug Selling Sites] Found," "'Picaderos' Taken Care of for $40,000," "Two More Assassinated.

Now 4 in Two Days; Left in Apartment Complex," "Student of Rapists Rescued," and "Minor Escapes Assault on Luis Olague [Street]."[12] It is then possible to state that crime advantageously competes with news from politics, culture, and economy as a fundamental social force. To that extent, the police reports appear as a primary purveyor of information about society. This choice is part of the phenomenon of violent journalism in its manipulation and selection of social reality.

Journalism is supposed to provide a "natural, self-evident, or realistic" frame for the assimilation of events, and this is represented by the structure of the news (the seminal "truth-effect" device).[13] The textual format is not only a way of arranging the information but, more important, it is a mode of reasoning. The generic convention of writing a news report about crime then follows a set of preestablished inquiries condensed in journalism's five basic questions: Who? What? When? Where? and How? It is a conventional practice, but also a hegemonic one from a cultural point of view. It is rather influential in the social construction of reality by revealing what the "news" is, but also by homogenizing the heterogeneous, effecting exclusions, promoting and suppressing social actors, agents, and views, while advancing programs and agendas. Indeed, news events are constructed. That is why the analysis of the structure of its discourse continues to be important inasmuch as it makes inferable an entire universe of meaning and some of the ideological conflicts newspapers reveal.[14]

A case in point is the apparently simple question of "what happened?"— the departure point of the journalistic narrative—which requires complex negotiations of agency and story plot making as can be seen in the following two examples:

Example 1

February 18, 2003

Three Bodies Found in Ciudad Juárez

CIUDAD JUÁREZ, CHIHUAHUA (*SUN*)   The remains of three bodies, who are assured to be women, were found yesterday in the area known as "Cerro del Cristo Negro" in the northwest sector of the border area where the cadavers of two other women were found at the end of last year.

This area is near the neighborhood "Lomas de Poleo," where in the spring of 1994 the bodies of nine young girls were found, crimes that were attributed at that time to the gang "Los Rebeldes" and to the Egyptian Abdul Latif Sharif.

The three bodies were found within a radius of approximately 100 meters from each other and, according to reports, two were decomposed; one of them still had on a brown colored skirt and black blouse and the other was nude.

A third body was found almost totally cleaned of its flesh, was nude and only had on a pair of white socks. The woman and the girl that found them say that they were playing in that area trying to find lost objects, when amongst the mountains of rocks and earth they discovered the remains of what has been confirmed as assassinated women.[15]

Example 2

April 12, 2004

Woman Strangled in Ciudad Juárez

It was confirmed in a police report that a newspaper delivery person transiting the area observed when the suspect struggled with the now slain woman.

CIUDAD JUÁREZ, CHIHUAHUA (*REFORMA*)   In the early hours of yesterday morning a woman was strangled in the street only a few meters from a newspaper delivery person who didn't intervene despite the fact that the body was abandoned in a busy avenue along the border. With this homicide the total number of victims this year comes to 17, of which according to the Combined Department of Investigation of the Murder of Women, only four were murdered according to a sexually abusive pattern. According to the Municipal Police, the events took place around 4:00 a.m. at the corner of Argentina Street and Hermanos Escobar Avenue in the neighborhood Colonias de Hidalgo, situated in the north of the city. In the report the agents stated on record that a newspaper delivery person that was passing through the area observed when someone, that he assures he could not identify in the darkness, was forcing himself on a woman. He also indicated that the witness avoided the immediate area until he arrived to the other side of the block and called the emergency telephone system 060 and reported only that he had seen a person on the ground.

Rescue personnel that arrived on the scene commented that the woman did not have on underwear and that the sport pants that she wore were raised up to her thighs. Flor Mireya Aguilar Casas, Deputy Chief of Justice in the Zona Norte, informed the newspaper that the victim was strangled by hand and dragged several meters, which caused scarring on her forehead and elbows. "After the post-mortem examination they are chemically analyzing the samples of fluids taken from the body of the victim in order to determine if there had been a rape or other sexual contact before her death, but we cannot speculate," said Aguilar Casas.[16]

The different scenarios constructed by the journalistic report on the femicides are embedded in a patriarchal narrative articulated by a sort of "syntax of blame and guilt" (to use the literary critic Susan Wells's terms). This effect is increased by the typical reference to a violent sexual act prior to the killing. In both examples this is alluded to by the focus on the nude or seminude condition of the victims. Typically there is an instrumental desire to assign responsibility for the murders on specific individuals. This concentrated, apparently factual, and noncontextualized journalistic narrative deflects any blame from society (the readers): the guilty one is a criminal or psychopath Other: the Egyptian Sharif or the gang "Los Rebeldes" in the first example or the unidentified (shadowy) man in the second.

By this rhetorical procedure social violence becomes subtly invisible. The rest of the community becomes, like the bystander in Example 2, a neutral observer or witness (almost a voyeur), or like the woman and the girl in Example 1, the "accidental" discoverers of crimes committed. In their chance encounter with death, the two females already know what occurred, because "they confirm the corpses they have found are assassinated women." Such a prior knowledge of human remains previously found in that area predates and surely is at odds with the naturalness and innocence of their play. They reflect the same innocence of society (who knows but pretends not to), by playing scavenger games at the place where others discard the "evidence" of their deadly "games." This last sentence—constructed on a contrast between chance and destiny, innocence and evil, life and death—is not different in its rhetorical strategy from apparently neutral constructions, which clearly reflect a specific way of framing reality.

In the journalistic discourse on the femicide, even the ambiguous nature of language contributes to this effect: the hundreds of women killed in the city become merely "Las muertas de Juárez," ("The dead women of Juárez"). Such an ambiguous expression refers to femicide as almost a natural occurrence and therefore dissipates direct responsibility while saving the readers of more troubling expressions with an emphasis on action and agency. Moreover, as all "natural cycles," the murders end up implicitly transformed into a repetitive event (the news is also the old news and the foretold news: a new corpse will appear tomorrow). The opposite procedure contributes to placing violence at the center of journalistic discourse. When it becomes the noun or referential object— gaining an actantial value as a grammar subject: "la violencia se cobra dos nuevas víctimas" ("the violence takes two new victims" [Imbert, 89])—it problematically refers to violence as an abstract force beyond human agency.

These discursive strategies appear without ground (in Derrida's terms)—that is, without an unquestioned point of departure for the interpretation beyond discourse itself. The origin of this deadly form of violence remains mostly indecipherable (ethnic revenge, patriarchal punishment, execution-style murders, satanic rituals, and so on). The frequent absence of identification and lack of progress in the investigation of many other cases confirm the "simulacrum" or "quasi-fictional" character of the "real" account of news reports. Because the typical journalistic report focuses on action and characters, the lack of information generates a void of knowledge in reference to, among other essential elements, the identity of the killer and often of the victim. The imperative is that of telling the story, any story, even sketchy details for "filling-in-the-blanks" because there is a public commitment to the act of telling. To somehow provide some information, some might resort to construct what Daniel Boorstin—the early theorist of simulation—has called "pseudo-events" (indirect information by reproduction of informal polls or interviews).

Besides disseminating disinformation and (a paranoid) anxiety, the effect is a "story of terrible deaths . . . a story of nobody having learned anything, a story of stupid repetition" (Wells, 190–91). Such stories are discontinuous, fragmented, shorn from their context, uprooted, which "will not organize public discourse [and which] will refer it to some impossible other place" (ibid., 166). Indeed, notorious structural defects in the production of news leads to confusion of the reader: information

placed without context; consultation of predictable sources of information, but omission of many more; limited information to serve a demand
to produce "something," be it speculation or rumor; abundance of press
releases and lack of firsthand research; and poor selection of sources and
experts. The implicit "inverted pyramid" organization of facts forces little
evocation of the real-world context (Schudson, 185). It aspires to contain
the violent act in discrete units (and avoids the context for the most part)
in a simplified causal relation.

The world of violence, according to this perspective, is a world of lin-
ear logic with segments of social behavior necessarily identified in terms
of clear-cut motives and causes; agents and victims; means, times, and
spaces. When all of this information is available, the typical structure of
the news report is considered successful and journalism's fundamental
mission—the accurate transmission of information—is (self-)fulfilled. In
their pursuit of objectivity and unambiguous causal relations, the reporter
and the newspaper editors may reproduce a vision of social reality that
refuses to examine the roots of the problem and the basic structures of
patriarchal society and its relationship to the economy, the use of urban
space, political power and class privilege, the role of the authorities, the
professional preparation of the security forces—all of which are important in the string of unsolved femicides.

It is then necessary to incorporate further contextualization or an interpretative layer, which would require journalists to do more independent
research, to test a hypothesis, interview more community members (using
primary sources rather than citing others or, moreover, pirating news
reports), look for the new instead of picking it up from official reports, and
so on. Despite the accumulation and presentation of facts, fragmentary
data, or incomplete reports—as if those pieces of information spoke for
themselves—that continue to populate the newspapers, the institutional
norms of journalism do not advocate blending fact and opinion, leaving
the interpretation part (if any) to the commentators, editorialists, or the
readers themselves. This proposition is hidden behind the newspapers'
internal division of the narration of the events: editorials and opinions on
one side and gathering and description of facts on the other.

Nevertheless, such a division of intellectual labor does not consider
that describing is also interpreting and that the selective use of anecdotal

information also requires a certain analytical discerning, just like contextual information or abstract data. This problem arises when newspapers use certain rhetorical strategies that approach the social by reporting the individual (that is, the specific example) oblivious to the (statistical) implications of a broader panorama. This is the case, for instance, when they seem to be more interested in highlighting information about women being killed. Likewise, when newspapers publish the official statistics of 410 cases of murdered women in Ciudad Juárez from 1993 to 2005, they may go as far as quoting independent sources that might even duplicate that number, but consistently fail to compare it with statistics nationwide and therefore may hint at false conclusions.

As critical as the murder of women in Ciudad Juárez is, in a recent report by the organization Justicia para Nuestras Hijas (Justice for Our Daughters) the figures of femicides in other areas appear as even more alarming based on purely quantitative terms: 1,500 in Chiapas in the past five years; 900 in Veracruz from 2000 to 2004; 112 in Baja California from 2002 to 2004; and 39 in Quintana Roo from January to September 2004.[17] This information casts an indirect light on the ways the press has contributed to territorialize the problem and keep it in spatial contention in a false seclusion (or focalization). And yet this is clearly a phenomenon that surpasses municipal boundaries and that requires other types of conceptualization and intervention, not as a problem confined to any given city but as a much larger national problem. By the same token, sensationalist news about the femicides that extend a mantle of victimization over women and women's struggles may also obscure or belittle the many strides and undeniable general advances of women in northern Mexico that are so profoundly changing this society.

The Crisis of Truth
and the Politics of "Not-Knowing"

The unconvincing official statements made about public security and the ambiguity and incompleteness of the information disseminated by the news media acquire a more profound historical resonance in the longstanding crisis of the "regimes of truth" in Mexican society. This crisis, which consequently accentuates the social relevance of rumor, cannot be the responsibility of institutions themselves but of the cultural and political system as a whole, as the very reading public itself is not exempt from this phenomenon. So the theoretical question about to what extent the distrust of the justice system indirectly affects the credibility of the press as a disseminator of the official information and as a social mediator is not an idle one. If consumption of printed news is an indicator of credibility and relevancy of the press, then we might have a problem.

Despite the high number of newspapers—Mexico City itself is the city with the most newspapers in the world, with twenty-four dailies— their readership is small and it has continued to decrease nationwide even more.[18] Some politicians cynically observed that this fact was one of the reasons that explain the diminished censorship toward the press since the Salinas de Gortari administration (1988–94). This negative tendency cannot be explained by increased access to the Internet, because computer usage is still low in the country. It could be attributed, instead, to simple economic reasons in terms of the population's declining purchasing power as well as to the unrivaled importance acquired by radio and TV news.

For a Mexican society that seemingly lives beyond "the age of truth"— if there ever was one—the press might mirror some of the problems of credibility faced by the justice system. Fully aware of the many errors in the administration of justice, in the series of contradictions and omissions in judicial proceedings, most of the press does not investigate, or it does so inconclusively, without copies of documents or reproduction of speeches or deliberations. Regarding the femicides, the information made public is far from complete. In many cases the only legal and factual certainty is the "evidence" provided by a dead body. There are doubts about everything else: the identity of the deceased, whether the accused (if any) were the true perpetrator(s), the motives, the evidence provided by "contaminated" crime sites, the process of prosecution, and so on.

There are contexts implied, but not explored or made explicit. The gaps of information are, as discussed earlier, filled up by the media by serving as a vehicle for political, economic, and cultural disputes over the dead bodies. In the resultant simulacrum, some provisional information is disseminated only to follow the trace of its effects throughout a well-known "roadmap" of public opinion. Following a common procedure to register it, the reporters inquire with specific social actors their reaction to recently published news, statements, or pieces of information. Then they proceed to interview opposite parties and, if pressed into it, a neutral or authorized opinion, subtly blending facts with opinions in the delimitation of the "real" by creating a sample of social agents and a field to represent "social reality." This procedure illuminates the fact that journalism is not only built upon hard data, but also on opinions, beliefs, and myths.

This is not the typical view of an institution based on Enlightenment ideals—that is, essentially monologic, accountable to norms of rational discourse, and committed to universal notions of truth. As such, it was a cultural practice associated with the narratives of institutions, practices, movements, identifications, and modes of affect and desire broadly defined as "modernity"—which in turn originates the specific audiences served by (the political, social, cultural, economic coverage of) the newspaper. Indeed, the press has always been associated with a more traditional "regime of truth" and modern logic (search for, simplification, and dissemination of the information) tied to a network of interest in and commitments to the legal pillars of modern society. The primary function of its narrative is supposed to render a succinct report of (primarily current) facts or events classified, organized, and judged in terms of interest, actuality, or relevance for the general public.

The news report is expected to be as accurate and unbiased as possible. Personal opinions are contained in specific sections within the newspaper's internal structure in which commentators, editorialists, reviewers, chroniclers, and so on respond to the need to insert a subjective dimension to the medium. However, similarly to the discourse of human rights, if everything else is relative, something is required to remain as the immutable record of change.[19] The entire conversation regarding a postmodern view of journalism and the impossibility of providing objective notions of truth hits home regarding the aforementioned politics of "not-knowing."[20] In the journalistic coverage of the Ciudad Juárez murders extending more than a decade into the past, most of the information disclosed to the public is fragmentary and nuclear, which reflects the state of affairs of public information. Some columnists translate such "not-knowing" as informative obscurantism and establish a link with the destruction of societal fabric.[21] An investigative stance is thus demanded of the press. Informing by reproducing the official bulletins—as if data and facts were isolated from interpretative contexts—does not suffice.

It is in this panorama that Jean Baudrillard's meditations ("The Perfect Crime") about the disappearance of truth amounts to the journalistic "politics of not-knowing," which more than substituting the "factual" merely seems to modulate it. However, the issue is not demanding that the press represent the nonrepresentational—the gaps of information—within the imperative of constructing a discourse of "the Real" that believes in its own transparency, but of giving consistency to a discourse that finds difficulty serving the basic purpose of informing.[22] Mexican society is then submerged in a state of not-knowing. This could be exemplified by one of the testimonies gathered by Sam Quinones ("Dead Women," 152), for whom "the perfect murder is, it turns out, unusually easy to commit, especially when the victim is no one important, an anonymous figure, and Juárez has enough of those. All of which leaves Sandra's people up on Capulin Street with a lifetime of wondering ahead of them. 'What we'd like is to know something,' says her aunt, María de Jesús Vásquez, pleading, holding out her hands. 'We don't know anything.'"

While the most evident consequence of those gaps is a collective public frustration and a sense of powerlessness in those affected by violence, the most pervasive effect of the journalistic simulacrum is the weakening of political actions by civil society itself. The politics of not-knowing also make evident the failure of the government's intelligence systems and the corruption of the judicial system. Efficacy of the governmental institutions and the presence of a critical press are among the essential elements of a modern nation-state. And it is precisely the lack of a reliable justice system that constitutes one of Mexico's most difficult obstacles to its development. Officials are not prosecuted for past crimes; bankers and politicians do not serve jail time, except in a very small number of cases. There is not enough accountability and legal responsibility. This clearly sends a signal to the rest of society of a potential or actual crisis of the State that may involve a void of power attempted to be filled up by alternative (namely illegitimate) sources of power.

Unlike the wanton murder, the targeted assassination, or the proven crimes of a serial murderer, the reiterative killing of women suggests a political reading, as it defies the legal and political bases of society. As the historian Achille Mbembe (11–12) has stated, "the ultimate expression of sovereignty resides, to a large degree, in the power and the capacity to dictate who may live and who must die. Hence, one's decision to kill or to allow another to live constitutes the limits of sovereignty, its fundamental attributes. To exercise sovereignty is to exercise control over mortality and to define life as the deployment and manifestation of power." The killings are then inscribed in a different order of power that challenges the foundations of society and redefines sovereignty. The state as such may indeed be surpassed: reiteration represents the power of proliferation and the rupture of social composition. In this sort of para-state, necropolitics and narcopolitics are opposed to politics, antijustice to justice, crime to public security, fear to peace, and "illegitimate" violence will only add to "legitimate" forms of violence.

Amid these oppositional and cumulative processes, some news media are also responsible for contributing to generate the idea of another Mexico, an obscure and lawless land that coexists and manifests itself on the country's violent surface. In this "México oscuro," terror and social paralysis are increasingly inhibiting social and political action aimed to lessen crime, corruption, and impunity. Notwithstanding, and against many odds, the news media will continue to have an important role in reversing this trend by supporting the dissemination of accurate information and crucial contextual analysis, and by doing so, supporting the demand for social justice and accountability in Mexican society.

Notes

Epigraph: Marcondes Filho, 8.

1. See "Las fronteras del país se convierten en zonas de alto riesgo para la mujer" (The borders of the country are converted into high-risk zones for women), El Diario de Yucatán, Mérida, September 18, 2005.

2. Similarly, in the United States the border has implicitly been represented as "a repository for fears about racial mixing, cultural purity, moral decadence, economic decline, and political threat; hence lurid accounts of violence, drugs, and illegal smuggling pervade journalistic representations of the border" (Heyman and Campbell, 206).

3. The analysis focuses mostly on the *textual* elements. Although it takes into account some varieties of *graphic* information (such as typographies, headings, and the semiotic placing of the textual elements), it does not focus on *infographic* elements (such as graphics, cartoons, or photographs), despite its relevance for scanning-type reading or limited-reading competency.

4. An alternative publicity campaign has sought to counterattack the city's bad reputation as a lawless place. Sponsored by the city and state governments, the Juárez es

mejor publicity campaign has been placed in the national media and on the Internet. This campaign, trying to "conceal the city's violent reality with an aura of communal harmony" (in Verónica Zebadúa's words) and very prominent in the Mexican printed and electronic media, has already been cancelled. The Web site is no longer available after about two years of existence. Notwithstanding, some publications still refer to this campaign, see Zebadúa's article for the Hemispheric Institute, available online at http://www.hemisphericinstitute.org/journal/2_2/pdf/zebadua.pdf.

5. Patricia Ravelo and Héctor Domínguez-Ruvalcaba have identified more than thirty hypotheses mentioned in the judicial investigations. See Ravelo Blancas and Domínguez-Ruvalcaba.

6. As in his study of the culture of violence in Spain, the scholar Gérard Imbert (203) has claimed: "To the imaginary of insecurity . . . the media responds with an imagery of violence in which the imaginary is confused with the real. Behind the imaginary of insecurity hides an imaginary of violence . . . a fear of being afraid of death" ("Al imaginario de la inseguridad . . . los medios responden con una imaginería de la violencia en la que lo imaginario se confunde con lo real. Tras el imaginario de la inseguridad se esconde un imaginario de la violencia . . . un miedo a tener miedo de la muerte").

7. "Al repetir el mismo enunciado en cada edición, se realiza el culto a la magnitud de la violencia en la sociedad y al poder justiciero del periodismo."

8. Some psychologists have even advised their anguish-laden patients in major Mexican cities to stop watching the TV news as a way to avoid adding more stress to their lives. Similarly, a few years ago the government took the facile decision of ordering off the air programs of "reality TV" focused on urban violence and crime from the two competing commercial TV networks (Televisa and TV Azteca), as if by doing so, these phenomena might ipso facto disappear.

9. Imbert (66) has described two contrasting processes of visualization or occultation (*visibilización/invisibilización*) in the press regarding the fascination with the images of violence. Depending on the acceptance of any of these two strategies, the newspaper can be categorized either as "sensationalist" (*popular*) or as "serious" (*de referencia*).

10. "Minor Decapitated and Raped" (Degüellan y violan a menor), September 17, 2005, *El Diario*; "Minor Was Not Raped: Autopsy" (Menor no fue violada: Autopsia), September 18, 2005, *El Diario*; and "Assassin Confesses" (Confiesa el asesino), September 21, 2005, *El Diario*.

11. *El Informador* is the most widely read daily in the city but, like other newspapers in Mexico, it does not reveal its daily publication figures because of an internal policy. As of 2005, its daily circulation is nonetheless estimated to be more than sixty-five thousand. The fact that a newspaper is not willing to disclose information about itself seems inconsistent with its societal role as an instrument of public information. Guadalajara, like Ciudad Juárez, has also been affected by the increase of delinquency and insecurity derived from drug trafficking since the late 1970s, when several drug cartels moved to the city and began to establish contact with local politicians and entrepreneurs. Murders, as a result of the ineffable "score-settling" (*ajustes de cuentas*) among rival groups, are not an uncommon occurrence. However, the issue of violent crimes or hid-

den violence does not appear as a consistent method to boost sales in the case of this newspaper. Likewise, a 1989 study from G. Fregoso Peralta of a sample of editorials of this newspaper from 1987 to 1988 reveals that the issue of security was not even among the top ten topics. Public services and works (23.5 percent), followed by electoral politics (13.6 percent), education and culture (13.0 percent), agriculture (11.6 percent), economy (10.3 percent), ecology (9.9 percent), and governmental politics (8.4 percent) were the top categories. As the indexes of violence and insecurity in the city have notoriously increased, to the nineties and the present decade as well, the thematic categories might have possibly changed.

12. "More Picaderos [Drug Selling Sites] Found" (Descubren otros picaderos), *El Diario*, April 10, 2005; "'Picaderos' Taken Care of for $40,000" (Cuidan por 40 md "picaderos"), *El Diario*, April 11, 2005; "Two More Assassinated. Now 4 in Two Days; Left in Apartment Complex" (Asesinan otros dos [sic]. Van 4 en dos días; los dejan en residencial), *El Diario*, October 21, 2005; "Student of Rapists Rescued" (Rescatan a estudiante de violadores), *El Diario*, June 10, 2005; and "Minor Escapes Assault on Luis Olague [Street]" (Escapa menor de agresión en la Luis Olague), *El Diario*, September 22, 2005.

13. With his "zero degree writing" notion, the semiologist Roland Barthes was implicitly paying homage to the cult of objectivity and neutrality surrounding journalism since at least the interwar period. However, as Imbert (83) has claimed: "The will to objectivity does not exempt one from the manipulation of message" (La voluntad de la objetividad no exime de la manipulación del mensaje).

14. However, such a semiotic analysis does not allow making inferences on how newspapers are really read. Complementary ethnographic, sociological, and interdisciplinary reception studies may offer indexes regarding both the process of readership (individual construction of meaning) and the influence newspapers have among readers by themselves and/or in combination with other media and formal or informal sources of information.

15. "Three Bodies Found in Ciudad Juárez," *La Crónica*, February 18, 2003. Available online at http://www.lacronica.com/buscar/traernotanew.asp?NumNota=208453.

16. "Woman Strangled in Ciudad Juárez," *Frontera.com*, April 12, 2004. Accessed at http://www.frontera.info/buscar/traernotanew.asp?NumNota=291488 (unfortunately this URL is no longer available).

17. For more information, see the report "Mexicanas asesinadas" by the organization Justicia para Nuestras Hijas, available online at http://www.nodo50.org/pchiapas/mexico/noticias/mujer2.htm.

18. This decline seems to occur elsewhere. As reported by the *New York Times Book Review*, daily readership for newspapers "dropped from 52.6 percent of adults in 1990 to 37.5 percent in 2000, but the drop is much steeper in the 20-to-49-year-old cohort, a generation that is, and as it ages will remain, much more comfortable with electronic media in general and the Web in particular than the current elderly are" (Posner, 8).

19. According to the philosopher Renata Salecl (*Spoils of Freedom*, 112): "In today's 'postmodern' world, where universality has been challenged in almost all areas of social life, human rights maintain the status of something unquestionable and sacred. They stand as the last remnant of the Enlightenment to retain its universal character. When,

for example, governments or opposition parties all over the world try to legitimize their politics, they invoke the universal rights of man. Human rights thus function as a normative imperative that is beyond politics and law." However, the modern presumption of universality in the defense of an ethical commitment to Truth and to truth-telling does not take into account the particular interpretations of Truth in the practice of journalism. From this standpoint critical views of the media are precisely based on their distancing from that goal and becoming partial in their account to specific interest groups, and/or by lack of commitment to an "objective" truth. The construction of reality from a given standpoint—unlike an absolute standpoint—hampers the neutrality and objectivity of the universal (ideological) tenets of the press. And yet, for all the differences between the modern and postmodern accounts of the press, there is an unavoidable ethical link: one that ties the newspaper to a general notion of Truth; and another one that ties the (postmodern) proliferation and democratization of media sources and communication technologies (that is, the Internet) to a more concrete (and therefore unstable and relativistic) notion of truth.

20. This notion differs from the liminal concept of "nonknowledge"—the consciousness of the absence of consciousness—that the French writer Georges Bataille (*Unfinished System*, 115) theorized as inbetween the concepts of "understanding" (connaissance) and "knowledge" (savoir) and experienced as the "persistent uneasiness of one who searches for knowledge" in a crucial point.

21. This sort of apocalyptic pronouncement finds echo, for instance, in a 2005 analysis of violence by the journalist Mauricio Merino in *El Universal*: "Disgracefully, we don't even have a completed diagnostic about the reality of our situation. Our information is fragmented and confused: serial assassinations that nobody manages to explain, like those that continue to occur in Ciudad Juárez; constant homicides between gangs and corrupt police officers, that apparently reveal the settling of scores or internal wars for the conquest of the drug market; kidnappings of fairly famous and fairly wealthy people; robbery of all types; drug trade with hands full; and a long, anguished and interminable list of assault, rape and murder that little by little becomes part of our daily life." ("Por desgracia, ni siquiera tenemos un diagnóstico acabado y completo sobre la situación en la que realmente estamos. Nuestra información es fragmentada y confusa: asesinatos en serie que nadie logra explicarse, como los que siguen ocurriendo en Ciudad Juárez; homicidios constantes entre bandas de delincuentes y policías corruptos, que aparentemente revelan ajustes de cuentas o guerras internas por la conquista de los mercados del narcotráfico; secuestros de personas más o menos famosas y más o menos acaudaladas; robos de toda índole; comercio de drogas a manos llenas; y una larga, angustiosa e interminable lista de asaltos, violaciones y asesinatos que poco a poco se va volviendo parte de nuestra vida cotidiana.")

Besides the informational demands, Merino adds that it is also necessary "to cut out the corruption that kills, literally, the police force, public officials and judges. We must, in the end, responsibly define the true causes of fear that we Mexicans feel for just living in our home country" (atajar la corrupción que mata, literalmente, a la policía, a los ministerios públicos y a los jueces. Tiene, en fin, que definir con responsabilidad las reales causas del miedo que sentimos los mexicanos por el solo hecho de vivir en nuestro país).

22. Clearly, facts will not reveal a transparent reality but will be an epistemic gain over the brute events of the everyday, the chaos and disorder of "the Real" (or what may seem as a chaotic reality).

Introduction to Chapter 6

In this chapter Miguel López-Lozano analyzes three novels that deal with the femicides of Ciudad Juárez. He points to the precarious value of women in globalized industrial capitalism and argues that the *maquiladora* industry is at the core of a process of dehumanization of women that has culminated in the femicides. The novels show a foreign perspective on border violence, which rather than seeming unauthorized and exogenous, underscores the global implications of the local tragedy. What the French, Mexican, and Chicana authors have in common is that they consider external economic factors — that is, multinational interests — to be the source of new forms of exploitation and killing.

Based on an ethical questioning of capitalism, López articulates a sort of post-Marxist economic critique of the structural causes of femicides. Global politics is a recurring theme in this book — from the women interviewed in chapter 2 (by Patricia Ravelo Blancas), who see international solidarity as the main source of support for local organizations, to the Tijuana transvestites in chapter 1 (by Debra A. Castillo, María Gudelia Rangel Gómez, and Armando Rosas Solís), who see international asylum as their last hope for salvation, to chapter 3 (by Héctor Domínguez-Ruvalcaba) and chapter 7 (by James C. Harrington) that reiterate this transnational perspective in their attempt to understand border contexts and the development of activism against violence. The novels studied by López continue this theme and connect it to another major axis in the volume: the media. The protagonists of the three novels investigate femicide not as members of the security forces but as journalists and human rights activists. This is important because the activist and the journalist have an ethical responsibility that is not attached to the state (as is the case of the police). Rather, they are committed to a universalist sense of justice. Accordingly, López calls for a transnational humanism that can lead to a better understanding of the causes and the ways to reduce the violence manifested throughout the border region.

CHAPTER 6

Women in the Global Machine
Patrick Bard's La frontera, *Carmen Galán Benítez's* Tierra marchita, *and Alicia Gaspar de Alba's* Desert Blood: The Juárez Murders

MIGUEL LÓPEZ-LOZANO

FOR MORE THAN A DECADE the disappearance and murder of hundreds of young women, among them many *maquiladora* employees, in Ciudad Juárez has brought international attention to the question of how gender interacts with the political, socioeconomic, and cultural dimensions of globalization. In this context Ciudad Juárez has become emblematic of a contemporary dystopia geared toward global production encouraged by such programs as the National Border Program (the Programa Nacional de Fronteras, PRONAF) and the Border Industrialization Program (the Programa de Industrialización Fronteriza, PIF) and enhanced by the signing of the North American Free Trade Agreement (NAFTA) in 1992. The femicides and the lack of official response have not escaped the literary imagination across Mexico, the United States, and Europe. Since the 1990s, a large number of book-length reports, some of them fictional, have been published that describe the femicides, often in sensationalistic terms.[1] See, for example, Simon Whitechapel's *Crossing to Kill* (1998), which investigates the alleged origins of the recent violence in the human sacrifices of the Aztecs, as well as Charles Bowden's *Juárez: The Laboratory of Our Future* (1998) and Víctor Ronquillo's *Las muertas de Juárez: Crónica de una larga pesadilla* (1999).

These texts have presented a graphic portrayal of border violence with the purpose of creating awareness of the femicides while pointing the finger at official corruption and the impact of savage capitalism in the border region. Although they are well intentioned, their narrative generally represents the point of view of the morally superior subject of Western civilization. Implicitly, the inhabitants of the Borderlands, as those of the developing world as a whole, are accused of moral and political corruption and backwardness. At the same time they are denied the possibility of being agents of their own historical self-construction.

The *Maquiladora* Stage

One of the earliest and most influential means of disseminating information about the femicides is Lourdes Portillo's documentary *Señorita extraviada, Missing Young Woman* (2001), which has been followed by an important series of documentaries from both sides of the border, such as *City of Dreams* (2001), *Juárez: Desierto de esperanza* (2002), *La batalla de las cruces* (2005), *Bajo Juárez* (2006), *On the Edge/En el borde* (2006), and *Juárez: La ciudad donde las mujeres son desechables* (2007), among others.[2] The commercial cinematic industry has also produced a number of films, such as *Las muertas de Juárez* (2002), *16 en la lista* (2004), *Pasión y muerte en Ciudad Juárez* (2002), and *Espejo retrovisor* (2002), as María Socorro Tabuenca Córdoba discusses in chapter 4 of this volume. In the United States commercial films have also been produced on this topic, including *The Virgin of Juárez* (2005), featuring Minnie Driver; and more recently *Bordertown* (2007), starring Jennifer López, Antonio Banderas, and Esai Morales; and a B-movie named *Juárez* (2008).[3] As in many of the novels, in these U.S. films it is someone from north of the border who must intervene to help the Mexican victims, who are represented as incapable of speaking for themselves.

This chapter addresses how the representation of violence has affected the literary imagination across geographical boundaries, by creating a narrative that denounces the institutionalization of misogyny, the lack of adequate official response to the disappearances, and the corruption of a legal system that does not serve all its citizens nor guarantee their safety. This chapter focuses on fictional representations of the femicides that explore several alternatives for explaining the increase of violence against women in Ciudad Juárez during the 1990s and that indirectly call attention to the neoliberal model of development and the lack of safeguards for the workers laboring in the hundreds of subassembly plants along the border. Although these themes are present in several works, Patrick Bard's *La frontière* (France, 2002), Carmen Galán Benítez's *Tierra marchita*

(Mexico, 2002), and Alicia Gaspar de Alba's *Desert Blood: The Juárez Murders* (United States, 2005) are representative examples of novels that generate awareness of the femicides while underscoring the by-products of globalization in a patriarchal context, in which men and women are stereotyped as victimizers and victims, enmeshed in a vicious circle of violence and deceit.[4]

These narratives shed light on the weakening of the social fabric of the family and the state, in the face of global capitalism in the burgeoning city of Ciudad Juárez. Employing elements of journalism and detective fiction, these novels help the reader to reconstruct and deconstruct the broader socioeconomic and cultural causes of the femicides rather than simply following the search for the individual killer as in the traditional whodunit. These novels establish lines of solidarity on both sides of the border and elsewhere by scrutinizing the construction of femininity as inferior in a patriarchal system of values and as disposable for the industrial apparatus. They analyze the relationship between these phenomena and the recent wave of femicides. In this manner the novels point to the human costs of the rapid industrialization of the border region by exploring the origins of the structural contradictions of working in a globalized economy—in particular, in the economy of subassembly, commonly known as the *maquiladora* industry—while living within a semifeudal system of gender segregation.[5]

Bard's *La frontière* is important because it was the first book-length narrative addressing the root reasons for the femicides. Galván Benítez's *Tierra marchita* is one of the first Mexican novels that portrays femicide against the backdrop of the violence of the drug subculture that today vexes Mexico's authorities and society. I close the chapter with Gaspar de Alba's *Desert Blood* because it incorporates a Chicano subjectivity from north of the border and provides an inside/outside perspective on border violence. All of these works emphasize the Mexican border as a zone of terror and question the wisdom of applying the neoliberal model of development to a global economy such as Mexico.

The process of industrialization experienced by Ciudad Juárez over the past four decades has contributed to the collapse of the agricultural model of production that used to be the main source of income for the region's wealth until the adoption of the subassembly industry in the

1960s. Soon the city went from being a transfer point to the United States to accommodating for both the returning workers from the *bracero* program as well as for waves of migrants from other parts of Mexico who began to inhabit the city's outskirts, occupying every square inch of the mountains and the desert. The arrival of the assembly plants required a large amount of labor, not necessarily qualified but keen to certain repetitious activities. In the initial stages of the *maquiladora* program, young women were hired because of their attention to detail and eagerness to work. The urban area expanded and the demand for services exceeded the planning and acting capacity of both municipal and state agencies, leading to the employment of unprecedented numbers of women.

The arrival of young Mexican women to the *maquiladoras* in large numbers transformed the demographic and cultural composition of Ciudad Juárez. Consequently, the form of economic and social development of the city was geared toward the reproduction of the most productive source of income: the *maquiladora*. The distribution of capital since the inauguration of the *maquiladora* program in 1965 has been engineered to develop the east side of the city. The west side — considered less desirable because of geographical impediments such as creeks, small rivers, and mountains — began to attract the city's labor force, giving birth to such *colonias* as Lomas de Poleo and Puerto de Anapra as well as the settling of immigrants and working classes in areas near the Cristo Negro, Cerro Bola, and the desert border with New Mexico, the same areas where the bodies of missing women have been found. At the same time the city and state government reallocated resources from public services to foster the *maquiladora* program in the name of modernization, thus sacrificing the development of the city as such. The three novels depict the violence in Ciudad Juárez as a product of the dark side of economic progress.

Production and Reproduction in Patrick Bard's *La frontière* (*The Border*)

Bard's *La frontière: Thriller* (2002) — published in Spanish as *La frontera una novela de denuncia acerca de las muertas de Ciudad Juárez* (2004) — precedes other European texts such as Maud Tabachnik's *J' ai regardé le diable en face* (2005) (translated into Spanish as *He visto al diablo de frente: Los crímenes de Ciudad Juárez*) and Roberto Clark's *KRFM Snuff*

Movie (2007) in using the theme of the Juárez femicides as a point of departure to bring attention to the incorporation of Third World women into global production before resolving issues of gender discrimination in the workforce. As in many of the novels dealing with the femicides, Bard's plot is predictable as are those of later films, such as *The Virgin of Juárez* (2004) and *Bordertown* (2007) in which an external agent, usually a journalist who plays the role of a detective, is sent to the Mexican border town to investigate the murders but in the process begins to unravel the various threads that have created a web of corruption and cover-up.

In this novel Bard introduces Toni Zambudio, a journalist from Spain's *El Diario* who will guide us through Juárez to investigate the rash of murders. In Ciudad Juárez the reporter becomes acquainted with the inhabitants of the shantytowns and deserted areas that have become notorious as grounds for dumping female bodies since the early 1990s. Zambudio is presented as a gritty reporter, a loner whose wife has abandoned him, taking with her their two children. *La frontera* explores several hypotheses about the femicides that have emerged since 1993 and that have fueled the imagination of the international media.[6] These include narco *santeros* performing human sacrifices, human organ trafficking, and finally transnational corporations maximizing profits at the cost of the exploitation of women from Third World societies, an important sector of the so-called industrial reserve army of labor.

Bard makes the point that women in the *maquiladora* have been objectified. Step by step he tells the gruesome way that women's bodies are taken apart and disposed of in the femicides. Corrupt policeman Alfonso Pazos informs Toni that many of the workers' last hours were spent in downtown bars partying. Pasos says that many *maquiladora* workers also work in informal sectors at night, adding: "Don't misunderstand me, Toni. I am not accusing the workers of being prostitutes, but some bars that are not officially cantinas that even can be Pink Zone elegant discos, are propitious for encounters and you know, the little gifts help to closer friendship" (Bard, 26).[7]

Throughout the novel with a third-person omniscient narrator, we follow Toni into the interstices of the border. In an opening note the narrator warns: "Juárez is just as violent as the novel depicts it" (ibid., 11).[8] The name of the opening chapter is "Juarez Is the City Where Not Even the Devil Wishes to Live." Along the same lines as journalist Charles

Bowden's description of Juárez as "a city woven out of violence," we see the stereotype of the border as a lawless land where obscure forces operate with formidable power over the state and society. Toni Zambudio's editor tells him that his assignment has "sex, violence in its purest state, a border city . . . all the elements of a noir novel" (ibid., 19).[9] This image of the border leads the journalist through a range of emotions from fear to attraction, with very little space for reflection. After his arrival Zambudio is consumed by the culture of the border: "He wanted to document, get lost in the city's bars and enter the areas that the victims and murderers frequented to give body to those stories of male striptease and of women's mud-wrestling and wet T-shirt contests" (ibid., 53).[10]

The scholar Rosalinda Fregoso has categorized the interpretative discourse regarding the femicides into two types: (1) the "moralizing" discourse in which, because of their behavior, the victims are blamed for their own demise, and (2) the "globalization" discourse in which all the problems of Juárez are based on the impact of late capitalism. In Juárez many of the maquiladora workers have been accused of leading a double life, with references to promiscuity and open prostitution of the victims. From an interview with a maquiladora manager: "Many of the murdered women were workers on weekdays and prostitutes on the weekends, to make more money" (cited in Fregoso, 138).[11]

In the early 1990s the local authorities used to blame the victims because of the way they were dressed and the places that they frequented. As we know today, many factory employees do resort to working in bars to complement the meager wages that they earn in the maquiladora. The reality that women have been killed at night after attending, serving, or performing at different nightclubs in Juárez provides the justification for municipal and state officials to blame the victim in order to brush off their own failure to apprehend the perpetrators. As the scholar Melissa Wright (457) has written regarding the "double life" of the workers as perceived in the patriarchal ideology: "By day, she might appear as the dutiful daughter, wife, mother, sister, and laborer, but by night she reveals her inner prostitute, slut, and barmaid. In other words, she might not be worth the worry." What is striking from the point of view of both factory employers and state officials is the idea that the murdered women are guilty of their own fate because they dare to work or go out at night.

Paralleling these official attitudes, through the narrator's eyes in Bard's *La frontera*, the attractive bodies of young Juárez residents entice the male gaze of the journalist to appropriate their spaces of desire: "Toni saw again barely pubescent female vampires who strolled down the downtown avenues stuffed in their mini-skirts and high heels with their voluptuous and sensuous lips painted blood red" (Bard, 26).[12] *La frontera* represents Juárez as a sex-driven orgiastic location, exoticizing the presence of the young girls. The city's nightlife attracts the attention of the reporter, who goes on an urban safari, constantly excited about the young *maquiladora* workers that frequent the bars and discos after their shift. Workers are dismembered and dumped as parts in diverse parts of the city. This process of taking the body of a woman apart has been an aspect that has called the attention of many writers, including Bard (46): "She was missing an arm. They have cut her breasts, she had been raped with several instruments and they have decapitated her."[13] But even before their death, the *maquiladoras* have deprived women of their humanity by converting them into *maquilocas*: "They use people like they were objects, robots or slaves. The assassins haven't done anything else; it was easy to do, since those women had already been objectified" (Bard, 145).[14]

The body is taken apart and with that the identity of the victim is erased. "Those girls are the perfect victims. They are a fresh meat supply. And the men, their bosses, husbands, fathers they treat them accordingly. What is so strange that they rape them, that they kill them, that they dismember them like dolls? It is the logical result of everything else" (ibid., 286).[15] While working for the *maquiladoras*, women become part of the global production machine, making it easier for the murderers to see them as dehumanized objects that are easy to discard. Since early in the investigation of the Juárez crimes, there has been reference to globalization, specifically to the impact of the *maquiladora* industry as one of the main factors contributing to the insecurity of the workers, which is conducive to crime. Interestingly, while *maquiladoras* have brought more opportunities for women to escape the inflexibility of traditional patriarchal values, this industry has also become the scapegoat for the lack of action from the authorities supposedly entrusted with securing the citizens' safety. Although the *maquiladoras* cannot be completely blamed for the wave of violence against women in Juárez, their practices have tended to reinforce or augment women's oppression through the exploitation of the culturally constructed stereotypes of women as abnegated, docile, and even sexless workers. In their customary practices, *maquiladoras* attempt to control the reproductive powers of their female employees in league with the legal and medical establishments.

In the opening scene of Bard's novel, we observe the overlapping of the public and the private, represented by the control of women's bodies regarding reproduction. "Production," "reproduction," and "repression" are thus themes that Bard identifies at the core of the problem of violence against the women of Juárez, as their bodily functions are tacitly subjected to the will of (transnational) industrial management. Through the gaze of the third-person narrator, the reader witnesses what occurs behind the walls of the *maquiladora* as a group of women in uniform prepare to be inspected by the factory's doctors. One worker, Dolores Guevara, tries to smuggle in a blood-stained sanitary napkin to pass the test that routinely is given to all female employees and applicants every twenty-eight days to ensure that they are not pregnant. Dolores has had three previous abortions to keep working in the *maquiladora*, but this time she wants to keep the baby. While Dolores struggles with the test, she ends up fired from the factory.

If in the *maquiladora* and in the city, women have been reduced to ambiguously sexual objects, when they are found dead, in many cases there is no evidence of their gender, as they are recognized only by their brand name clothes and shoes, ironically produced in the global assembly machine: "Lee Jeans size 38. Underwear Fruit of the Loom. Tennis shoes brand Reebok. An authentic showcase of the global textile industry" (Bard, 23).[16] Another victim was only identified as coming from Central America from the clothing label that read "Made in Honduras." This is another reminder of how globalization is the victimizer on many levels, because it creates the victims as both producers and consumers of cheap products.

In *La frontera*, Toni meets Guadalupe Vidal, the president of the NGO Alianza de Mujeres, which has been gathering data about the femicides. In this fiction a common characteristic of all the murdered women is that they were pregnant and their wombs emptied after a brutal session of torture and terror. Throughout the novel we are told how customarily the fictional Candados Lock Company dumps chemical residue in the public drainage. We are also informed how some of the containers used for depositing hazardous waste are sold in the Anapra colony to hold drinking water used for daily consumption. The ASARCO smelter plant from north of the border also dumps its toxic fumes over the Anapra colony. When the worker Dolores is killed, Toni crosses the border and goes to San Diego and Brownsville, searching for clues about a trans-border cover-up operation. In this story, international corporations in league with the CIA have engineered the femicides to kill women who are pregnant with babies that have been exposed to chemicals known to cause birth defects.

Inasmuch as this fiction is about the femicides, it is also about the protagonist linking his ethnic identity to the border. After being arrested for public drunkenness the journalist reveals that he was born in Juárez to a half-Tarahumaran mother and a Spanish Civil War refugee father who worked as a university professor. In a flashback the narrator reveals how Toni's mother died at the hands of a policeman who is robbing the local bank. Toni's father then takes Toni back to Spain in 1976, after Generalíssimo Francisco Franco's death. Thus Toni has an inside/outside perspective on the Juárez culture.

At the end of *La frontera*, Toni has discovered the real reasons for the killings, but he is intercepted by a corrupt CIA agent at the moment that he is going to publicly discover the conspiracy. The agent kills Zambudio, whose body is never found. Although the main killer is caught, there are copycats that emulate the doings of the CIA operative, thus pointing to the impossible solution of the crimes. Bard's novel advances a fantastic theory: that the murders are a maneuver to cover up the ecological negligence of a transnational corporation. In his depiction the U.S.–Mexican border is an apt location for the transformation of global capitalism because it is represented as a wild zone where anything goes. *La frontera* revisits all the stereotypes ranging from the border area plagued by violence, sexuality, and pollution in both physical and moral terms.

Culture and Femicides in Carmen Galán Benítez's *Tierra marchita*

One of the earliest Mexican literary works to mention the femicides, Carmen Galán Benítez's *Tierra marchita* (2000), captures the climate of the border in a border thriller (*novela negra fronteriza*), a genre that has become very popular in recent decades. What distinguishes Galán Benítez's text from the rest of the literature dealing with the impact of the femicides is her dense reading of the rapid and violent transition of Ciudad Juárez from a midsized agricultural town to a hyperpopulated city, where international investment in the form of *maquiladoras* and illegal trafficking have become synonymous with this border economy.

The femicides are not the central theme of *Tierra marchita*. Rather, they represent a by-product of both narco trafficking and the impact of the *maquiladora* industry on the modus vivendi of the border community. Through the novel's central plot, Galán Benítez examines the construction of the invisibility of gender in a society assailed by mass consumption and lack of proper responses from the authorities. As the sociologists Patricia Ravelo and Alfredo Limas Hernández (47) have written regarding the nature of the femicide: "Femicide in Juárez presents us with symptoms of social fragmentation at the core of juarense society."[17] *La frontera, Tierra marchita,* and *Desert Blood* coincide with research in the social sciences in attributing the current crisis in Juárez to the brutal transformation of an economy and society and its values because of the rapid industrialization and concomitant migration.

Regarding this issue, the sociologist Luis H. Méndez (9), exploring the dynamics of the *maquiladora* industry, concludes that "the symbolic border territory of the *maquiladora* is defined from their economic status, and as such, it has an unstable character legitimated by a metalegal power that, by locating itself outside the territory, diminishes the possibility of strengthening the habitat, and, consequently, of consolidating identity."[18] As a result, in the border areas where neoliberal policies of investment have displaced the powers of the state, we see a mushrooming of illegal activities alongside the disruption of the traditional life of northern Mexico and the substitution of its institutions and values with those of the *maquiladora* and the multinational corporations they represent.

In Galán Benítez's novel the femicides are introduced as a salient example of the impact of rapid modernization in the Borderlands, where the movement of merchandise and people in search of the "American Dream" serves as an apt cauldron for the flowering of drug trafficking and human exploitation. Thus *Tierra marchita*'s narrator discusses the femicides in the larger context of life in Juárez during Mexico's crisis of the 1990s, where the canalization of resources for the creation of an industrial force began to seriously affect the life of this border town. To introduce the femicides, the narrator weaves a story of the cycle of abuse and neglect when Cuca, a bartender, beats her daughter Luz because she has ceased attending school because of her association with a young man, Toño, who steals cars to sustain his drug addiction. Luz runs away to live with Toño and takes refuge in the Anapra colony, where after several days of sex and drugs, the young woman takes a job at the *maquiladora*, where her boss, Gonzalo, seduces her and gives her money that she is reluctant to accept.

Through Luz's experiences we see many of the elements of what the sociologist Leslie Salzinger has termed "the sexualization of factory life"—that is, the permutation of traditional gender roles now transposed onto the *maquiladora*. Hence, if Luz begins with an abusive home life and a rocky relationship with her boyfriend, she ends up having an abusive and unequal relationship with her boss in the factory. As readers, we might hope that Luz will find her way back from prostitution, drug consumption, and labor exploitation, but soon after she finds a nice boyfriend who helps her to turn her life around, a gang of delinquents kidnaps, rapes, mutilates, and ultimately kills her and her friend Gloria. The delinquents also videotape the horrendous acts, thus suggesting the idea that the Juárez murders are being committed to create snuff films.[19]

The hypothesis that the snuff industry is related to the Juárez femicides parallels theories offered by Mexican investigators, such as Deputy Marcela Lagarde ("Mujeres asesinadas eran elegidas por internet"), who sustains that many of the victims were chosen through the Internet: "Many of the young girls were students in computer schools that at the time of enrolling, they have their photo taken, and these photos circulate through the Internet where they are chosen, kidnapped, raped, mutilated and then killed, all while being videotaped for pornographic consumption."[20] This hypothesis resembles one that suggests we are dealing with satanic cults or killings related to the snuff film industry. These hypotheses form part of what Patricia Ravelo Blancas and Héctor Domínguez-Ruvalcaba have termed the "politics of monsters" theory, in which the blaming of individual criminal masterminds rather than a corrupt institutional structure ends up justifying the state and hegemonic groups' inability to effectively investigate the crimes.

Regarding the notions that the femicides are related to snuff films or satanic cults, these researchers conclude: "However, in none of the research to date have we found enough evidence to support the two hypotheses" (Domínguez-Ruvalcaba and Ravelo Blancas, 126).[21] This description of the femicides as the work of serial murderers, satanic cults, and pornographers ultimately mystifies violence, thus hindering the search for those who are responsible for the crimes. In the novel Galán Benítez avoids this theoretical pitfall by emphasizing the broader socioeconomic context in which the femicides take place. The author informs us that the most important changes occurred in the 1980s, when the *maquiladoras* began to displace the agricultural economy of Ciudad Juárez.

In a flashback we see how the clientele in the bar that is the center of much of the novel's action start looking for cocaine instead of alcohol. This change of values is also evident in the streets when BMWs, Mercedes Benz, and armored vehicles become the transportation of choice of the upwardly mobile population: "Imported cars, wasteful lifestyle" (Carros importados, vida dispendiosa) (Galán Benítez, 185). The senseless modernization of border life is also evidenced by the unplanned growth of the city as Ciudad Juárez is overtaken by the waves of immigrants eager to partake in the *maquiladora* boom: "Without a blueprint, only respecting the paths formed by spaces that have not been taken to found a home of sheet metal, cinder blocks, and cardboard, the streets of Anapra are dark in this moonless night" (ibid., 186).[22] Unlike Bard's *La frontera*, Galán Benítez's *Tierra marchita* does not have a conspiracy theory linking the murders to a single cause. As in Bard's novel, the fact that victims are young women who have migrated to Juárez to work is emphasized, as is the dismemberment of their bodies. For the narrator then, 180 known victims all had a different story, only united by the common characteristics of their deaths: "Recent immigrants / young. / With signs of violence. / Their bodies are abandoned in deserted areas. / or parts of their bodies" (ibid., 183).[23]

As in *La frontera*, the residents of the border are represented as lacking the critical distance to interpret their own situation and thus they require the presence of an outside authority who offers theories about the femicides. In *Tierra marchita* this takes the form of a journalist, who explains to Cuca the meaning of drug consumption and violence along the border. For Cuca the not knowing about her daughter's fate has pushed her to learn more about life in Ciudad Juárez. The journalist criticizes the idea that drugs alone are to blame for the violence as he theorizes about the commodification of drugs, which he notes *"were introduced to mass consumption through the culture of drug trafficking*; with the collusion of governments, speculators of capital, hitmen, corruption of farmers, false prosperity. Their products arrived stained with blood" (ibid., 184, my emphasis).[24] The journalist also plays another angle worth exploring. Similar to Toni Zambudio, Joel is a Juárez native who has been forced to leave the city, providing the inside/outside perspective. The journalist criticizes the authorities for blaming all the problems of Juárez on the drug culture.

From his insider/outsider perspective as a former drug user, Joel points the finger not to drugs themselves—which have always existed—but to corruption and consumerism. *Tierra marchita* does not give the journalist all the answers, however. Cuca's voice is also heard, and her ideas about the situation in Juárez are expressed. From her perspective the current situation is bad because people have accepted living in isolation; they lack concern for what happens in the rest of the city—the meaning of community has lost its meaning. It is after her daughter's disappearance that the former bartender becomes active in the search for other people's loved ones. This makes her come to the realization that "if Juárez has any hope at all, it lies in this grassroots notion of community formation" (ibid., 183).[25]

While *Tierra marchita* is a well-written novel with ample documentation and strong plot construction, it is a view from Central Mexico about the Borderland that offers little optimism for the future of this region. We glean that everyone in Juárez is involved in the drug business, and there is not much difference between victims and victimizers in a dehumanized situation where maximizing profits is the only law of the land. Across the Rio Grande/Rio Bravo divide literary interest has been expressed, demonstrating solidarity of Chicana authors toward the victims of the femicides. Like *La frontera* and *Tierra marchita*, Alicia Gaspar de Alba's *Desert Blood* also focuses on the broader cultural context in which the femicides have occurred.

Gender and Globalization
in Alicia Gaspar de Alba's *Desert Blood*

In the opening chapter of *Desert Blood*, the reader is presented with a scene where a nameless woman faces terror and torture from a faceless perpetrator who has kidnapped her. From this point on, the third-person omniscient narrator focuses on the male gaze as a form of control along the lines of snuff films in which a woman is videotaped while being raped and killed for the viewer's voyeuristic pleasure. The reader is then introduced to the way in which the *maquiladora* workers are selected as victims, picked up in a bar in Juárez, and then forcefully taken to an abandoned factory where heavy metal music coupled with mental and physical torture create an atmosphere of heightened tension.

This narrative line is ultimately revealed to be interrelated with the story of protagonist Ivon Villa, who is searching for the mother of a baby she was going to adopt along with her partner Brigit. She is also searching for her sister, Irene, who has been kidnapped and presumably destined to be sacrificed on the Internet. When we are first introduced to Ivon, however, she is unaware of the recent history of border violence against women. She is traveling from Los Angeles to El Paso to pursue the adoption, and she reads a magazine article about the bodies of more than a hundred murdered women who have been found in the desert. The novel thus traces the process of her consciousness raising and growing cynicism. Soon after Ivon's arrival to the Borderlands, the cadaver of Cecilia, the mother of the baby that Ivon and her partner were going to adopt, is found with her throat slashed and the unborn child ripped from her womb. The body is found near the Juárez airport, in one of the dumping grounds where the corpses of several female *maquiladora* workers had appeared in recent years. Later in the novel, Ivon's younger sister, Irene, also disappears in Juárez, leading to an intricate web of official corruption on both sides of the border.

Although the theories regarding the causes of the mortal violence against women continue to be debated in academic, legal, and human rights arenas, Gaspar de Alba's literary rendering aids in our understanding of gender politics while simultaneously criticizing the neoliberal model of development that has been adopted in the Borderlands in recent decades. In particular, *Desert Blood* examines the ambiguous impact of

NAFTA on Mexico's economy, since this international treaty allowed the transnational manufacturing industry the opportunity to expand its productive base through the reduction of tariffs and the creation of incentives for the installation of more subassembly factories in highly concentrated manual labor areas such as Ciudad Juárez.[26] The novel introduces the English-speaking reader to some of the most disturbing details of the femicides that have appeared over the past decade. Like *Tierra marchita*, *Desert Blood* suggests that the rapid industrialization along the border is an important contributing factor to the violence. Through the eyes of a Chicana lesbian detective figure, a subject of multiple identities, Gaspar de Alba demonstrates how the femicides are just the visible tip of the iceberg. She offers a window into the broader issues of the politics of gender and violence along the border.

As the research of Susan Tiano and Vicki Ruiz, Leslie Livingston, Leslie Salzinger, María Patricia Fernández-Kelly, and Melissa Wright has supported, foreign-owned subassembly factories use the patriarchal values of the host culture in their hiring practices, profiling the "ideal *maquiladora* employee" as someone whose "nimble hands and acute gaze, attention to detail and patience" can adapt to the "painstaking labor of electronic assemblage" (Livingston, 126). As Tiano (*Patriarchy on the Line*) has pointed out, since the 1960s, *maquiladoras* have specifically been interested in hiring young unmarried women.[27] Along with the aforementioned characteristics, employers also sought traits associated with traditional Mexican women, such as a willingness to serve, docility, and shyness, which would inhibit them from forming alliances with other workers to unionize and demand better working conditions.

Aware of these hiring practices, the novelist Gaspar de Alba scrutinizes how the *maquiladoras*, as the main actor in the socioeconomic orientation and decision making of border society, reinforce traditional cultural values that contribute to homicidal misogyny. *Desert Blood* underscores the irony of NAFTA's implementation for women, as the economic freedoms associated with industrialization clash with the values of patriarchal culture. One character in the novel postulates: "Juárez is not ready for the liberated woman, at least not in the lower classes [...]. They are expected to alter their value system, to operate within the cultural and political economy of the First World, at the same time that they do not move up on the social ladder" (Gaspar de Alba, 252). Despite the advances in the hiring of women in the current climate of neoliberal-ism, the cultural infrastructure of northern Mexican society continues to limit women to traditional gender roles.[28] Mexican women's mobility from the private to the public sphere as a result of the transition from an agriculturally oriented to an industrialized economy has been a key issue in the discussion of the femicides, and *Desert Blood* further elaborates on the alienation of women's bodies in the age of globalization.

Gaspar de Alba's novel focuses on how female bodies are processed as part of the patriarchal system as reproductive agents and by the *maqui-ladora* industry as producers of global wealth for the hundreds of fac-tories that occupy the industrial corridors of Ciudad Juárez.[29] Gaspar de Alba examines how the industrial apparatus exercises control over female productivity, while also monitoring women's reproductive power with the complicity of the medical establishment. Similarly to Bard's *La frontera* in which Dolores and her daughter have become pregnant and are forced to abort to keep their jobs, *Desert Blood* thematizes this issue when it is revealed that Elsa, the mother of a child that Ivon and Brigit do finally end up adopting, had been artificially inseminated without her consent while receiving a physical exam to qualify for employment. This addresses the issue that women aspiring to begin or continue working on the assembly line are sometimes asked to present proof that they are not pregnant. *Desert Blood* creates a fictional scenario in which the medical and industrial establishments join forces to exploit naïve factory workers by using them as specimens to test new forms of fertility control.

Desert Blood does not represent this control of women's fertility as an anomaly, but rather as a part of a larger system geared toward terrorizing women to keep them under control. Regarding the violence targeting women's sexuality, in Gaspar de Alba's novel, as in the real cases of femi-cide, victims have been found with signs of mutilation often specifically focused on their reproductive organs. As Ivon ponders the meaning of the femicides, she refers to an "overt sexualization of their bodies—not just murder but violation and mutilation of the maternal organs, the breasts and nipples, the wombs and vaginas" (Gaspar de Alba, 333).

As in Bard's *La frontera*, there is a theory that the femicides are being committed for political reasons. Ivon draws an explicit connec-tion between the *maquiladoras'* control of female reproduction and the femicides themselves, focusing on the fear of a brown nation that has been a constant in Chicano/a narratives: "They can have babies. That's a power that needs to be controlled from the minute they set foot in the *maquiladora* system. Isn't pregnancy reason enough to get fired or not hired at all? Isn't it the reason why the women's periods are monitored so closely by the *maquilas*, because the companies don't want to be paying maternity leave and cutting into their profits? How many potentially pregnant bodies are employed at these *maquilas*? It's probably more cost effective to kill them off" (ibid., 254). As a means of drawing attention to the bigger picture of the interrelation between industry, misogyny, and violence, Gaspar de Alba thus portrays the femicides as yet another facet of industrial exploitation.

Throughout the novel Gaspar de Alba dramatizes the different theories that have appeared in an effort to explain the femicides and links these to her argument regarding the use of women for profit. One such hypothesis proposes that young women have been killed to harvest their organs for the black market, "because they're healthy, they haven't developed bad habits yet that will have a negative impact on their organs" (ibid., 95). Although the theme of organ trafficking is not explored in-depth in *Desert Blood*, this passage points to the idea that with global capitalism, a pregnant worker is worth more dead than alive.

When describing the forsaken places in which the dismembered and disemboweled bodies of the victims have been dumped, as in Bard's *La frontera*, *Desert Blood*'s narrator associates *maquiladora* workers with consumerism, implying a loss of the human dimension of each specific victim: "Someone in the group found a plastic Mervyn's bag that had a trachea and a bra inside it. Someone else spotted a spinal column in some weeds, and then a skull turned up with a silver tooth in it engraved with the letter 'R'" (Gaspar de Alba, 25).[30] Step by step the reader is introduced to a macabre spectacle in which female body parts begin to appear all over Ciudad Juárez and surrounding areas.

The repulsive crime scenes reflect an utter lack of respect for women's bodies, which are perceived unequivocally as "waste": "Tucked into the mesquite brushes, *in a nest of garbage and human hair*, the body was lying face down, legs spread-eagled, wrists handcuffed over her head, a *blood-stained blue smock* thrown over her head and shoulders. The exposed part of the back, like the legs and the buttocks, had been picked over by the scavengers, what was left of the cartilage charred black by the sun. [. . .]

The ground stank of urine and rotten flesh" (ibid., 244, emphasis mine). Gaspar de Alba's novel offers various examples of how women's bodies are equated with machine parts, as their remains appear scattered in pieces in desolate areas near industrial locations: "Many of the young women had been raped, several were mutilated, and a large number had been dumped like worn-out machine parts in some isolated spot" (ibid., 4).

As in the film *Señorita extraviada*, in which the director Lourdes Portillo denounces a complicity of the police, drug smugglers, and politicians in the commission of the crimes as well as their cover-up, in her novel Gaspar de Alba also exposes a large network of accomplices from both sides of the border. In *Desert Blood* border patrol captain Jeremy Wilcox represents the quintessential figure of the psychopath who profits from the annihilation of women. He is the leader of a pornographic violence ring that distributes their live-stream snuff videos via the Internet. Despite the fact that a direct link between the femicides and the snuff industry has not been established, the role of pornography as a devaluation and objectification of women plays a crucial role in the novel's representation of gendered violence along the border.

The novel describes how a teenaged *maquiladora* worker named Mireya escapes the tedium of the assembly line by going to a bar after her shift. She is then picked up by Jeremy Wilcox and later found murdered in the desert. The protagonist reacts with a mixture of horror and fascination about Mireya's fragmented body: "She was staring at Mireya's mutilated breasts, the *maquila* smock and identification tag next to the body. *The irony of it: an assembly worker disassembled in the desert*" (Gaspar de Alba, 255, emphasis mine). Significantly, the killer leaves his sadistic signature in all his "productions" by leaving pennies in the orifices of the murdered women or making them eat coins before they are killed.[31] The specific use of pennies harks back to the idea that the logic of industrialism assigns a low value to women: "They're just highly exploitable, shift-wage *maquiladora* labor that will make millions of dollars of profit for the multinational corporations that employ them here in Juárez. Thanks to NAFTA, they're all as expendable and replaceable as pennies, anyway" (ibid., 254). Here Gaspar de Alba clearly links the femicides to the systemic problems of global capitalism in which women are consistently exploited and undervalued.

Over recent decades the ideology behind *maquiladora* investment along the border has strengthened the patriarchal notion that women workers are cheap, docile, easily replaceable labor due to the nature of jobs in the subassembly plants and the high rate of turnover. Melissa Wright ("Dialectics of Still Life," 455, emphasis mine) has observed that in the corporate mentality of the border, women only represent worth when they are young: "Mexican women represent *waste in the making*, as the materials of their body gain shape through discourses that explain how she is untrainable, unskillable, and always a temporary worker."[32] *Maquiladora* workers are thus considered disposable, "waste in the making," and their experience working on the assembly line does not lead to professional advancement to higher paid jobs in machine operation or in management (Peña, 38). Women's high rate of turnover is attributed to an intrinsic labor incompetency as well as women's reproductive role and domestic obligations. Because of this, the *maquila* becomes a machine that feeds on female bodies and then disposes of them as their productive capabilities diminish.

At the end of *Desert Blood*, Ivon recovers her sister and resumes her life as an academic north of the border, while Ciudad Juárez continues to be represented as irredeemable. As in most detective novels, there is a measure of poetic justice in that the villain, Jeremy Wilcox, is killed. However, there is little doubt that the patriarchal order has not been fundamentally altered. Despite Ivon's statements about the snuff videos, the police conceal the truth about the involvement of corrupt officials: "Pornographers, gang members, serial killers, corrupt policemen, foreign nationals with a taste for hurting women, immigration officers protecting the homeland—what did it matter who killed them? This wasn't a case of 'whodunit,' but rather of who was allowing these crimes to happen? Whose interests were being served? Who was covering it up? Who was profiting from the deaths of all these women?" (Gaspar de Alba, 333). Thus, like *Tierra marchita*, *Desert Blood* is not focused exclusively on the pathological individuals directly responsible for the femicides, but rather on the broader social structures that allow such crimes to be committed and the perpetrators to remain unpunished. By emphasizing the exploitation of female workers both in life and death, *Desert Blood* elaborates on the systematic use of women in developing economies.

Most of the texts discussing the femicides, including those analyzed in this chapter, follow Charles Bowden's initial representation in his 1996 article in *Harper's* magazine of the workers being killed because of their racial origin and economic background. A quarter of the women assassinated in Juárez since January 1993 have been *maquiladora* workers, but that does not account for the majority of the crimes. In most of the novels that depict these murders, the women are portrayed exclusively as victims, not as subjects endowed with agency to potentially contribute to the betterment of their working and living conditions. The few citizens who do find redemption in the novel find it only with the aid of a foreign protagonist or by migrating further north to the United States. Although the misogyny of the patriarchal system is blamed for creating a general atmosphere in which violence against women is tolerated, *La frontera*, *Tierra marchita*, and *Desert Blood* point specifically to industrial capitalism as a key factor in these crimes.

In this manner this selective corpus of works draws attention to the subordination of women to economic development and clearly establishes how globalization, while opening the door for women to enter the labor market, ultimately perpetuates and aggravates their second-class citizen status in border society. Novels like these perpetuate the deeply ingrained stereotype of the border as a zone of terror in which justice, dignity, and humanity fail to flourish. Nonetheless, they help us to understand various forms of explicit and implicit violence that constrain the lives of hundreds of thousands of women, men, and children who live and work along the U.S.–Mexican border.

Notes

This chapter has been made possible through professional dialogue with several academic communities. The author thanks so many friends for their encouragement and contribution to the completion of the chapter, among them Melissa Wright, Patricia Ravelo Blancas, Susan Tiano, Susana Báez, Héctor Domínguez-Ruvalcaba, and Ignacio Corona.

1. Coined after the 1989 murder of nine women at the University of Toronto's School of Engineering, the term *femicide* is defined as a systematic attack on women because of their gender. The scholar Julia Estela Monárrez Fragoso ("Serial Sexual Femicide," 157, emphasis mine) has elaborated: "Femicide comprises a progression of violent acts that range from emotional, psychological, and verbal abuse through battery, torture, rape, prostitution, sexual assault, child abuse, female infanticide, genital mutilation, and domestic violence—*as well as all the policies that lead to the deaths of women, tolerated by the state.*"

2. For a good discussion of Portillo's film, see De la Mora and Henríquez.

3. The impact of the femicides for the discussion of gender has had an important effect on the cinema of María Novaro, whose film *Sin dejar huella* (2000) presents two women running away from the violence on the border, contrasting with her earlier film, *El jardín del Edén* (1998), in which the border was perceived as a location where women had an opportunity to construct their own identity.

4. In addition to the three novels discussed in this chapter, there is a larger corpus of novels that have thematized the femicides, including Roberto Bolaño's posthumous *2666* (Chile, 2004); Maud Tabachnik's *J'ai regardé le diable en face* (France, 2005), translated into Spanish as *He visto al diablo de frente*; Malú Huacuja del Toro's *La lágrima, la gota y el artificio* (Mexico, 2006); Kama Gutier's *Ciudad final* (Spain–United States, 2007); Roberto Clark's *KRFM Snuff Movie* (Spain, 2007); and Stella Pope Duarte's *If I Die in Juárez* (United States, 2008).

5. According to anthropologist Devon G. Peña's (46) definition, *maquiladoras* are neither a question of import nor export but partial assembly: "*Maquilas* are not factories (in the classic sense of horizontally integrated production systems), but rather are simply processors or assemblers of components usually manufactured in the home-base countries of transnational corporations."

6. Henceforth I use the Spanish title; all translations from Spanish into English are mine.

7. "No me malinterprete, Toni. No acuso a las obreras de ser prostitutas, pero algunos bares que no son oficialmente cantinas que incluso pueden ser discotecas elegantes de la Zona Rosa, son propicios para los encuentros y, ya sabe, que los regalitos ayudan a estrechar la amistad."

8. "Juárez es tan violenta como la pinta la novela."

9. "Sexo, violencia en estado puro, una ciudad de frontera. . . . Todos los ingredientes de una auténtica novela negra."

10. "Quería documentarse, perderse por la ciudad y sus bares, introducirse en los medios que frequentaban las víctimas y asesinos para dar cuerpo a aquellas historias de locales de strip-tease masculino y de espectáculos de lucha femenina en lodo y concursos de camisetas mojadas."

11. "Muchas de las mujeres asesinadas trabajaban entre semana de obreras y en los fines de semana como prostitutas para hacerse de mayores recursos."

12. "Toni volvía a ver a las vampiresas apenas púberes que merodean por las avenidas del centro la noche de su llegada embutidas en minifaldas y encaramadas en zapatos de tacón de aguja, con los pulposos labios ensangrentados de carmín."

13. "Le faltaba un brazo. Le habían cortado los pechos, la habían violado con diversos objetos y decapitado."

14. "Utilizan a las gentes como si no fueran más que objetos, robots o esclavos. Los asesinos no han hecho otra cosa; era fácil, esas mujeres ya estaban instrumentalizadas." The term *maquiloca* connotes a woman who has been "infected" by the liberal customs associated with working on the assembly line (Ravelo Blancas, "Feminicidio"). *Maquiloca* thus refers pejoratively to a young woman who has lost her traditional values

because of the influence of the *maquiladora* industry—that is, someone who has become "Americanized."

15. "Esas chicas son las víctimas perfectas. Se ofrecen como una reserva de carne fresca. Lo que por otra parte son, y los hombres, sus jefes, sus maridos, sus padres, las tratan en consecuencia. ¿Qué tiene de extraño que las violen, que las maten, que las desmembren como a muñecas? Es el resultado lógico de todo lo demás."

16. "Pantalones vaqueros marca Lee, talla 38. Ropa interior Fruit of the Loom. Tenis Reebok. Un auténtico muestrario de la industria textil mundializada."

17. "El feminicidio en Juárez nos presenta síntomas ineludibles de una fragmentación social en las entrañas de la sociedad juarense."

18. "El territorio simbólico maquilador fronterizo está definido desde lo económico, por tanto, tiene un carácter inestable legitimado por un poder metalegal que, al ubicarse fuera del territorio, disminuye las posibilidades de fortalecer hábitos y, en consecuencia, de consolidar identidades."

19. The scholar Beverly Labelle (189) has defined this genre as a "movie which purports to show the actual murder and dismemberment of a young woman, used as an aphrodisiac." Since the 1980s, there have been rumors that Mexican immigrants are being killed for the production of pornographic videos.

20. "Muchas de las jóvenes eran estudiantes de academias de informática [. . .] que al apuntarse se les hacen fotos, estas fotos circulan por Internet, se las escoge, se las secuestra, se las viola, mutila, y se las mata, todo esto es grabado en video para consumo pornográfico."

21. "Sin embargo, en ninguna de las investigaciones realizadas se han encontrado evidencias contundentes para comprobar las dos primeras hipótesis, pese a que algunos sectores de la sociedad las han explorado."

22. "Sin trazo, tan sólo respetando los senderos formados por espacios que no han sido tomados para fundar un hogar de láminas, tabique, cartón, las calles de Anapra son oscuras en esta noche sin luna."

23. "Recientemente inmigradas / Jovencitas. / Con huellas de violencia. / Abandonan sus cuerpos en despoblado. / O cachos de sus cuerpos."

24. "*Introducidas al consumo masivo a través de la cultura del narcotráfico*; gobiernos coludidos, especuladores de capital, matones, corrupción de campesinos, falsa prosperidad. Sus productos llegan manchados de sangre" (my emphasis).

25. "Para ser felices es necesario construir una buena comunidad."

26. The number of *maquiladora* workers is calculated at nearly a million in 3,800 *maquiladoras* along the length of the border. The growth of the *maquiladoras* has affected the size of Ciudad Juárez, with an increase in population from 407,000 in 1970 to 1.5 million people as of 2003 (Quinones, "Dead Women," 141).

27. In her book *For We Are Sold*, the scholar María Patricia Fernández-Kelly (5–6) found that managers preferred hiring childless women because they believe that motherhood interferes with optimal job performance, contributing to higher rates of absenteeism and distracting women from the demands of the assembly line.

28. Sociologist Susan Tiano's *Patriarchy on the Line* broke ground by discussing

how women entered the *maquiladora* in the 1980s. More recently, scholars Robert Fiala and Susan Tiano, Sandra Salzinger, Devon Peña, and Melissa Wright have focused on female fertility in the *maquiladora* in the 1990s and early twenty-first century. Patricia Ravelo Blancas has studied the same issues after the femicides.

29. In *The Terror of the Machine*, Peña (37) points out that since the initial introduction of the assembly line, the factory has been a hostile environment for women having children: "In the early years, the Ford Motor Company did not hire married women. Single women who married were summarily fired." As Fiala and Tiano (5) have observed, the continual construction of "women's identities as housewives whose primary obligation is to the home and family, promotes an image of waged work as a temporary pastime to occupy young women until they find a husband and begin their families."

30. The description of this scene echoes an account in journalist Víctor Ronquillo's *Las muertas de Juárez* (13, emphasis mine) in which we are told how a female body was found: "The sweatshirt was a faded pink color that contrasted with the dirt that almost covered it. This garment was the vestige of a crime scene. More than 20 meters from there appeared the remains of a spinal cord, a rosary of disarticulated bones. The skull was right above the ground, behind some bushes. One final dose of horror: the detail of a *platinum tooth with a letter R engraved on it.*" ("La sudadera era de color rosa, un deslavado rosa que saltaba sobre la tierra, que la cubría casi por completo. La prenda era del vestigio de un crimen. A más de 20 metros de donde fue encontrada aparecieron los restos de la columna vertebral, un rosario de huesos desarticulados. El cráneo estaba a flor de tierra, tras de unos huisaches. Una dosis más de horror: el detalle de un *diente de platino con una letra R grabada*").

31. Gaspar de Alba (v) states in a disclaimer at the beginning of the book that she "added a metaphorical dimension to the story, using the image of American coins, particularly pennies, to signify the value of the victims in the corporate machine."

32. Elsewhere, Wright ("Manifesto against Femicide," 558) has reiterated this idea: "This pattern of coming and going reveals a cycle of consumption and [the] discarding of women, as if they are always located in a cycle of waste."

Part IV

The Legal Status of Femicides

Introduction to Chapter 7

James C. Harrington addresses one of the central concerns regarding femicides in Mexico: the difficulties of enforcement of human rights laws along the border, specifically those related to such violations as negligence, falsification of evidence, and false accusations. Harrington deals with the role of international institutions of justice and explains the factors that lead to their ineffectiveness. He develops a transnational legal framework that addresses existing loopholes in the Mexican and American legislation on border issues. The chapter presents the opportunity to reflect on the limits of national ideologies regarding the enforcement of human rights and the protection of human beings beyond the concept of territorial sovereignty.

Harrington argues that the implementation of such a transnational legal framework based on international law can contribute to eliminating jurisdictional confusions and diminishing the scandalous levels of impunity and corruption on either side of the border.

Because the globalization of the economy is fundamentally connected to the murder of (predominantly female) *maquiladora* workers, as Miguel López-Lozano has pointed out in chapter 6, a global perspective on the application of human rights law is an urgent task. The political web that activism is now weaving throughout transnational solidarity networks and the worldwide broadcasting of violence from the border region, as discussed in the chapters by Patricia Ravelo Blancas and Héctor Domínguez-Ruvalcaba, are political and cultural expressions that require a more solid international legal system. Harrington develops an analysis that points out the direction that reinforcement of universal law must take.

CHAPTER 7

¡Alto a la Impunidad!

Is There Legal Relief for the Murders of Women in Ciudad Juárez?

JAMES C. HARRINGTON

THE FORMER MEXICAN PRESIDENT Vicente Fox repeatedly affirmed the need to bring Mexico "in line with international obligations" it had assumed but had yet to realize. The international system of human rights protection depends on the will of governments to adhere to customary international law and treaties.[1] Mexico has ratified more than fifty human rights treaties and has accepted compulsory jurisdiction of the Inter-American Court of Human Rights and the United Nations Human Rights Committee.[2] However, reports show that egregious abuses continue, and a large gap exists between the international human rights norms to which Mexico has committed itself and the current state of affairs ("Annual Report 2002" and "World Report 2005: Mexico").

Although first developed to govern relationships between states, international human rights treaties increasingly regulate states' treatment of persons within their borders (Leary). Adoption of the Universal Declaration of Human Rights was the catalyst for the evolution of various international treaties aimed at internally protecting fundamental rights. Specially designed supranational legal mechanisms "enforce" most human rights treaties, although economic sanctions are sometimes used. For example, international regulatory and judicial bodies—such as the United Nations (UN), the International Labor Organization (ILO), the Inter-American Commission on Human Rights, and the Inter-American Court of Human Rights—seek to enforce treaty compliance. Although these bodies have made considerable efforts to monitor compliance, their enforcement mechanisms are inadequate and noncompliance is common (Hathaway, "Do Human Rights Treaties Make a Difference?"). As Mexico's current sociopolitical climate shows—which is typical of many nations—ratifying treaties in itself does not necessarily lead to better human rights practices, but it does open the avenue toward that goal.

Beyond just strengthening international enforcement processes, treaty norms need to become part of the domestic legal system and culture. The ultimate goal is the legal internalization of human rights treaties, both legislatively ("binding domestic legislation or even constitutional law") and judicially (Goldman et al., 90). Various nations have implemented legal means to enforce human rights and punish violations that occur in foreign countries. The United States has enacted the Alien Tort Claims Act, which allows recovery of damages in United States courts for personal injuries, pursuant to the Law of Nations and customary international law. This chapter looks at only two options: the Inter-American Court of Human Rights of the Organization of American States (OAS) and the United States courts.

Lack of Protection for Women in Ciudad Juárez and the State of Chihuahua

Ciudad Juárez has about 1.2 million residents. Its location along the U.S.–Mexico border has enabled it to undergo significant economic development, but it has also attracted organized crime, especially drug trafficking, which has generated high levels of violence. In the mid-1970s Mexico's Border Industrialization Program set up *maquiladoras*, assembly plants for export products, along the border with the United States. A large number of transnational companies moved in to take advantage of such conditions as cheap labor costs, low or nonexistent taxes, political patronage, and minimal regulation.

The dramatic growth of *maquiladora* enterprises around Ciudad Juárez increased even more with the passage of the North American Free Trade Agreement (NAFTA) in 1994. The *maquiladora* industry is a strong magnet for poor people from other parts of Mexico, who migrate to Juárez looking for work or as a step toward entering the United States. For years women comprised the majority of *maquiladora* workers, although that figure is now about 50 percent. Women face pervasive discrimination in the *maquiladoras*: low wages, segregation, inadequate social benefits, and cumpulsory pregnancy tests (UN, Inter-American Commission on Human Rights, "Situation of the Rights of Women," para. 90). The *maquiladoras* control the economy of Juárez, but they typically do not look after the safety of their female employees, inside or outside their premises. They generally disregard improvements to public lighting on their property and ignore security for their employees on the transport services taking them to and from work. Nor do the *maquiladoras* use their influence or work with the authorities to improve public safety and to solve gender-based crimes against their employees.

Murders, Sexual Violence, Kidnappings, and Disappearances

This pattern of murders with sexual brutality is a horrific form of violence against women, which we can define as: "any act or conduct, based on gender, which causes death or physical, sexual or psychological harm or suffering to women, whether in the public or the private sphere. . . . [It includes] . . . physical, sexual and psychological violence: . . . (a) that occurs in the community and is perpetrated by any person, including, among others, rape, sexual abuse, torture, trafficking in persons, forced prostitution, kidnapping and sexual harassment in the workplace, as well as in educational institutions, health facilities or any other place; and (b) that is perpetrated or condoned by the state or its agents regardless of where it occurs" (UN, *Inter-American Convention on the Prevention, Punishment, and Eradication of Violence against Women*, arts. 1, 2).[3] Young women of Juárez and Chihuahua have been abducted, held captive, tortured, and sexually assaulted in a horrendous manner before being murdered and left among rubble on wasteland and empty fields. In some instances their remains have been found by passersby days, or even years later. Other times, the women's bodies have never been found, and their relatives live in anguish, never knowing what happened to them. The evidence indicates that the killers choose young women who are poor because they have no power in society, itself characterized by high crime rates and public insecurity because of drug trafficking and organized crime that operates in the environs.

Although the murders of women can be attributed to many different motives and perpetrators, a great number of cases share common features that indicate gender-based violence. When the victim's gender is a significant factor in the crime, it influences the motive behind the crime, the type of violence inflicted, and the manner in which the authorities respond. Even though the general level of violence in Ciudad Juárez and Chihuahua affects men, women, and children generally, it is possible to identify a pattern of violence in the abductions and homicides of women—the violence clearly has a detectable gender dimension. The victims are usually workers in the *maquiladoras*, waiters, laborers in the informal economy, or students. Most live in poverty, often with children to support. They have no option but to travel alone on the long bus rides from the poor suburbs surrounding Ciudad Juárez to and from their place of work or study.

Lack of Responsiveness by Officials

The Mexican authorities, both in the state of Chihuahua and at the federal level, have treated the deaths of the women and girls of Ciudad Juárez as acts of random violence. They deny any pattern of violence against women, rooted in discrimination. Their refusals to recognize this systemic violence and to implement effective policies against it have left women and teenage girls without protection.[4] This also has deprived families who have lost daughters, mothers, and sisters of a judicial remedy. Even when officials have occasionally acknowledged a pattern of murders against women, they have denied it was gender-based and at times blamed the victims or arrogantly suggested that, because the young women were from lower social status, they were expendable. They have also attempted to publicly discredit individuals and organizations advocating for the victims and their families, marginalizing their criticisms.[5] Moreover, the authorities have refused to accept responsibility for investigating and punishing offenses committed under previous political administrations. Simply put, the authorities have failed to prevent, investigate, and punish the murders of Ciudad Juárez. Also, they have refused to address the pain of the families who do not know where their loved ones are and whose daughters have mysteriously gone missing only to be found later, brutally murdered.

The families and nongovernmental organizations (NGOs) working on their behalf have denounced the manner in which officials have behaved and have sought justice through other means.[6] They have brought the

Juárez and Chihuahua cases to the world's attention and have forced the authorities to account for their behavior, at least at the national and international levels. The persistence of the families and human rights organizations has attracted the attention of various human rights mechanisms within the United Nations and the Inter-American Commission on Human Rights.

For a while, as more murders continued to be reported, local, national and international pressure increased — ironically without the participation of the Mexican press. Meanwhile, with each new case local authorities have announced an "end to the problem," once they have arrested one or several suspects, and sometimes applied torture until the suspect "confessed." Every new case of a murdered woman, however, further undermines the credibility of the authorities, who seem more preoccupied with political repercussions than with protecting citizens and ensuring justice is done. In most cases when a young woman has gone missing, there are no witnesses or clear evidence of kidnapping or other offenses, especially in the first few hours after she has vanished. The families, not knowing what has happened, are in a state of anxiety, all too aware of the pattern of abductions and homicides.

Despite this, the officials consistently refuse to open even a preliminary criminal investigation to determine whether a crime, such as unlawful detention or kidnapping, has taken place. They disregard the pattern that ought to guide their actions from the outset. The authorities perceive no duty to open a criminal investigation immediately once a woman is reported missing in circumstances suspiciously similar to those of other abductions. Neither do they commit necessary resources and political will to investigate a reported abduction nor are local authorities linked to other state investigative mechanisms. They reject giving the families the opportunity to collaborate in the investigation. The fact that the authorities, at any level, have not managed to solve or stamp out these crimes against women has engendered deep distrust of the judicial apparatus and politicians. Rumors persist that officials are protecting those responsible, that drug traffickers and others involved in organized crime are implicated, or that people living in the United States might be behind the crimes. Other theories suggest motives connected with Satanism, pornography, or organ trafficking.

The Case against Mexican Authorities

Officials at the federal, state, and local levels point their fingers at each other or, more typically, claim that structural limitations in the Mexican justice system account for the perceived lack of investigation and prosecution. Just as the federal government tried to stay aloof from the murders of Ciudad Juárez, so too did Chihuahua state officials, attempting to leave everything in the hands of the local police. Much like the judicial structure of the United States, Mexico has parallel federal, state, and local criminal justice systems. Until 2003, Mexican federal authorities disclaimed jurisdiction over the murders and disappearances because they were not federal crimes. In 2003, however, the federal government changed course and announced it had a duty to clear up the cases in question and to promote dialogue with relatives, victims, and civil society, as well as to institute collaborative initiatives with NGOs. While sounding the right note, the old refrain applies: "Between what is said and what is done, there is a wide gap."[7]

Likewise in 2003, facing international pressure, the attorney general of Mexico set up the Joint Investigating and Prosecuting Agency, combining federal and state investigative resources to criminally prosecute and punish any official responsible for allowing abuses through negligence, complicity, torturing detainees, or using threats or coercion against witnesses, lawyers, or human rights defenders. Not much came of this, although there have been other highly acclaimed but ineffective steps taken by law enforcement authorities toward a more equitable solution. Regardless of which authorities are involved, there is a salient, well-documented pattern of how officials interact with the Juárez abductions and killings.

Impunity

The impunity rate for cases of women murdered with or without sexual violence is difficult to ascertain, mainly because information held by the authorities is extremely variable and contradictory, for various disingenuous reasons. The problem is whether prosecutions and arrests, when they do occur, and the manner in which they are done, actually operate to fight impunity or to encourage it.

Invisibility of Women Who Go Missing

Even when the authorities do concern themselves with cases of mutilated, raped, and murdered women, they ignore the question of women
who have "disappeared," whose numbers are now greater than six hundred (UN, "Report of Special Rapporteur on Extrajudicial, Summary, or
Arbitrary Executions," para. 85).

"High Risk" Missing Person Cases:
Leads Ignored and Delays in Investigating

Despite all that has happened, when a woman is reported missing,
the authorities do not initiate a criminal investigative action any more
quickly than they do otherwise, even in cases the authorities acknowledge
are "high risk." So bad are their ineptness and callousness that, when
police receive a missing person report, they do not even undertake such
activities as immediately distributing photographs of the victims, even in
places where they were seen last. Nor do they use the media to publicize
photographs or encourage the community to help with the search. That
the bodies of the deceased typically have been found by happenstance
rather than by the police reflects the superficiality of their investigations.
Sometimes, in fact, officials, reflecting a societal sexism, make their own
evaluation as to whether a missing woman is a "good girl" or someone
who might have gone off on her own. This sexism undermines dealing
effectively with this saga of violence ("Annual Report 2002").

A missing person report is not treated as a formal complaint or notice
of a crime that sets police machinery in motion. It is simply an administrative report. Although it should be the officials' duty to establish whether
the missing person was a victim of a crime, they impose on the families
the burden of demonstrating the woman did not leave voluntarily. The
fact that there is a pattern in which women are kidnapped and murdered
should lead the officials to open criminal investigations immediately on
the assumption that the woman, especially if a girl, has gone missing
because of a criminal offense. Once an investigation has begun, the relatives can exercise *la coadyudancia* (a kind of *amicus curiae* assistance to
the investigating officials). This gives them the right to see and question
all the procedural police formalities and suggest leads for the police to

follow up on. A criminal investigation has the effect of obliging the officials to justify their actions. Without the investigation the missing person has no legal protection, and the family has no full right to justice but is dependent on the goodwill of the authorities.

Police Inefficiency, Incompetence, and Negligence

The National Human Rights Commission of Mexico (Comisión Nacional de Derechos Humanos, CNDH) has painstakingly delineated a litany of police inefficiency, incompetence, indifference, insensitivity, and negligence regarding the Juárez murders, especially in failing to protect evidence and improperly conducting forensic examinations. The CNDH issued its report after five years of official inaction and concluded that several levels of the judicial authorities and the state and municipal governments of Chihuahua were guilty of negligence and dereliction of duty. A Special Rapporteur for the UN Commission on Human Rights made similar findings ("Report of Special Rapporteur on the Independence of Judges and Lawyers on the Mission to Mexico").

Allegations of Torture during Criminal Investigations

Some arrests and convictions indeed have occurred, but the victims' families and NGOs have raised serious questions about the nature of charges brought against alleged suspects, and postarrest procedures. Detainees awaiting sentence in "serial murders" cases have claimed that torture was used to coerce information and confessions. The strong suspicion is that the authorities use trumped-up confessions and convictions to make it appear they are doing something to resolve the situation, even though the murders continue.

Amnesty International and other organizations have called repeatedly on the authorities to stop taking self-incriminating statements without the accused's attorney or a judge being present, and then using the statements in court. The fact that judges accept such confessions legitimizes torture as an investigative tool, however unreliable it may be. The absence of an independent judiciary and the unwillingness of judges to implement international human rights standards means the courts do not effectively protect the rights of the accused to a fair trial and to be free from torture.

This also casts a long shadow of suspicion over the integrity of the judicial system. This and the lack of transparency raise the twin specters of corruption and impunity.

The International Responsibilities of Mexico

Various international and national legal principles are at issue in the Juárez murders. This section focuses on those that seem the most viable for legal action in either the Inter-American human rights schema or U.S. courts.

General Rights of Women

Violence against women implicates the violation of a range of fundamental human rights, civil and political as well as economic, social and cultural (UN, *Inter-American Convention on the Prevention, Punishment, and Eradication of Violence against Women*, arts. 3–6; UN, *Convention on the Elimination of All Forms of Discrimination against Women*; UN, *General Recommendations Adopted by Committee on Elimination of Discrimination against Women*, para. 7).

Due Diligence and the Duty to Protect and Ensure Rights

Mexico's failure to respond effectively to the abductions and murders could incur responsibility and liability under regional and international standards Mexico has ratified, such as the *American Convention on Human Rights* and the *International Covenant on Civil and Political Rights*. That failure to respond effectively also would contravene other standards, including those dealing specifically with violence against women.

Both the *American Convention* and the *International Covenant* guarantee the rights to life, physical integrity, liberty, and personal safety. These standards require not only that officials not violate these rights, but also that they do what is necessary to protect those rights when threatened by private individuals' criminal actions. Under the *American Convention* (art. 1) states have a duty to ensure the exercise of human rights within their territory. The Inter-American Court outlined that obligation in a case of forced disappearance in Honduras in which the identity of those responsible was not known (*Velásquez-Rodríguez*, para. 172). The Inter-American Court used the concept of "due diligence" to measure the degree of effort a state must undertake to ensure the exercise of human rights, even where people with no connection with the state commit abuses: "due diligence" requires the state to take reasonable steps to prevent human rights violations, use the means at its disposal to carry out serious investigations, identify those responsible, impose appropriate punishment, and ensure adequate reparation for the victims, whether the state itself commits the transgression or "allows private persons or groups to act freely and with impunity to the detriment of the rights recognized by the Convention" (*Velásquez-Rodríguez*, paras. 174, 176). That requires a serious investigation and not "a mere formality preordained to be ineffective." "Where the acts of private parties that violate the Convention are not seriously investigated, those parties are aided in a sense by the government, thereby making the State responsible on the international plane" (ibid., paras. 177, 185–88). The Inter-American Court ruled that, although it had not been possible to attribute the disappearance to state officials, the state's failure to act with due diligence was in itself a breach of the duty to ensure the victim's rights to life, liberty, and personal integrity (ibid., paras. 185–88). The UN Human Rights Committee, which monitors compliance with the *International Covenant on Civil and Political Rights*, has also stated that the duty to "ensure" the rights in the *International Covenant* requires appropriate measures be taken to prevent and investigate abuses perpetrated by private persons or entities, punish those responsible, and provide reparations to the victims (UN, Human Rights Committee, Draft General Comment on Article 2 of the *International Covenant on Civil and Political Rights*, para. 7). Both the *International Covenant* and the *American Convention on Human Rights* assert the obligation to respect, protect, and ensure rights without discriminating because of sex and to guarantee equality for men and women in the enjoyment of rights and the protection of the law (*International Covenant*, arts. 2[1], 3, 26; *American Convention*, arts. 1, 24). When the law does not provide women with sufficient protection against violence, either because of the way in which offenses are defined or how the law is enforced, the state has responsibility by virtue of these antidiscriminatory provisions to rectify the situation.

Due Diligence and Mitigating Violence against Women

The international community has adopted several instruments that have enshrined the concept of "due diligence" with the specific intention of combating violence against women. The UN *Declaration on the Elimination of Violence against Women* (art. 4c) reaffirms the state's due diligence obligation to prevent, investigate, and punish violence against women, whether perpetrated by the state or private persons.

Although the *Convention on the Elimination of All Forms of Discrimination against Women*, which Mexico ratified in 1981, does not explicitly refer to violence against women, the UN committee that monitors its implementation has stated that gender-based violence is a form of discrimination as defined by the convention. According to the *General Recommendations Adopted by the UN Committee on the Elimination of Discrimination against Women* (para. 6), gender-based violence is "violence that is directed against a woman because she is a woman or that affects women disproportionately. It includes acts that inflict physical, mental or sexual harm or suffering, threats of such acts, coercion and other deprivations of liberty."

The Optional Protocol to the *Convention on the Elimination of All Forms of Discrimination against Women*, which Mexico ratified in 2002, created another mechanism for vying against violence by giving women the right to seek redress at an international level for violations of their rights under the convention. The victims or their representatives may submit a complaint directly to the committee once they have exhausted all other remedies. The committee then can carry out its own investigation and decide the case in question.

The Inter-American system offers a legal framework for reducing violence against women. It is the only system with a binding treaty on the issue: the *Inter-American Convention on the Prevention, Punishment and Eradication of Violence against Women* (known as the "Convention of Belém do Pará"). The convention protects women's right to a life free from violence, at home and in the community, and while in state custody. The treaty explicitly codifies the obligation to act with "due diligence" in all legal and administrative measures without delay (UN, *General Recommendations Adopted by Committee on Elimination of Discrimination against Women*, art. 7). The convention makes it possible for the Inter-American Commission on Human Rights to receive petitions and take action. The doctrine established almost twenty years ago by the Inter-American Court regarding the responsibility to respond with "due diligence" to abuses committed by private persons has been applied by the commission to cases of violence against women. Considering a domestic violence case in Brazil, the commission concluded "the failure to prosecute and convict the perpetrator [that is, "to take effective action to sanction such acts"] is an indication that the State condones the violence suffered" (Inter-American Commission on Human Rights, Report No. 54/01, Case 12,051, paras. 55, 56).

Other Standards That Apply to Violence against Women

Mexico is also a party to other international human rights treaties, which, if complied with, could help prevent the violence against women in the state of Chihuahua. International standards on protecting children are relevant, because a third of the victims of the abductions and murders were under eighteen years of age. The UN's *Convention on the Rights of the Child* (arts. 2, 19), for example, places an obligation on the state to protect children against all forms of physical and mental abuse, ill treatment, and exploitation, including sexual abuse, whoever may be responsible and irrespective of sex or social origin.

A nation may also incur responsibility and liability under international norms that prohibit torture, if authorities do not take adequate measures to prevent and punish rape and other forms of sexual violence committed by private persons that amount to "cruel, inhuman or degrading treatment or punishment" (UN, *International Covenant on Civil and Political Rights*, General Comment No. 20 Concerning Prohibition of Torture and Cruel Treatment or Punishment, art. 7, para. 2). Both the *Inter-American Convention to Prevent and Punish Torture* (arts. 2, 3) and the *UN Convention against Torture* (art. 1.1) establish state responsibility for torture or ill treatment carried out by private individuals, if committed with the consent or acquiescence of a public official. The cases of Chihuahuan women who have gone missing share several important elements of the definition of a "disappearance" in the *Inter-American Convention on Forced Disappearance of Persons* and the *UN Declaration on the Protection of All Persons from Enforced Disappearance.* Under these standards a "disappearance" is depriving a person of freedom "perpetrated by agents of the state or by persons or groups of persons acting with the authorization, support, or acquiescence of the state" (OAS, *Inter-American Convention on Forced Disappearance*, art. 2). In several instances it appears officials may have been involved in carrying out or covering up abductions of women, but the authorities have not duly investigated them. Even where they have no direct involvement, Mexican officials have demonstrated a general pattern of negligence and ineffectiveness comparable to the pattern of "tolerance by the state" that the Inter-American Court and Commission have found culpable in other cases. Regardless of whether these cases strictly fall within the standard notion of a "disappearance," relatives of the "disappeared" have the right to know what happened to their relatives and to mourn and bury them in accord with their beliefs and traditions (*Velásquez-Rodríguez*, para. 181; and *Villagrán-Morales* case, paras. 173–77).

Using the Courts: Where and How?

Obviously, the Mexican courts have not been effective in enforcing criminal law, let alone international norms, in their jurisdictions. They have been impotent, if not complicit. Even where a judicial official might seek justice, there are serious problems with the independence and strength of the Mexican judiciary, and it is unlikely any judge would confront local authorities. There would be great personal risk, as seen by the killings of at least two attorneys and an investigative journalist. There are two options that may be worthwhile, although each faces formidable obstacles: the Inter-American Court of Human Rights and the United States courts.

Inter-American Court of Human Rights

As for invoking the assistance of the Inter-American Court, the *American Convention on Human Rights* requires that the process begin by lodging a petition against a country (Mexico, in this case) with the Inter-American Commission. Before presenting a petition to the court, the commission must determine the petition meets the following criteria: (1) domestic law remedies have been pursued and exhausted; and (2) the petition has been lodged within six months from the date when the party alleging violation of rights received notice of the final domestic law judgment. Sometimes the commission will try to settle the case before that step (OAS, *American Convention on Human Rights*, art. 46).

Standing is very liberal: any person, group of persons, or NGO legally recognized in one or more OAS member states may lodge a petition with the commission, alleging violations by a state party (ibid., art. 44). Certainly, the most viable legal theory is to link the special protections allotted to women and the elimination of discrimination and violence against women with the concept of "due diligence" the Inter-American Court used in the *Velásquez-Rodríguez* and *Villagrán-Morales* cases, together with the concept of "state tolerance" the Inter-American Commission adopted in the *Maia* case.

The pattern of noncompliance with the minimum requirements of "due diligence" has been so pronounced regarding the Juárez murders that it calls into question whether the authorities have the will to put an end to the violence, and thus effectively tolerate the situation. Given their abysmal performance, there is strong suspicion of police complicity in the violence or in covering it up. By international standards the Mexican authorities have grossly failed "due diligence" in two critical areas: (1) prompt, thorough, effective, coordinated, and impartial investigations that comply with international standards; and (2) punishing those responsible while ensuring they receive a fair trial. That dereliction has had the collateral effect of undermining crime prevention for the most vulnerable members of Chihuahuan society.

As for the investigations, there has been "a pattern of intolerable negligence" (see the *Villagrán-Morales* case) such that, despite evidence pointing to what actually happened, the majority of cases go unpunished. Criminal investigations are not commenced with any urgency; vital clues are not investigated or followed up; evidence is allowed to become contaminated; key testimonies are unjustifiably discredited; and allegations that suspects were tortured are not properly investigated or recorded. In addition, criminal investigations do not occur about reported harassment of witnesses, and procedures for identifying bodies, forensics, and autopsies do not comply with standards necessary to solve crime.

As to fair punishment, those few who have been accused and convicted were in custody for several years in violation of minimum fair trial standards. Allegations of torture to secure confessions and other aspects of the criminal proceedings raise serious questions about the legitimacy and effectiveness of the authorities' measures to identify and punish those responsible. This later point includes speedy trials and refraining from publicly asserting in the media that suspects are guilty before their trials have run their course. This also assumes that judges are trained on issues about violence against women and human rights, and that the judiciary is independent and protected from coercion. The fact that Mexican authorities are plainly aware of these serious deficiencies and have done little, if anything, to correct them would add a claim of "state tolerance" that should strengthen the case overall. And the intersection with the various, clear international protections for women against violence would make the case even stronger.

Another normative possibility is NAFTA, which affects the *maquiladoras* and includes generalized protections about labor conditions and worker safety or the duties of the owners and treaty signatories, like Mexico. NAFTA was the first trade agreement linked to workers' rights provisions in a major way. Its companion "side agreement," the North American Agreement on Labor Cooperation (NAALC), went into effect with NAFTA. Under NAALC the signatories agreed to enforce their respective labor laws and standards, while promoting eleven workers' rights principles. However, under NAALC sanctions as an enforcement tool are applicable to only three of the labor principles (pertaining to minimum wages, child labor, and occupational safety and health) (Bolle, 4–5). NAALC is a structurally noninvasive way of promoting workers' rights: it does not require any country to adopt new worker protection laws or conform to any international standards—only to enforce what it already has on the books. In this sense NAALC is relatively weak (ibid., 4–5). Even though it has a self-enforcing mechanism, to the extent it enforces rights, it is not a vehicle for judicial action in and of itself. However, one could point to NAALC as acknowledging again the internationally recognized duties of employers to provide workplace safety for women and to avoid all forms of gender discrimination—violence obviously being at the top of the list. These standards might be another route to enhancing liability of the Mexican government (and even perhaps of Mexican officials or a *maquiladora* owner, under the Alien Tort Claims Act or in a negligence action, described next).

United States Courts

The courts of the United States may provide a forum for certain civil cases for damages that a victim or aggrieved party, such as a family member, could bring forward. Generally, a civil action may be commenced in a U.S. federal court under the Alien Tort Claims Act (ATCA) (28 U.S.C. sec. 1350) to recover damages for personal injuries, pursuant to the Law of Nations and/or customary international law, if:

- *The plaintiff (complaining party) is an individual alien or foreign national, who is neither a U.S. citizen nor owes permanent allegiance to the United States.*
- *The claim asserted by the plaintiff is for a personal injury that constitutes a violation of the Law of Nations or a U.S. treaty.*
- *The conduct of the perpetrator caused the plaintiff to suffer actual harm.*
- *The perpetrator is a foreign government official and/or a private person acting color of law—that is, acting as representatives of the state.*
- *The action is commenced within ten years of the event(s) complained of. (Holton)*

The ATCA standing requirement is stricter than that for the Inter-American Commission and Court—the person bringing suit must be an aggrieved individual, and the complaint must be levied against a specific individual official rather than a state. An additional hurdle is that the court must obtain personal jurisdiction over the perpetrator, which generally means the defendant has to be found in the United States or has such "minimum contacts" with the United States that a court may exercise jurisdiction consistent with the due process requirements of the U.S. Constitution.

Officials. ATCA has a provision specifically referring to extrajudicial killings and torture, which arguably would apply to Mexican officials, who can be identified. Until the U.S. Supreme Court speaks authoritatively on the issue, federal appellate courts are free to define the extent of ATCA coverage. As noted below, the U.S. Ninth Circuit Court of Appeals in California has taken one of the strongest leads. The Fifth Circuit Court of Appeals, which oversees Texas, however, has imposed hurdles that complicate ATCA suits (*Carmichael v. United Technologies Corp.*, 112–15). There would most likely be a problem bringing an ATCA claim against Mexican officials on a theory of failure to investigate and prosecute because of the great difficulty in proving causation—the failure to investigate and prosecute one crime caused the commission of another crime.

Another challenge in bringing an ATCA lawsuit is that a U.S. court may define the issue as a "political question." While the prospects of "due diligence" and "state tolerance" claims might have currency in the Inter-American Commission and Court, it is likely a U.S. federal court would rule that the way Mexico chooses to allocate its resources with respect to investigation and prosecution of crimes would be deemed a "political question," not proper for review by American courts. Although tying the issue of failure to prosecute in with murders *by* Mexican officials might help clear these hurdles somewhat, strong evidence would be required to trump the "political question" defense. ATCA requires a violation of international law or U.S. treaty, and international law rarely addresses random individualized acts of violence. One would have to show the Juárez murders were part of a systematic violation of customary international law. In most cases, that requires official action or state action.

Owners of maquiladoras. Is there any liability that would attach to owners of *maquiladoras* that would subject them to ATCA jurisdiction in U.S. courts? The issue of liability of nonstate actors, especially corporations, is currently at the cutting edge of international law. U.S. courts are beginning to seriously address the issue of corporate liability under ATCA. Traditionally, American courts have not recognized corporations as official actors against whom an ATCA claim can be brought (*Bao Ge v. Li Peng*). However, the U.S. Ninth Circuit recently declined to dismiss claims brought under ATCA, alleging that several corporations aided and abetted the Myanmar military's perpetration of various atrocities in support of an oil pipeline project (*Doe I v. Unocal Corp.*). A few years earlier a New Jersey federal district court held that Ford Motor was subject to ATCA claims because, when it used forced labor provided by the German government during World War II, it was a de facto state actor. The court dismissed the claims on other grounds (*Iwanowa v. Ford Motor Co.*). To successfully hold a private company liable, the claim would have to rise to the level of aiding and abetting Mexican government officials in violation of international law, as in *Unocal*, or being a de facto state actor when it violated the law, as in *Iwanowa*, or somehow tie into one of the few categories of violations of international law recognized for ATCA claims for which nonstate actors are liable. ATCA claims for (de facto) state actors include genocide; slavery or slave trade; murder or causing the disappearance of individuals; torture or other cruel, inhumane degrading treatment or punishment; prolonged arbitrary detention; systematic racial discrimination; and a consistent pattern of gross violations of internationally recognized human rights. ATCA claims for nonstate actors are fewer: piracy, slave trade, attacks on or hijacking of aircraft, genocide, war crimes, and perhaps certain acts of terrorism (Holton; *Doe I v. Unocal Corp.*). As noted, another normative possibility is NAFTA, which affects the *maquiladoras* and includes generalized protections about labor conditions and worker safety or the duties of the owners or treaty signatories. This might be a route to enhancing liability for a *maquiladora* owner (or even a Mexican official) under ATCA.

    Texas state courts. Another legal strategy is possible litigation in a Texas state court, perhaps in El Paso, against a *maquiladora* owned by a company that operates in both Texas and Mexico for negligence where the negligence occurred in Mexico and the plaintiff is a Mexican citizen. There is precedent for this. In *Dow Chemical Company v. Alfaro*, eighty-two Standard Fruit employees who lived in Costa Rica brought suit against Dow Chemical and Shell Oil. Dow and Shell manufactured and furnished Standard Fruit with dibromochloropropane (DBCP), a toxic pesticide. The employees claimed that as a result of exposure to DBCP, they suffered personal injuries, including sterility. The workers alleged the companies were liable and filed suit in a Houston state court. Shell's headquarters were in Houston, and Dow, with headquarters in Michigan, conducted extensive business in Houston. Subsequent to the *Dow* case, however, the Texas Legislature made it more difficult for this genre of litigation. It amended Texas law to include a *forum non conveniens* (inconvenient forum) principle. Thus the requirements of such an action are now the following:

1. A law of the foreign state or country or Texas gives a right to maintain an action for damages for the death or injury.

2. The action is begun in Texas within the time provided by Texas law.
3. For a resident of a foreign state or country, the action is begun in Texas within the time provided by the laws of the foreign state or country in which the wrongful act, neglect, or default took place.
4. In the case of a citizen of a foreign country, the country has equal treaty rights with the United States on behalf of its citizens.

In addition, if the Texas court finds, in the interest of justice and for the convenience of the parties, that the action would be more properly heard in a forum outside Texas, the court must decline to exercise jurisdiction. Thus if a *maquiladora* in Ciudad Juárez provides unsafe working conditions for women, such as having them work late and then dropping them off by bus at some distance from their homes so they must walk a long and dangerous distance, the company could be liable in negligence for their injury or death, given the well-documented danger in Ciudad Juárez for women. If the woman or her family wanted to bring a personal injury or wrongful death claim or a group of female workers wanted to assure their safety in the future, they should be able to sue the *maquiladora* in Texas state court, if it or its parent company does business in Texas, within two years of the death, injury, or anticipated injury and according to the time parameters in Mexican law for negligence actions. The company would most likely challenge jurisdiction as an inconvenient forum. In the Juárez situation this should not be difficult to defeat because the plaintiff could make a credible showing that no alternate forum exists for such an action in Mexico and that Mexico does not provide an adequate remedy.

One could make similar claims against a *maquiladora* that refuses to cooperate with a Mexican police investigation into deaths and disappearances that directly affect the company's female employees, and so on. There are a number of possibilities. Here, too, the NAALC standards and principles of protecting women from gender-based discrimination could come into effect and help set operative standards in a negligence action. Often, a damage action against a corporate entity, if successful, has a greater impact and more ameliorative effect in enhancing protection of aggrieved persons than relying on the police power of the authorities.

Conclusion

I hope this chapter rises to more than a study "full of sound and fury, signifying nothing." Rather, may it outline a possible roadmap that could point the way to some modicum of justice for the victims of the murders in Ciudad Juárez, and may it motivate someone to set foot on that path, for the sake of those who have died and disappeared, so that their deaths and disappearances will protect others in the future.

Appendix. Legally Binding Applicable International Human Rights Instruments to Which Mexico Is a Party

Civil and Political Rights

- *International Covenant on Economic, Social, and Cultural Rights*
- *American Convention on Human Rights*

Economic, Social, and Cultural Rights

- *International Covenant on Economic, Social, and Cultural Rights*
- *Additional Protocol to the American Convention on Human Rights on Issues of Economic, Social, and Cultural Rights (also known as the "San Salvador Protocol")*

Combating Torture

- *Convention against Torture and Other Cruel, Inhuman, or Degrading Treatment or Punishment*
- *Inter-American Convention to Prevent and Punish Torture*

Rights of Women

- *Inter-American Convention Relating to the Concession of the Civil Rights to Women*
- *Inter-American Convention Relating to the Concession of Political Rights of Women*

- *Convention on the Nationality of Women*
- *Convention on the Nationality of Married Women*
- *Convention on the Political Rights of Women*
- *Convention on the Elimination of All Forms of Discrimination against Women*
- *Inter-American Convention on the Prevention, Punishment, and Eradication of Violence against Women*

Rights of the Child

- *Convention on the Rights of the Child*
- *Convention (No. 90) Related to Nocturnal Work of Minors in Industry*
- *Convention (No. 182) on the Prohibition of the Worst Forms of Child Labor*

Discrimination

- *International Convention on the Elimination of All Forms of Racial Discrimination*
- *Inter-American Convention for the Elimination of All Forms of Discrimination against Persons with Disabilities*

Labor Rights

- *Freedom of Association and Protection of the Right to Organise ("Convention 87")*
- *Convention Concerning Equal Remuneration for Men and Women Workers for Work of Equal Value ("Convention 100")*
- *Convention Concerning Discrimination in Respect of Employment and Occupation ("Convention 111")*
- *Convention Concerning Protection and Facilities to Be Afforded to Workers' Representatives in the Undertaking ("Convention 135")*

Notes

The title for this chapter comes from events of December 2001, when after the bodies of women were found in a cotton field near Juárez, more than three hundred civil society groups from all over Mexico launched a campaign, Alto a la Impunidad: Ni una muerta más (Stop the impunity: Not one more murder), to exert pressure on Mexican authorities and increase attention worldwide.

1. Although some important protections are found in customary international law, such as prohibitions on slavery and genocide, this chapter focuses on norms established in international treaties. However, the distinction between customary international law and treaties may not be too crucial, because many human rights norms are now codified in treaties. See, for example, UN, Office of the High Commissioner for Human Rights, *Convention on the Prevention and Punishment of the Crime of Genocide*; and UN, *Supplementary Convention on the Abolition of Slavery, the Slave Trade, and Institutions and Practices Similar to Slavery*.

2. See the appendix, "Legally Binding Applicable International Human Rights Instruments to Which Mexico Is a Party," at the end of this chapter for a list of legal instruments ratified by Mexico. See also Héctor Fix-Fierro, *Los derechos políticos de los mexicanos* (2006); UN, Committee on the Elimination of Discrimination against Women, "Inquiry into Rapes, Murders, Abductions in North Mexico," Report on Mexico Produced by the Committee on the Elimination of Discrimination against Women under Article 8 of the Optional Protocol to the Convention, Reply from the Government of Mexico (jurisdiction of UN, Human Rights Committee); and OAS, *American Convention on Human Rights*, "Pact of San José" (mandatory jurisdiction of Inter-American Court of Human Rights).

3. Leary; Inter-American Court, Advisory Opinion OC-2/82 ("Upon concluding these human rights treaties, the States submit themselves to a legal order within which, for the common good, they assume various obligations, not in relation to other States, but rather to individuals under their jurisdiction").

4. Much of the information here comes from Amnesty International (*Intolerable Killings*) and various UN documents (for example, the Committee on the Elimination of Discrimination against Women, "Inquiry into Rapes, Murders, Abductions in North Mexico").

5. The Partido de Acción Nacional (the PAN, National Action Party) governed Chihuahua from 1992 until 1998, when it lost the elections to the Partido Revolucionario Institucional (the PRI, Institutional Revolutionary Party), which has governed the state since then.

6. The families have sought justice through other means: freedom of association and protection of the right to organize, to bargain collectively, and to strike; prohibition of forced labor; minimum employment standards, including minimum wages and overtime pay; elimination of employment discrimination; equal pay for women; compensation for occupational injuries and illness; protections of migrant workers, children, and young persons; and prevention of occupational injuries and illnesses.

7. "Del dicho al hecho, hay mucho trecho."

References

Books, Journals, and Newspaper Articles

"Abuso y corrupción policíaca contra transgéneros." *Frontera gay*, November 1999, 3.

Alcalá Iberri, María Socorro. *Las muertas de Juárez*. Mexico City: Libra, 2004.

Alvidrez López, David. "Brutal crimen en Cuauhtémoc: Violan, torturan y asesinan a mujer frente a sus hijos, abusan de una menor." *Diario de Chihuahua*, July 4, 1995, 1A.

Andreas Peter. *Border Games: Policing the U.S.–Mexico Divide*. Ithaca, N.Y.: Cornell University Press, 2000.

"Annual Report 2002." *Amnesty International*. Available online at http://www.reliefweb .int/rw/lib.nsf/db900SID/JDAB-5SHJEK?OpenDocument.

Anzaldúa, Gloria. *The Borderlands/La frontera: The New Mestiza*. San Francisco: Aunt Lute, 1992.

Appadurai, Arjun. *Modernity at Large: Cultural Dimensions of Globalization*. Minneapolis: University of Minnesota Press, 1996.

Arce, Luz. *El infierno*. Santiago, Chile: Planeta, 1993.

Avila López, Betzabé, and Lorena Orihuela Bobadilla. "Significaciones imaginarias en torno a los asesinatos de mujeres en Ciudad Juárez." *El cotidiano* 120 (2003): 26–34.

Bajtín, Mijaíl. *La cultura popular en la edad media y el renacimiento: El contexto de Francois Rabelais*. Madrid, Spain: Alianza Editorial, 1987.

Balderas Domínguez, Jorge. *Mujeres, antros y estigmas en la noche juarense*. Mexico City: Conaculta-Ichicult, 2002.

Baldwin, Elaine, Brian Longhurst, Scott McCracken, Miles Ogborn, and Greg Smith, eds. *Introducing Cultural Studies*. Athens: University of Georgia Press, 1999.

Balli, Cecilia. "Ciudad de la Muerte." In *Rio Grande*. Edited by Jan Reid. Austin: University of Texas Press, 2004.

Bard, Patrick. *La frontière: Thriller*. Paris: Seuil, 2002.

Barthes, Roland. *El grado cero de la escritura: Nuevos ensayos críticos*. Translated by Nicolás Rosa. Mexico City: Siglo XXI, 1997.

Bataille, Georges. *El erotismo*. Barcelona, Spain: Tusquets, 1979.

——. *The Unfinished System of NonKnowledge*. Translated by Michelle Kendall and Stuart Kendall. Minneapolis: University of Minnesota Press, 2001.

Baudrillard, Jean. *L'échange symbolique et la mort*. Paris: Gallimard, 1976.

——. "The Perfect Crime." In *The Politics of Human Rights*. Edited by Obrad Savic, 273–80. London: Verso, 1999.

——. *Selected Writings*. Edited by Mark Poster. Stanford, Calif.: Stanford University Press, 1988.

BBC. "Mexico's Transvestite Ban Draws Gay Protest." *BBC.com*. November 5, 2000. Available online at http://news.bbc.co.uk/2/hi/americas/2402571.stm.

Benítez, Rhory, et al. *El silencio que la voz de todas quiebra*. Chihuahua, Mexico: Ediciones del Azar, 1999.

Bhabha, Homi. *The Location of Culture*. New York: Routledge, 1994.

Biron, E. Rebecca. *Murder and Masculinity: Violent Fictions of Twentieth-century Latin America*. Nashville, Tenn.: Vanderbilt University Press, 2000.

Blum, Deborah. *Sex on the Brain: The Biological Differences between Men and Women*. New York: Viking, 1997.

Blumenthal, Ralph. "Hoping the Good News Holds, El Paso Prepares for Major Growth at Fort Bliss." *New York Times* 154, no. 53222 (2005): 20.

Bolle, Mary Jane. "NAFTA Labor Side Agreement: Lessons for the Worker Rights and Fast-Track Debate." Library of Congress. Congressional Research Service. Available online at http://ncseonline.org/nle/crs/abstract.cfm?NLEid=1465.

Boorstin, Daniel. *The Image: A Guide to Pseudo-Events in America*. New York: Vintage Books, 1992.

Bourdieu, Pierre. *Pensamiento y acción*. Buenos Aires, Argentina: Libros del Zorzal, 2002.

Bowden, Charles. *Down by the River: Drugs, Money, Murder, and Family*. New York: Simon & Schuster, 2002.

———. *Juárez: The Laboratory of Our Future*. New York: Aperture, 1998.

———. "While You Were Sleeping: In Juárez, Mexico, Photographers Expose the Violent Realities of Free Trade." *Harper's* 273, no. 1759 (1996): 44–52.

"Brutal asedio policiaco, denuncian travestis y transexuales de Tijuana." *Frontera gay*, November 1999.

Butler, Judith. *El género en disputa: El feminismo y la subversión de la identidad*. Mexico City: Paidós–PUEG, 2001.

———, Ernesto Laclau, and Slavoj Žižek. *Contingency, Hegemony, Universality: Contemporary Dialogues on the Left*. New York: Verso, 2000.

Cameron, Deborah, and Elizabeth Frazer. *The Lust to Kill: A Feminist Investigation of Sexual Murder*. New York: New York University Press, 1987.

Campbell, David. *National Deconstruction*. Minneapolis: University of Minnesota Press, 1998.

Cantú, Lionel. "De Ambiente: Queer Tourism and the Shifting Boundaries of Mexican Male Sexualities." *GLQ* 8, nos. 1–2 (2002): 139–66.

Caputi, Jane. *The Age of Sex Crime*. Bowling Green, Ohio: Bowling Green University Press, 1987.

Carrier, Joseph. *De los otros: Intimacy and Homosexuality among Mexican Men*. New York: Columbia University Press, 1995.

Castillo, Debra A., María Gudelia Rangel Gómez, and Bonnie Delgado. "Border Lives: Prostitute Women in Tijuana." *Signs* 24, no. 2 (1998): 387–422.

Castillo, Debra A., and María Socorro Tabuenca Córboba. *Border Women: Writing from la Frontera*. Minneapolis: University of Minnesota Press, 2002.

Certeau, Michel de. *La invención de lo cotidiano: I Artes de hacer.* Translated by Alejandro Pescador. Mexico City: Universidad Iberoamericana, 1996.

Colaizzi, Giulia. "El cuerpo ciborguesco, o del grotesco tecnológico." In *Bajtín y la literatura: Actas del IV Seminario Internacional del Instituto de Semiótica Literaria y Teatral.* Edited by Mario García-Page Sánchez, José Nicolás Romera Castillo, and Francisco Gutiérrez Carbayo, 103–26. Madrid, Spain: Visor, 1994.

Concha-Eastman, Alberto. "Urban Violence in Latin America and the Caribean: Dimensions, Explanations, Actions." In *Citizens of Fear: Urban Violence in Latin America.* Edited by Susan Rotker, 37–54. New Brunswick, N.J.: Rutgers University Press, 2002.

Connel, R. W. *Masculinities.* 1995. Reprint, Cambridge: Polity Press, 2005.

Conover, Ted. *Coyotes: A Journey through the Secret World of America's Illegal Aliens.* New York: Random House, 1987.

Crary, Jonathan. *Techniques of the Observer: On Vision and Modernity in the Nineteenth Century.* Cambridge: MIT Press, 1990.

Crosthwaite, Luis Humberto, John William Byrd, and Bobby Byrd. *Puro Border: Dispatches, Snapshots, and Graffiti from La Frontera.* El Paso, Tex.: Cinco Puntos Press, 2003.

De la Mora, Sergio. "Lourdes Portillo/Terrorisme de genre à la frontière Méxique-USA: Assassinat de femmes et justice dans 'Señorita extraviada' (Demoiselle perdue) de Lourdes Portillo." *Cinémas d'amérique latine* 12 (2004): 116–32. Available online at http://www.elojoquepiensa.udeg.mx/ingles/revis_01/secciones/cinejour/artic_05 .html.

Dobash, Rebeca E., and Russell P. Dobash. *Rethinking Violence against Women.* Thousand Oaks, Calif.: Sage Publications, 1998.

"Doble injusticia: Feminicidio y tortura en Ciudad Juárez y Chihuahua." *Witness and Comisión Mexicana de Defensa y Promoción de los Derechos Humanos.* March 3, 2008. Available online at http://hub.witness.org/en/DobleInjusticia.

Domínguez-Ruvalcaba, Héctor. "La educación de los hombres o cómo producir victimarios." *Metapolítica* special issue (2003): 27–32.

Ellis, Bruce G. "The Evolution of Sexual Attraction: Evaluative Mechanisms in Women." In *The Adapted Mind: Evolutionary Psychology and the Generation of Culture.* Edited by Jerome H. Barkow, Leda Cosmides, and John Tooby, 267–87. New York: Oxford University Press, 1992.

Elsuertudo. Online posting. September 5, 1998. Http://groups.google.com/group/alt.sex .prostitution.tijuana.

Erip. Online posting. February 1, 1999. Http://groups.google.com/group/alt.sex.prostitu tion.tijuana.

———. Online posting. September 2, 1997. Http://groups.google.com/group/alt.sex.pros titution.tijuana.

Fairclaugh, Norman. *Language and Power.* London: Longman, 1990.

Feldman, Allen. *Formations of Violence.* Chicago: Chicago University Press, 1991.

Fentanes, Julio. "Propone Diego Cevallos Comisión mixta para los crímenes de mujeres:

Pide El Jefe no politizar este caso porque es policiaco, no político." *El Diario*, May 10, 1998, A4.

Fernández-Kelly, María Patricia. *For We Are Sold: I and My People*. Albany: State University of New York Press, 1983.

Ferreira-Pinto, João B., Rebeca L. Ramos, and Alberto G. Mata Jr. "Dangerous Relationships: Effects of Early Exposure to Violence in Women's Lives on the Border." In *Life, Death, and In-between on the U.S.–Mexico Border*. Edited by Martha Oehmke Loustaunau and Mary Sánchez-Bane, 61–76. Westport, Conn.: Bergin & Garvey, 1999.

Fiala, Robert, and Susan Tiano. "Maquila Employment and Fertility in Mexicali, Mexico: A Study of the Dynamics of Productive and Reproductive Relations." Latin American and Iberian Institute Research Papers Series. No. 39. Albuquerque: University of New Mexico, 2003.

Fisher, Helen. *El primer sexo: Las capacidades innatas de las mujeres y cómo están cambiando el mundo*. Madrid, Spain: Taurus, 1999.

Fix-Fierro, Héctor. *Los derechos políticos de los mexicanos*. Mexico City: Universidad Nacional Autónoma De México (UNAM), 2006.

Franco, Jean. "Baile de fantasmas en los campos de la Guerra Fría." In *Nuevas Perspectivas desde/sobre América Latina: El desafío de los estudios culturales*. Edited by Mabel Moraña, 171–84. Santiago, Chile: Cuarto Propio, 2000.

———. "Killing Priests, Nuns, Women, Children." In *Critical Passions: Selected Essays*. Edited by Mary Louise Pratt and Kathleen Newman, 9–17. Durham, N.C.: Duke University Press, 1999.

Fregoso Peralta, Gilberto. "La página editorial de *El Informador* (Decano de la prensa jalisciense)." *Comunicación y Sociedad* no. 7 (1989): 11–54.

Fregoso, Rosa Linda. "Voices without Echo: The Global Gendered Apartheid." *Emergences: Journal for the Study of Media and Composite Cultures* 10, no. 1 (2000): 137–55.

Foucault, Michel. *El orden del discurso*. Translated by Alberto González Troyano. Mexico City: Ediciones populares, 1982.

———. *Hermenéutica del sujeto*. La Plata, Argentina: Altamira, 2002.

Fuentes, Carlos. *La frontera de cristal*. Mexico City: Aguilar, Altea, Taurus, Alfaguara, 1995.

Galán Benítez, Carmen. *Tierra marchita*. Mexico City: Consejo Nacional para la cultura y las artes, 2002.

García, Antonio. "Escenifican obra de Ensler en el teatro Sala Chopin," "Las muertas de Juárez, víctimas de una sociedad clasista: Alvarado. Los monólogos de la vagina busca sensibilizar a la comunidad." *La Jornada*, December 9, 2000, 4.

García Canclini, Néstor. *Consumidores y ciudadanos: Conflictos multiculturales de la globalización*. Mexico City: Grijalbo, 1995.

García García, M.D.L., J. Valdespino, J. Izazola, and others. "Bisexuality in Mexico." In *Bisexuality and HIV/AIDS*. Edited by Rob Tielman, Manuel Carballo, and Aart Hendriks, 41–58. Buffalo, N.Y.: Prometheus, 1991.

Gaspar de Alba, Alicia. *Desert Blood: The Juárez Murders.* Houston, Tex.: Arte Público, 2005.

Gauntlett, David. *Media, Gender, and Identity: An Introduction.* London: Routledge, 2002.

Goldman, Robert Kogod, Claudio Grossman, Claudia Martin, and Diego Rodríguez-Pinzón, eds. *The International Dimension of Human Rights: A Guide for Application in Domestic Law.* Washington, D.C.: Inter-American Development Bank, 2001.

González Rodríguez, Sergio. *Huesos en el desierto.* Barcelona, Spain: Anagrama, 2002.

———. "Noche y día: Las muertas de Juárez." *Reforma.* June 7, 1997, 84.

Greenblatt, Stephen. *Marvelous Possessions. The Wonder of the New World.* Chicago: University of Chicago Press, 1991.

———. *Tales of Love.* New York: Columbia University Press, 1987.

Gutiérrez Castañeda, Griselda. *Violencia sexista: Algunas claves para comprender el feminicidio en Ciudad Juárez.* Mexico City: UNAM/Programa Universitario de Estudios de Género/Facultad de Filosofía y Letras, 2004.

Gutiérrez, Griselda, ed. *Violencia sexista: Algunas claves para la comprensión del feminicidio en Ciudad Juárez.* Mexico City: UNAM, 2004.

Hall, Stuart. "Cultural Identity and Diaspora." In *Identity and Difference.* Edited by Kathryn Woodward, 29–36. London: Sage, 1997.

———. "Encoding/decoding." In *Culture, Media, Language: Working Papers in Cultural Studies, 1972–79.* Edited by Stuart Hall, Dorothy Hobson, Andrew Lowe, and Paul Willis, 99–132. London: Hutchinson, 1980.

Hanssen, Beatrice, Julia Constantino, and Mónica Mansour. "Los límites de la representación feminista: El lenguaje de la violencia de Elfriede Jelinek." *Debate feminista* 25, no. 13 (2002): 237–76.

Hardt, Michael, and Antonio Negri. *Empire.* Cambridge: Harvard University Press, 2000.

Hathaway, Oona. "Do Human Rights Treaties Make a Difference?" *Yale Law Journal* 11 (2002): 1935–2042.

Heise, Lori. L., Jacqueline Pitanguy, and Adrienne Germain. "Violence against Women: The Hidden Health Burden." World Bank Discussion Paper No. 225, 3. Washington, D.C.: World Bank, 1994.

Henríquez, Alejandro. "Lourdes Portillo's '*Señorita Extraviada:*' The Poetics and Politics of Femicide." *Studies in Latin American Popular Culture* 23 (2004): 123–36.

Heyman, Josiah M., and Howard Campbell. "Recent Research on the U.S.–Mexico Border." *Latin American Research Review* 39, no. 3 (2004): 205–19.

Hierro, Graciela. *De la domesticación a la educación de las mexicanas.* Mexico City: Editorial Torres Asociados, 1990.

———. *Ética y feminismo.* Mexico City: UNAM, 1990.

Holton, Tracy Bishop. "Cause of Action to Recover Civil Damages Pursuant to the Law of Nations and/or Customary International Law." In *21 Causes of Action 2D 327,* no. sec. 51, 2007.

Ianni, Octavio. "La violencia en las sociedades contemporáneas." *Metapolítica* 5, no. 17 (2001): 56–69.

182 REFERENCES

Iglesias, Norma. *Entre yerba, polvo y plomo: Lo fronterizo visto por el cine mexicano.* Mexico City: Colegio de la Frontera / Instituto Mexicano de Cinematografía, 1992.

Imbert, Gérard. *Los escenarios de la violencia.* Barcelona, Spain: Icaria Editorial, 1992.

Izard, Ralph. "Conference Report. Images of Mexico in the U.S. Media." Accessed at http://www.columbia.edu/cu/ilas/events/MexicoInUSMediaSymposium.html (unfortunately this URL is no longer available).

Jameson, Fredric. *Postmodernism, or, The Cultural Logic of Late Capitalism.* Durham, N.C.: Duke University Press, 1991.

Janoff, Victor. "Life under Siege." *Xtra West.* October 19, 1995, 15.

Kristeva, Julia. *Poderes de la perversión.* Mexico City: Siglo XXI, 1988.

———. *Powers of Horror: An Essay on Abjection.* New York: Columbia University Press, 1982.

———. *Sol negro: Depresión y melancolía.* Caracas, Venezuela: Monte Ávila Editores Latinoamericana, 1997.

Kruger, Barbara. "Untitled" [photomontage]. In *Literary Theory: An Anthology.* Edited by Julie Rivkin and Michael Ryan. Malden, Mass: Blackwell, 2000.

Labelle, Beverley. "Snuff—the Ultimate in Woman Hating." In *Femicide: The Politics of Woman Killing.* Edited by Jill Radford and Dianna E. H. Russell, 189–94. New York: Twayne, 1992.

Lagarde, Marcela. *Claves feministas para el poderío y la autonomía de las mujeres.* Managua, Nicaragua: Puntos de Encuentro, 1998.

———. *Identidades de género y derechos humanos: La construcción de las humanas.* Aguascalientes, Mexico: Universidad Autónoma de Aguascalientes, 1997.

———. *Los cautiverios de las mujeres: Madresposas, monjas, putas, presas y locas.* Mexico City: UNAM, 1990.

———. "Mujeres asesinadas eran elegidas por internet." Accessed at http://www.almar gen.com.mx/homicidios/2004/internet.htm (unfortunately this URL is no longer available).

Laufer, Peter. "Mexican Media: The Oral Tradition." *Internews.* July 30, 2002, 1–85.

Laumann, Eduard O., John H. Gagnon, Robert T. Michael, and Stuart Michaels, eds. *The Social Organization of Sexuality: Sexual Practices in the United States.* Chicago: University of Chicago Press, 1994.

"La_vida_loca." Online posting. June 11, 1999. Http://groups.google.com/group/alt.sex .prostitution.tijuana.

Leary, Virginia. *International Labor Conventions and National Law.* Boston: Brill Academic Publishers, 1982.

Lee Holmes, Marsha. "Get Real: Violence in Popular Culture and in English Class." *English Journal* 89, no. 5 (2000): 104–10.

"Legal Survey, Mexico." *International Lesbian and Gay Association.* Available online at http://www.asylumlaw.org/docs/sexualminorities/Lesbs.pdf.

Limas Hernández, Alfredo. "Sexualidad, género, violencia y procuración de justicia." *Revista metapolítica* special issue (2003): 64–67.

Livingston, Jessica. "Murder in Juarez: Gender, Sexual Violence, and the Global Assembly Line." *Frontiers: A Journal of Women's Studies* 25, no. 1 (2004): 59–76.

Lorey, David E. *The U.S.–Mexican Border in the Twentieth Century.* Wilmington, Del.: SR Books, 1999.

Lugo, Alejandro. *Fragmented Lives, Assembled Parts: Culture, Capitalism, and Conquest at the U.S.–Mexico Border.* Austin: University of Texas Press, 2008.

Lumsden, Ian. *Homosexuality, Society, and the State in Mexico.* Toronto: Canadian Gay Archives, 1991.

Luna Andrés de. *Erótica: La otra orilla del deseo.* Mexico City: Tusquets, 2003.

Maciel, David R. "Introduction." In *Mexico's Cinema: A Century of Film and Filmmakers.* Edited by Joanne Hershield and David R. Maciel, xi–xiv. Wilmington, Del.: SR Books, 1999.

MacKinnon, Catharine A. *Only Words.* Cambridge: Harvard University Press, 1993.

Marcondes Filho, Ciro. *O capital da notícia.* São Paulo, Brazil: Atica, 1985.

Martín-Barbero, Jesús. "La ciudad que median los medios." In *Espacio urbano, comunicación y violencia en América Latina.* Edited by Mabel Moraña, 19–35. Pittsburgh, Pa.: Instituto Internacional de Literatura Iberoamericana, 2002.

Martínez, Oscar J. *Border People: Life and Society in the U.S.–Mexico Borderlands.* Tucson: University of Arizona Press, 1994.

Martínez, Wilebaldo, et al. "Perfil epidemiológico y nuevos desafíos de la salud en nuestro entorno." Mimeograph. Ciudad Juárez: Academia de Salud Pública Universidad Autónoma de Ciudad Juárez, 2005.

Mbembe, Achille. "Necropolitics." *Public Culture* 15, no. 1 (2003): 11–40.

Méndez, Luis H. "Violencia simbólica en el territorio maquilador fronterizo." *El cotidiano* 125 (2004): 7–20.

Merino, Mauricio. "La indefinición del miedo." *El Universal.* July 23, 2005. Available online at http://www.eluniversal.com.mx/editoriales/29891.html.

"Mexican Town Cracks Down on Drag Queens." *Sapa-AFP.* November 4, 2002. Accessed at http://www.q.co.za/2001/2002/11/4-mexico.html (unfortunately this URL is no longer available).

"Mexico: Intolerable Killings: Ten Years of Abductions and Murders of Women in Ciudad Juárez and Chihuahua." *Amnesty International.* Available online at http://web.amnesty.org/library/index/ENGAMR410262003.

Monárrez Fragoso, Julia Estela. "La cultura del feminicidio en Ciudad Juárez, 1993–1999." *Frontera norte* 23, no. 12 (2000): 87–117.

———. "Feminicidio sexual en Ciudad Juárez: 1993–2001." *Debate feminista* 25 (2002): 279–305.

———. "El feminicidio sexual sistémico: Víctimas y familiares en Ciudad Juárez 1993–2003." Dissertation, El Colegio de la Frontera, 2005.

———. "Serial Sexual Femicide in Ciudad Juárez, 1993–2001." *Aztlán* 28, no. (2003): 153–79.

Money, John. *Principles of Development Sexology.* New York: Continuum, 1997.

Monsiváis, Carlos. *Amor perdido*. Mexico City: SEP, 1986.

———. *A ustedes les consta: Antología de la crónica en México*. Mexico City: Era, 1980.

———. *Los rituales del caos*. Mexico City: Era, 1995.

———. "Víctimas de crímenes sexuales, más allá de las estadísticas." *Revista metapolítica* special issue (2003): 50–56.

MuleLip. Online posting. January 20, 1999. Http://groups.google.com/group/alt.sex.pros titution.tijuana.

———. Online posting. January 24, 1999. Http://groups.google.com/group/alt.sex.prosti tution.tijuana.

Mulvey, Laura. *Visual and Other Pleasures*. Bloomington: Indiana University Press, 1989.

Múñiz, Elsa. *Cuerpo, representación y poder: México en los albores de la reconstruccón nacional, 1920–1934*. Mexico City: Porrúa/UNAM, 2002.

Nathan, Debbie. "Death Comes to the Maquila." *The Nation* 20, no. 264.2 (1997): 18–22.

———. "Missing the Story." *Texas Observer* 94, no. 16 (2002). Available online at http://www.texasobserver.org/issue.php?iid=98.

Novo, Salvador. *Return Ticket*. Mexico City: Cultura, 1928.

Nuestras Hijas de Regreso a Casa. 2007. Available online at http://www.mujeresdejuarez.org/.

Parra, Eduardo Antonio. "La carga del miedo." *El ángel*. March 13, 2005. Available online at http://gruporeforma.reforma.com/coberturas/elangel/.

Parra Molina, José Antonio. "Representa Juárez un peligroso coctel social: Investigador español da a conocer resultado de análisis sobre los crímenes de mujeres." *Norte de Ciudad Juárez*. August 1, 1998, 1.

Pecora, Norma. "Superman/Superboys/Supermen: The Comic Book Hero as Socializing Agent." In *Men, Masculinity, and the Media*. Edited by Steve Craig, 61–77. Newbury Park, Calif.: Sage Publications, 1992.

Pedroso, Rosa Nívea. "Elementos para una teoría del periodismo sensacionalista." *Comunicación y sociedad* 21 (1994): 139–58.

Peña, Devon. G. *The Terror of the Machine: Technology, Work, Gender, and Ecology on the U.S.–Mexico Border*. Austin: University of Texas Press, 1997.

Pérez Espino, José. "Homicidios en Ciudad Juárez: La invención de mitos en los medios y la lucrativa teoría de la conspiración." In *Violencia sexista: Algunas claves para la comprensión del feminicidio en Ciudad Juárez*. Edited by Griselda Gutiérrez, 47–62. Mexico City: Universidad Nacional Autónoma de México, 2004.

Petersen, Roger D. *Understanding Ethnic Violence: Fear, Hatred, and Resentment in Twentieth-Century Eastern Europe*. Cambridge: Cambridge University Press, 2002.

Pineda Jaimes, Servando. "Los mitos de las Muertas de Juárez." *Al Margen*. August 12, 2004. Available online at http://www.almargen.com.mx/homicidios/2004/imagen.htm.

Posner, Richard A. "Bad News." *New York Times Book Review*. July 31, 2005, 1, 4–11.

Prieur, Annick. *Mema's House, Mexico City: On Transvestites, Queens, and Machos*. Chicago: University of Chicago Press, 1998.

Quinones, Sam. "The Dead Women of Juárez." In *Puro Border: Dispatches, Snapshots, and Graffiti.* Edited by Luis Humberto Crosthwaite, John William Byrd, and others, 139–58. El Paso, Tex.: Cinco Puntos, 2003.

———. *True Tales from Another Mexico.* Albuquerque: University of New Mexico Press, 2001.

Radford, Jill, and Dianna E. Russell. *Femicide: The Politics of Woman Killing.* New York: Twayne Publishers, 1992.

Ramos, Roberto. "Hallan cuerpo de una mujer brutalmente asesinada." *El Diario.* October 5, 1998, C1.

Rangel Gómez, Gudelia, Linda Rebhun, and Yasmina Katsulis. "Migración, trabajo y riesgo de VIH entre trabajadores(as) sexuales en Tijuana, México." Colegio de la Frontera–Tijuana.

Ravelo Blancas, Patricia. "Aportes para una epistemología de la conciencia feminista." *Cuadernos del norte: Sociedad, política y cultura* 28 (1993): 14–19.

———. "Entre las protestas callejeras y las acciones internacionales: Diez años de activismo por la justicia social en Ciudad Juárez." *El cotidiano* 125 (2004): 21–32.

———, and Alfredo Limas. "Feminicidio en Ciudad Juárez: Una civilización sacrificial." *El cotidiano* 111 (2002): 47–57.

———, and Domínguez-Ruvalcaba, Héctor. "La batalla de las cruces: Los crímenes en la frontera y sus intérpretes." *Desacatos* 13 (2003): 122–53.

Reding, Andrew. *Mexico: Treatment of Homosexuals.* April 1998. INS Resource Information Center. Available online at http://uscis.gov/graphics/services/asylum/ric/qa _pdfs/QAMEX98.pdf.

———. *Mexico: Update on Treatment of Homosexuals.* May 2000. INS Resource Information Center. Available online at http://uscis.gov/graphics/services/asylum/ric/qa _pdfs/QAMEX00.pdf.

———. *Sexual Orientation and Human Rights in the Americas.* World Policy Institute. Available online at http://www.worldpolicy.org/projects/globalrights/sexorient/2003-LGBT-Americas.pdf.

Research Directorate Immigration and Refugee Board. "Mexico: The Treatment of Sexual Minorities." Ottawa. April 1999. Available online at http://www.unhcr.org/ refworld/type,COUNTRYREP,,MEX,3ae6a82510,0.htm.

Richardson, Chad. *Batos, Bolillos, Pochos, and Pelados: Class and Culture on the South Texas Border.* Austin: University of Texas Press, 1999.

Ripoll, Laura. "Prostitución masculina en el DF: Ellos también venden caro su amor." *La Jornada.* November 17, 2002. Available online at http://www.jornada.unam.mx/ 2002/11/17/mas-ripoll.html.

Robinson. Online posting. September 7, 1998. Http://groups.google.com/group/alt.sex .prostitution.tijuana/browse_frm/month/1998-09.

———. Online posting. February 8, 2000. Http://groups.google.com/group/alt.sex.prosti tution.tijuana/browse_frm/month/2000-02.

Rodríguez, Armando. "'Testimonios de horror: Confiesa 'El Gaspy' con frialdad, José Gaspar Ceballos Chávez, uno de los choferes acusados del homicidio de mujeres en

Ciudad Juárez, dio detalles sobre la violación y muerte de Brenda Patricia Méndez Vázquez." *El Diario*. April 11, 1999, A7.

Ronquillo, Víctor. *Las muertas de Juárez*. Mexico City: Planeta, 1999.

Rosaldo, Renato. "Surveying Law and Borders." In *The Latino/a Condition: A Critical Reader*. Edited by Richard Delgado and Jean Stefancic, 631–38. New York: New York University Press, 1998.

Rotker, Susana. "Cities Written by Violence. An Introduction." In *Citizens of Fear: Urban Violence in Latin America*. Edited by Susana Rotker and Katherine Goldman, 7–24. New Brunswick, N.J.: Rutgers University Press, 2002.

Rust. Online Posting. June 9, 1998. Http://groups.google.com/group/alt.sex.prostitution .tijuana.

Salecl, Renata. "Focus: Cut-and-Dried Bodies or How to Avoid the Pervert Trap." In *Jenny Holzer*. Edited by David Joselit, Joan Simon, and Renata Salecl, 78–89. London: Phaidon Press, 1998.

——. *(Per)versions of Love and Hate*. London-New York: Verso, 1998.

——. *The Spoils of Freedom: Psycoanalysis and Feminism after the Fall of Socialism*. New York: Routledge, 1994.

——. "Worries in a Limitless World." *Cardozo Law Review* 26, no. 3 (2005): 101–19.

Salzinger, Leslie. *Genders in Production*. Berkeley: University of California Press, 1995.

Sartori, Giovanni. *Homo videns: La sociedad teledirigida*. Translated by Ana Díaz Soler. Madrid, Spain: Ediciones Santillana, 2005.

Sau, Victoria. *Ser mujer: El fin de una imagen tradicional*. Barcelona, Spain: Icaria, 1993.

Schudson, Michael. *Discovering the News*. New York: Basic Books, 1978.

Schutz, Alfred. *El problema de la realidad social*. Buenos Aires, Argentina: Amorrortu, 1974.

Segato, Rita Laura. "Territorio, soberanía y crímenes de segundo Estado: La escritura en el cuerpo de las mujeres asesinadas en Ciudad Juárez." In *Ciudad Juárez: De este lado del puente*. Edited by Instituto Nacional de las Mujeres, 75–93. Mexico City: Instituto Nacional de las Mujeres-Epiketa, 2004.

Sherwin, Susan. "Philosophical Methodology Are They Compatible?" In *Women Knowledge and Reality: Explorations in Feminist Philosophy*. Edited by Ann Garry and Marilyn Pearsall, 21–35. Boston: Unwin Hyman, Inc., 1989.

Sinclair, John. "Culture and Trade: Some Theoretical and Practical Considerations." In *Mass Media and Free Trade: NAFTA and the Cultural Industries*. Edited by Emile G. McAnany and Kenton T. Wilkinson, 30–60. Austin: University of Texas Press, 1996.

Smith, Sharon. "The Image of Woman in Film: Some Suggestions for Future Research." *Women and Film* 1 (1972): 13–21.

Staudt, Kathleen. *Violence and Activism at the Border*. Austin: University of Texas Press, 2008.

Stevenson, Rodert Louis. *Strange Case of Dr. Jekyll and Mr. Hyde*. Cambridge: Chadwyck-Healey Ltd, 2000.

Suárez, Marcela. "Introduction." In *Impunidad: Aproximaciones al problema de la injus-*

ticia. Edited by Marcela Suárez, 5–8. Mexico City: Universidad Autónoma Metropolitana, 2002.

Tabuenca Córdoba, María Socorro. "Baile de fantasmas en Ciudad Juárez al final/principio del milenio." In *Más allá de la ciudad letrada: Crónicas y espacios urbanos*. Edited by Boris Muñoz and Silvia Spitta, 411–37. Pittsburgh, Pa.: Instituto Internacional de la Literatura Iberoamericana, 2003.

——, and Julia Monárrez, eds. *Bordeando la violencia contra las mujeres en la frontera norte de México*. Mexico City: Miguel Ángel Porrúa/Colegio de la Frontera, 2007.

Tiano, Susan. *Patriarchy on the Line*. Philadelphia, Pa.: Temple University Press, 1994.

Tiano, Susan, and Vickie Ruiz. *Women on the U.S.–Mexico Border: Responses to Change*. Colorado Springs, Colo.: Westview Press, 1991.

Tomasini Bassols, Alejandro. "Violencia, ética, legalidad y racionalidad." In *Estudios sobre violencia: Teoría y práctica*. Edited by Witold Jacorzynski, 21–38. Mexico City: Centro de Investigaciones y Estudios Superiores en Antropología Social/Miguel Ángel Porrúa Editores, 2002.

"Transfobia dentro de la comunidad Lésbico-Gay-Trans Género." *Sal del closet*. August 15, 2003. Available online at http://www.saldelcloset.com/recursos/centrosdeapoyo/iitrans foro.shtml.

Urrea, Luis Alberto. *Across the Wire: Life and Hard Times on the Mexican Border*. New York: Anchor Books, 1993.

Valero Flores, Luis Javier. "Las muertas de Juárez." *La Jornada*. June 14, 1998, 52.

Vasconcelos, José. *Ulises criollo: La vida del autor escrita por él mismo*. 1936. Reprint, Mexico City: Editorial Jus, 1958.

Velásquez, Emilio. "Denuncian transgéneros abusos de autoridades y violaciones a sus derechos humanos." *Frontera gay*. February 2000, 7.

Velásquez-Rodríguez v. "Honduras Case. Inter-American Court of Human Rights." Judgment. July 29, 1988. Available online at http://www.corteidh.or.cr/seriecpdf_ing/seriec _04_ing.pdf.

Vigil, James Diego. *Barrio Gangs: Street Life and Identity in Southern California*. Austin: University of Texas Press, 1988.

Virilio, Paul. *Ground Zero*. London-New York: Verso, 2002.

Washington Valdez, Diana. "Ciudad Juárez: Así empezó todo." *La Jornada*. October 31, 2003. Available online at http://www.nodo50.org/pchiapas/mexico/noticias/juarez2 .htm.

——. *La cosecha de mujeres: Safari en el desierto mexicano*. Mexico City: Océano, 2005.

——. "Las muertas de Juárez: Modus operandi." *Proceso* 148, no. 8 (2005): 44–49.

Wells, Susan. *Sweet Reason: Rhetoric and the Discourses of Modernity*. Chicago: University of Chicago Press, 1996.

White, Hayden. *Metahistoria: La imaginación histórica en la Europa del siglo XIX*. Translated by Stella Mastrangelo. Mexico City: Fondo de Cultura Económica, 1992.

Whitechapel, Simon. *Crossing to Kill*. New York: Virgin, 1998.

Williams, Linda. "Corporealized Observers: Visual Pornographies and the 'Carnal Density of Vision.'" In *Fugitive Images. From Photography to Video.* Edited by Patrice Petro, 3–41. Bloomington: Indiana University Press, 1995.

Woods, Tryon P. "Globalizing Social Violence: Race, Gender, and the Spatial Politics of Crisis." *American Studies* 42, no. 1 (2002): 142.

"World Report 2005: Mexico." *Human Rights Watch.* Available online at http://www.hrw .org/english/docs/2005/01/13/mexico9873.htm.

Wright, Melissa W. "Crossing the Factory Frontier: Gender, Place, and Power in a Mexican Maquiladora." *Antipode: A Journal of Radical Geography* 29, no. 3 (1997): 278–302.

———. "The Dialectics of Still Life: Murder, Women and Maquiladoras." *Public Culture* 11 (1999): 453–74.

———. "Manifesto against Femicide." *Antipode* 33, no. 3 (2001): 550–66.

———. "Maquiladora Mestizas and a Feminist Border Politics: Revisiting Anzaldúa." *Hypatia* 13, no. 3 (1998): 114–31.

Zemelman, Hugo. "Sujetos y subjetividad en la construcción metodológica." In *Subjetividad: Umbrales del pensamiento social.* Edited by Emma León and Hugo Zemelman, 21–35. Barcelona, Spain: Anthropos/Centro Regional de Investigaciones Interdisciplinarias/UNAM, 1997.

Zermeño, Sergio. "Maquila y machismo." *Revista memoria* 183. May 2004. Available online at http://www.rebelion.org/noticia.php?id=4556.

Žižek, Slavoj. *El acoso de las fantasías.* Mexico City: Siglo XXI, 1999.

———. *Tarrying with the Negative: Kant, Hegel, and the Critique of Ideology.* Durham, N.C.: Duke University, 1993.

Interviews

Acosta, Rosario. Interview with Patricia Ravelo. Ciudad Juárez, November 2003.

Andrade, Norma. Interview with Patricia Ravelo. Ciudad Juárez, November 2003.

Arce, Evangelina. Interview with Patricia Ravelo. Ciudad Juárez, November 2003.

Chávez Cano, Esther. Interview with Patricia Ravelo. Ciudad Juárez, November 2003.

Davenport, Hazel. Interview with Emilio Velázquez. Tijuana, September 2005.

Flores, Paula. Interview with Patricia Ravelo. Ciudad Juárez, January 2004.

Gabriela. Interview with Gudelia Rangel. Tijuana, March 1994.

González, Josefina. Interview with Patricia Ravelo. Ciudad Juárez, January 2004.

Karla. Interview with Emilio Velázquez. Tijuana, September 2005.

Monárrez, Benita. Interview with Patricia Ravelo. Ciudad Juárez, January 2004.

Morales, Ramona. Interview with Patricia Ravelo. Ciudad Juárez, January 2004.

Ortiz, Marisela. Interview with Patricia Ravelo. Ciudad Juárez, January 2004.

Pineda, Servando. Interview with Jorge Pineda. Ciudad Juárez, March 2005.

Rosa. Interview with Emilio Velázquez. Tijuana, September 2005.

Yadira. Interview with Emilio Velázquez. Tijuana, September 2005.

Yolanda. Interview with Emilio Velázquez. Tijuana, September 2005.

Legislation and Legal Cases

Alien Tort Claims Act. 28 U.S.C. sec. 1350.

Bao Ge v. Li Peng. 201 F.Supp.2d 14 (D.D.C. 2000).

Carmichael v. United Technologies Corp. 835 F.2D 109. 5th Cir. 1988.

Doe I v. Unocal Corp. 395 F.3d 932. 9th Cir. 2002. 395. F.3d 978 9th Cir. 2003.

Dow Chemical Company v. Alfaro. 786 S.W.2d 674 Tex. 1990.

Inter-American Commission on Human Rights. *Report No. 54/01.* Case 12,051. María da Penha Fernandes Maia. Brazil. Available online at http://www.cidh.org/women/Brazil12.051.htm.

Iwanowa v. Ford Motor Co. 67 F. Supp. 2D 424 D.N.J. 1999.

Organization of American States (OAS). Additional Protocol to the *American Convention on Economic, Social, and Cultural Rights,* O.A.S. T.S. No. 69, (1989) 28 I.L.M. 156. Entered into force 16 November 1999. Also known as the San Salvador Protocol. Available online at http://www.oas.org/juridico/english/treaties/a-52.html.

——. *American Convention on Human Rights.* Also known as the "Pact of San José." Available online at http://www.oas.org/juridico/english/Sigs/b-32.html.

——. *Inter-American Convention on Forced Disappearance of Persons.* Available online at http://www.oas.org/juridico/english/Treaties/a-60.html.

——. *Inter-American Convention on the Prevention, Punishment, and Eradication of Violence against Women.* Also known as the "Convention of Belém do Pará." Available online at http://www.oas.org/cim/English/Convention%20Violence%20Against%20Women.htm.

——. *Inter-American Convention to Prevent and Punish Torture.* Available online at http://www.oas.org/juridico/english/Treaties/a-51.html.

United Nations (UN). Commission on Human Rights. *Report of Special Rapporteur on the Independence of Judges and Lawyers on the Mission to Mexico.* Available online at http://www.unhchr.ch/Huridocda/Huridoca.nsf/0/c0120deaf3b91dd2c1256b760 03fe19d?Opendocument.

——. Committee on the Elimination of Discrimination against Women. "Inquiry into Rapes, Murders, Abductions in North Mexico." *Report on Mexico Produced by the Committee on the Elimination of Discrimination against Women under Article 8 of the Optional Protocol to the Convention. Reply from the Government of Mexico. Available online at http://www.un.org/womenwatch/daw/cedaw/cedaw32/CEDAW-C-2005-OP .8-MEXICO-E.pdf.*

——. *Convention against Torture and Other Cruel, Inhuman, or Degrading Treatment or Punishment.* Available online at http://untreaty.un.org/english/treatyevent2001/pdf/07e.pdf.

——. *Convention on the Elimination of All Forms of Discrimination against Women.* Available online at http://www.un.org/womenwatch/daw/cedaw/text/econvention.htm.

——. *Convention on the Rights of the Child.* Available online at http://www2.ohchr.org/english/law/crc.htm.

———. *Declaration on the Elimination of Violence against Women.* Available online at http://www.unhchr.ch/huridocda/huridoca.nsf/%28symbol%29/a.res.48.104.en.

———. *Declaration on the Protection of All Persons from Enforced Disappearance.* Available online at http://www.un.org/documents/ga/res/47/a47r133.htm.

———. *General Recommendations Adopted by Committee on Elimination of Discrimination against Women.* General Recommendation 19. Available online at http://www.un.org/womenwatch/daw/cedaw/recommendations/recomm.htm#recom19.

———. Human Rights Committee. *Draft General Comment on Article 2 of the International Covenant on Civil and Political Rights.* Available online at http://www.unhchr.ch/tbs/doc.nsf/0/9b1f4ddaca5b86fec1256faco03f3524/$FILE/G0344835.doc.

———. Inter-American Commission on Human Rights. *The Situation of the Rights of Women in Ciudad Juárez, Mexico: The Right to Be Free from Violence and Discrimination.* Available online at http://www.cidh.org/annualrep/2002eng/chap.vi.juarez.htm.

———. *International Covenant on Civil and Political Rights.* General Comment No. 20 Concerning Prohibition of Torture and Cruel Treatment or Punishment (Article 7). Available online at http://www.unhchr.ch/tbs/doc.nsf/0/6924291970754969c12563ed004c8ae5?Opendocument.

———. *International Covenant on Civil and Political Rights.* Available online at http://www2.ohchr.org/english/law/ccpr.htm.

———. Office of the High Commissioner for Human Rights. *Convention on the Prevention and Punishment of the Crime of Genocide.* Available online at http://www.unhchr.ch/Huridocda/Huridoca.nsf/%28Symbol%29/E.CN.4.RES.2003.66.En?Opendocument.

———. *Report of Special Rapporteur on Extrajudicial, Summary, or Arbitrary Executions.* By Asthma Jahangi. Available online at http://www2.ohchr.org/english/issues/executions/index.htm.

———. *Supplementary Convention on the Abolition of Slavery, the Slave Trade, and Institutions and Practices Similar to Slavery.* Available online at http://www.unhchr.ch/html/menu3/b/30.htm.

———. *Universal Declaration of Human Rights.* Available online at http://www.un.org/Overview/rights.html.

Villagrán-Morales v. Guatemala. Inter-American Court of Human Rights Judgment. November 19, 1999. Available online at http://www.escr-net.org/caselaw/caselaw_show.htm?doc_id=417163.

Selected Videography

Bajo Juárez: La ciudad devorando a sus hijas. Directed by Alejandra Sánchez. Foprocine, 2006.

The Border. Directed by Paul Espinosa. Espinosa Productions, 2000.

Border Echoes/Ecos de una frontera. Directed by Lorena Mendez-Quiroga. Peace at the Border Films, 2007.

Borderline Cases: Environmental Matters at the United States–Mexico Border. Directed by Lynn Corcoran. Bullfrog Films, 1997.

Bordertown. Directed by Gregory Nava. Nuyorican Productions/El Norte Productions/Capitol Films, 2007.

City of Dreams. Directed by Bruno Sorrentino. Filmakers Library, 2001.

Espejo retrovisor. Directed by Héctor Molinar. Cine Producciones Molinar, 2002.

Juárez: Desierto de esperanza. Directed by Cristina Michaus. Tenzin S.C., 2002.

Juárez: La ciudad donde las mujeres son desechables. Directed by Alex Flores and Lorena Vassolo. Las Perlas del Mar, 2007.

Juárez, México. Directed by James Cahill. Dodging Bullets, 2005.

Juárez: Stages of Fear. Directed by Cesar Alejandro. Gorilla Productions, 2006.

La batalla de las cruces. Directed by Rafael Bonilla and Patricia Ravelo. CIESAS-Campo Imaginario, 2005.

Las muertas de Juárez. Directed by Enrique Murillo. Laguna Films, 2002.

Las paraditas. Directed by York Shackleton. Auteúr Films, 2001.

Maquila: A Tale of Two Mexicos. Directed by Saul Landau and Sonia Angulo. Cinema Guild, 2000.

Maquilápolis. Directed by Vicky Funari and Sergio de la Torre. California Newsreel, 2006.

Ni una más. Directed by Alejandra Sánchez. CUEC, 2002.

On the Edge/En el borde. Directed by Steev Hise. Detrital Films, 2006.

Pasión y muerte en Ciudad Juárez. Directed by Javier Ulloa and Luis Estrada. Cine Producciones Molinar, 2002.

Performing the Border. Directed by Ursula Biemann. Women Make Movies, 1999.

Preguntas sin respuesta: Los asesinatos y desapariciones en Ciudad Juárez. Directed by Rafael Montero. IMCINE/TV Azteca/UNAM, 2005.

Señorita extraviada/Missing Young Woman. Directed by Lourdes Portillo. Women Make Movies, 2001.

Sin dejar huella. Directed by María Novaro. Altavista Films, 2000.

16 en la lista. Directed by Rodolfo Rodoberti. Cine Producciones Molinar, 1998.

The Virgin of Juarez. Directed by Kevin James Dobson. First Look Pictures, 2006.

About the Contributors

DEBRA A. CASTILLO is Stephen H. Weiss Presidential Fellow, Emerson Hinchliff Professor of Hispanic Studies, and professor of comparative literature at Cornell University. She specializes in contemporary narrative from the Spanish-speaking world (including the United States), gender studies, and cultural theory. She is the author of several books, including *The Translated World: A Postmodern Tour of Libraries in Literature* (1984), *Talking Back: Strategies for a Latin American Feminist Literary Criticism* (1992), *Easy Women: Sex and Gender in Modern Mexican Fiction* (1998), and (with María Socorro Tabuenca Córdoba) *Border Women: Writing from La Frontera* (2002). She is also the translator of Federico Campbell's *Tijuana: Stories on the Border* (1994) and the coeditor of various volumes of essays. Her most recent book is *Re-dreaming America* (2004).

IGNACIO CORONA is an associate professor in the Department of Spanish and Portuguese at The Ohio State University. He specializes in Mexican and Latino/a American Cultural Studies. He has published articles on the intersection of journalism, political discourse, and literary discourse. He is the author of *Después de Tlatelolco: Las narrativas políticas en México, 1976–1990, un análisis de sus estrategias retóricas y representacionales* (2001); the coeditor (with Beth E. Jörgensen) of *The Contemporary Mexican Chronicle: Theoretical Perspectives on the Liminal Genre* (2002); and the coeditor (with Alejandro L. Madrid) of *Postnational Musical Identities: Cultural Production, Distribution, and Consumption in a Globalized Scenario* (2008).

HÉCTOR DOMÍNGUEZ-RUVALCABA is an associate professor in the Department of Spanish and Portuguese at the University of Texas at Austin. He is the author of *La modernidad abyecta: Formación del discurso homosexual en Latinoamérica* (2001) and *Modernity and the Nation in Mexican Representations of Masculinity: From Sensuality to Bloodshed*

(2007). He has published numerous articles on homosexuality, masculinities, and violence. His areas of academic interest are masculinity and queer studies in Latin America, United States–Mexico border violence, and cultural and political implications of organized crime in Mexico.

JAMES C. HARRINGTON is the director of the Texas Civil Rights Project and an adjunct professor at the University of Texas Law School. He is the author of *The Texas Bill of Rights: A Commentary and Litigation Manual* and of myriad law review articles, commentaries, and book reviews on human rights and civil liberty.

MIGUEL LÓPEZ-LOZANO is an associate professor of Mexican and Chicano Literature in the Department of Spanish and Portuguese at the University of New Mexico. He has published articles in journals in Cuba, Germany, Mexico, and the United States. He is the author of *Utopian Dreams, Apocalyptic Nightmares: Globalization in Recent Mexican and Chicano Narrative* (2008), which focuses on dystopian visions of urban spaces in the Mexican and Chicano novel. He is currently engaged in two different research projects: one on the work of Mexican women writing ethnographic indigenist novels during the 1930–1960 period, and another one on representations of the Mexican border in the arts around the globe.

MARÍA GUDELIA RANGEL GÓMEZ is a researcher at the Colegio de la Frontera (COLEF) in Tijuana, where she has been the director of academic affairs and the director of the Department of Population Studies. She has several studies on public health and is currently the principal investigator of the project "HIV Risk and Access to Health Care." She is the author of *Condiciones de salud en la frontera norte de México* (2008), *Las migraciones Guanajuato-Estados Unidos: Un acercamiento a las distintas dimensiones del fenómeno* (2007), and (with Norma Ojeda de la Peña) *Mujer y salud sexual* (1996).

PATRICIA RAVELO BLANCAS is a professor at the Center for Research and Advanced Studies in Social Anthropology (CIESAS) and a visiting professor at the University of Texas at El Paso and the Universidad Pedagógica Nacional, Unidad Juárez. She is the author of *Trabajo, enfer-*

medad y resistencia entre costureras de la Ciudad de México: Un estudio acerca de sus representaciones, experiencias y subjetividad (2001), coeditor (with Sara E. Pérez-Gil) of *Voces disidentes: Debates contemporáneos en estudios de género* (2004), coeditor (with Héctor Domínguez-Ruvalcaba) of *Entre las duras aristas de las armas* (2006), and coeditor (with Florence Peña and Sergio Sánchez) of *Cuando el trabajo nos castiga: Debates sobre el mobbing en México* (2007), among others. She is the producer of the documentary *La batalla de las cruces: Una década de impunidad y violencia contra las mujeres* (2005).

ARMANDO ROSAS SOLÍS is a history librarian at Universidad Autónoma de Baja California in Tijuana, México.

MARÍA SOCORRO TABUENCA CÓRDOBA is a researcher at the Colegio de la Frontera Norte (COLEF) in Ciudad Juárez, for which she also served as director from 1995 to 2007. She is a member of the editorial board of *Revista diálogo cultural entre las fronteras de México*. She has published many articles in Mexico and the United States and is the author and coauthor of various books, including *Mujeres y fronteras: Una perspectiva de género* (1998), *Lo que el viento a Juárez* (2000), and (with Debra Castillo) *Border Women: Writing from la Frontera* (2002).

Index